Laurence Cockcroft is a developme[...] of Transparency International, the g[...] against corruption, and was formerl[...] He is the author of *Global Corruptio[...] in the Modern World* and *Africa's Way: A Journey from the Past* (both I.B.Tauris).

Anne-Christine Wegener is a political scientist and anti-corruption analyst based in Frankfurt. She was previously deputy director and programme manager at Transparency International UK, focusing on defence and security.

'This is an important book on an uncomfortable subject. Corruption is big business and hugely damaging. Defeating it will take a focused effort by governments, and that will only happen if people wake up to what is going on.'

Paul Collier, author of *Exodus: Immigration and Multiculturalism in the 21st Century*

'In *Unmasked*, Cockcroft and Wegener provide a needed antidote to the idea that corruption is a malady confined to the developing world. In this clear-headed analysis, they systematically show how the West's political donors, big business, offshore havens, and organised crime have created a parallel universe of corrupt deals and conflicts of interest that cost all of us dearly. If you care about transparency and a clean society, put this book on your reading list.'

David E. Kaplan, Global Investigative Journalism Network

'This thorough analysis of contemporary corruption in the developed world goes beyond the scandals that regularly attract attention and probes the complex forces that undermine politics, business and contemporary life. This path-breaking book combines fine research with a highly readable text making it accessible to a broad audience. This work will advance in important ways our understanding of what we must do to address this corrosive corruption.'

Louise I. Shelley, author of *Dirty Entanglements: Corruption, Crime and Terrorism*

'This is a tour de force, exposing the essence of how our global predatory economic system has captured and corrupted our supposedly democratic societies. Cockcroft and Wegener brilliantly describe how, far from simple cash exchanges in brown envelopes, corruption is a rampant cancer sitting in the heart of our countries' democratic systems of checks and balances. At a moment of ever-more corporate scandals, rising demagoguery of populist politicians, and massive voter outrage, confusion and disengagement, this could not be a more prescient and urgent read for all those who wish to see democracy mean something – where those elected by the people, actually serve the interests of the people.'

Simon Taylor, Co-founder and Director, Global Witness

UNMASKED

CORRUPTION IN THE WEST

LAURENCE COCKCROFT AND ANNE-CHRISTINE WEGENER

I.B. TAURIS

LONDON · NEW YORK

Published in 2017 by
I.B.Tauris & Co. Ltd
London • New York
www.ibtauris.com

References to websites were correct at the time of writing.

ISBN: 978 1 78453 608 4
eISBN: 978 1 78672 079 5
ePDF: 978 1 78673 079 4

A full CIP record for this book is available from the British Library
A full CIP record is available from the Library of Congress

Library of Congress Catalog Card Number: available

Typeset by Out of House Publishing
Printed and bound by CPI Group (UK) Ltd, Croydon, CR0 4YY

For our children: Mathilda, Lola and Philippa
and grandchildren: Meredith and Adam

Contents

Tables and Figures

Preface

Corruption in the West is overlooked and underplayed. This book sets out to correct the record by showing that influence is bought and power is sold on both sides of the Atlantic. This is true for many areas including politics, sports and the business world. By now, corruption as a subject has moved up the global agenda and is increasingly being recognised as a threat in Europe and America. It is mainly the corruption of influence rather than the corruption of brown paper envelopes.

As the authors of this book, we have been engaged in advocacy work in relation to corruption under the banner of Transparency International (TI). Laurence Cockcroft was a co-founder of TI in the early 1990s, and chairman of its UK chapter from 2000 to 2008. Anne-Christine Wegener was the deputy director of the TI Defence and Security Programme, based in the UK, for five years and has been working on other sectoral anti-corruption issues since, currently with Germany's international development cooperation agency, GIZ. In 2013, we decided to write the book from a sense that while corruption was a serious global problem, it was important to maintain a focus on the West, and that corruption needed to be unmasked in order to be recognised much more widely.

We also realised that corruption means different things to different people, both professionally and morally. In conversations with lawyers, one will often be assured that fraud is a very different matter to corruption. People in business may well argue that cartels are 'not really' corrupt. Those in banking may argue that exaggerated 'risk-taking' can never reach the stage of being corrupt. However, in this book we have taken a very broad definition of corruption that ranges from bribery to forms of political lobbying, to the dramas played out in international sports in late 2015 to the crises in banking circles since 2007/8.

We have been writing at a time when the international attention to corruption – at least measured by the actions proposed at summits of the G8 and G20 – has never been higher. But the content of our book suggests that the reality within the countries of the EU, and of the US and Canada, falls well short of these ambitious agendas, and shows how important it is to bridge the gap and match action to words. This is particularly true at a time when the values of liberal democracy are under fire as never before, on the European continent itself, in parts of the developing world and from radical Islamist circles for whom corruption is a key rallying call.

Our concern has also been to show that corruption does not only impact directly on lives in the developing world but also in the West, although often in more subtle ways. Doctors may be pressurised to prescribe a certain drug, traders in financial markets may be tempted by the very high returns from rate-fixing, an automobile engineer may design exhaust systems that deliberately evade emissions standards. So the issue is real for many citizens in the West, even if often behind a mask of normality. There is every reason why the 'developed' societies of the West should be prepared to face these questions, for their own future.

Addressing corruption is never a light-hearted business. There are very powerful forces at work whose ability to determine policy and business outcomes should never be underrated. We hope this book succeeds in defining these powers and showing how they can be challenged.

Acknowledgements

In writing this book we have found a surprising willingness in many circles to acknowledge the scale of the problem of corruption in the West. As a consequence, we have received valuable support from colleagues in the 'anti-corruption' world, from professionals whose work is or has been to fight forms of corruption, who work in the sectors treated in this book, and from the academic world where the issue of corruption is under ever-more intensive scrutiny.

Among those in the anti-corruption world of civil society we are particularly grateful to Frank Vogl of Transparency International; Sheila Krumholz of the Center for Responsive Politics; Lindsay Ferris, then at the Sunlight Foundation in Washington, DC; and Rick Messick, senior contributor to the Global Anticorruption Blog. In the European Parliament, we have been kindly assisted by Claude Moraes MEP, the chair of the Civil Liberties, Justice and Home Affairs Committee.

On the wider EU front, the director of Europol, Rob Wainwright, kindly arranged for us to meet several of his team, among whom David Ellero, working on north–south links in organised crime within Europe, was particularly helpful. In the US we had invaluable conversations with Judge Jed Rakoff of the Southern District Court of New York, and Elise Bean of the Levin Center at Wayne Law School in Detroit and formerly head of Senator Levin's team at the Senate Permanent Investigations Committee. Likewise it was very helpful to talk with Feras Sleiman in the office of Senator Elizabeth Warren (D-Mass) in relation to her stance on key financial regulatory issues. We also appreciated a discussion with Dan Glickman, formerly secretary of state for agriculture and currently co-chair of the Bipartisan Policy Center in Washington, DC.

In the academic world, we were privileged to have discussions at the Edmond J. Safra Center for Ethics at Harvard University including its director (from 2010 to 2015) Professor Lawrence Lessig and several of his associates including Bill English, Dr Laurence Tai (regarding financial regulation) and Brooke Williams (regarding the influences behind think tanks). At the American University in Washington, DC, Professor James Thurber has been a source of both encouragement and guidance. We also very much appreciated a long discussion with John Dickie, expert on the history of the Italian mafia at University College London.

Among journalists and writers, we are grateful to Nick Mathieson of the Bureau of Investigative Journalism in London, whose reporting on the finance and banking sector is invaluable, and to David Kaplan of the Global Investigative Journalism Network in Washington, whose international network of investigative journalists not only is formidable but is also extremely powerful.

We also benefited greatly from discussions on the issue of 'secrecy jurisdictions' with John Christensen of Tax Justice Network, and Jack Blum in the US, a long-time investigator and analyst of these jurisdictions.

Among those in the professional world that tackle corruption, we were very glad to have discussions with Sir Ian

Andrews, former chair of the Serious Organised Crime Agency of the UK. We also greatly benefited from discussions with Carl Dolan and Daniel Freund at Transparency International EU, with Anna-Maija Mertens, managing director of Transparency International Deutschland; Miklos Marschall, deputy managing director of Transparency International; Gareth Sweeney, editor of Transparency International's *Global Corruption Report: Sport*; and in London with Leah Wawro at the Transparency International Defence and Security Programme. We are also grateful to Neill Stansbury, founder of the Global Infrastructure Anti-Corruption Centre, for his knowledge and insight on corruption in the construction business.

We received very valuable research support from Cosimo Stahl and Maxilian Heywood, when both were graduate students at the School of East European Studies at University College London, thanks to Professor Alena Ledeneva, Professor of Politics and Society.

Laurence Cockcroft is particularly grateful to John Riggan in Philadelphia (for his powerful enthusiasm); to Roger Frank, financier in New York (for his honest appraisal of the issues in the financial sector); to Alan Kaufman, formerly of the hedge fund world and now a successful mushroom grower in Princeton, New Jersey; and to Sir John Gieve, formerly deputy governor of the Bank of England for his positive and critical appraisal. Anne-Christine Wegener is particularly grateful to Mark Pyman for everything there is to know about defence corruption (and beyond); to Dr Ben Weinberg at GIZ for his input and enthusiasm on the subject of sports governance; to Diana Tesic, sports lawyer; to Nick Maxwell for his generous sharing of literature on pharmaceutical corruption; and to Bill Hughes (ex Director General of SOCA) for his critical and insightful comments on corruption and the police. She is also immensely thankful to Elena Panfilova, deputy chair of Transparency International, for her encouragement and lively exchanges on all matters corruption and non-corruption (and for a lovely birthday surprise meeting and dinner), and to all friends who offered support, ideas and kind and/or critical words.

We are very grateful to Jo Godfrey at I.B.Tauris for her patience, thinking and clear guidance throughout the development of this book.

Finally, we are both, as always, indebted to our spouses Shamshad and Paul for their support and tolerance of this project and later discerning but always constructive and invaluable input.

1

Corruption and its Perils

In Europe and North America, corruption exists and determines outcomes on a scale that is scarcely recognised but embraces fields as diverse as politics, sport and climate change.

It has permeated society in the West in ways that cannot be ignored, and corruption is increasingly recognised by the public. As part of a global survey of citizens' attitudes to corruption, carried out by Transparency International, interviewees recently expressed an extraordinarily high level of distrust in key institutions in both Europe and America. When asked: 'Do you regard political parties as corrupt or very corrupt?', nine out of ten Italians, three-quarters of Americans, and almost the same percentage of Czechs replied 'yes'.[1] Parliaments did not fare much better: two-thirds of Canadians and more than half of British citizens found their parliaments or legislatures to be 'corrupt' or very corrupt.[2]

For the most part, these responses do not reflect a personal experience of bribery. Rather, they reflect a general view that government itself is corrupt and represents the interests of small elites who control decision making and the allocation of resources. This perception has led to the rise of protest parties of the What has happened to the spacing? in Europe, and increasingly aggressive criticism of the politics centred on Washington, DC in the USA.

In this context, corruption is regarded as much more than a question of bribery or slightly more subtle financial pay-offs. For the most part, contemporary corruption in the West is not the corruption of brown envelopes but the corruption of influence, in which politics and institutions (including sports associations) are captured by people or interest groups for illicit gain and their own organisation's benefit. Looked at another way, it is the buying of influence and the selling of power.

Corruption is one of the principal drivers of the inequality at both the global and the national level, and is increasingly recognised as a major problem for both the world economy and national politics. It is no accident that in the US midterm elections of 2014 (federal level), one per cent (32,000) of the wealthiest one per cent of donors – the one per cent of the one per cent – gave 30 per cent of disclosed political contributions, and that those with firm connections to Wall Street were the largest contributors.[3] The consequence of this pattern of financial support is a vicious circle in which corruption by influence reinforces the position of the top one per cent.

Because corruption in Europe and North America is not centred around bribery but is rather a struggle for the capture of resources, it may appear that it has a less dire effect on the public than direct bribery. This conclusion would not be justified. A patient forced to pay a bribe to receive health care at a hospital in the developing world, which should be free of charge, will be likely to complain at least in private. A patient being prescribed a more expensive drug without his knowing, but for which he has to pay, is unlikely to find out and complain. Both patients will be cheated by a system of corruption: but where a network linking health managers to pharmaceutical companies gains influence, it can skim off profits or illicit gains without having to resort to a hierarchy of bribes.

This more subtle form of corruption, as we will see in the following chapters, is alive in different countries in different ways but affects all walks of life, from politics to justice, from banking and finance to the corporate world (notably in pharmaceuticals, construction and defence), in the world of sport and even in the case of action designed to combat climate change.

None of these sectors, as we will show in the following chapters, is immune from influence bought by money, and from elected politicians and well-placed bureaucrats selling power, although some are significantly more prone to such backroom deals than others.

On the political front, voters are dismayed that big funders can determine the scale of political campaigns, or that parties can enrich their leaders from party funds. Campaign finance in the US is a cogent example of the danger of money not only in influencing particular decisions, but in determining who gets to make the decisions in the first place, by targeting individual congressmen at both the state and the federal level. A very large increase in direct and indirect financial contributions to the campaigns of candidates for political office has been created by the Citizens United case. Decided by the Supreme Court in 2010, the ruling on the case removed nearly all obstacles on corporate and individual contributions to independent vehicles such as Political Action Committees (PACs), and eased limits on individual contributions made directly to candidates. Although in the 2016 US presidential campaign, neither Donald Trump (R) nor Bernie Sanders (D) used this 'liberalisation' in their campaigns, other candidates including Hillary Clinton did so on a big scale. The same was true for many candidates for Congress and at the state level. The outcome of this huge increase in the inflow of political contributions is one in which policy can be bought for a price and elected members fear that unless they toe the funders' line they will have few resources to fight their next campaign. The corruption consists of the role that 'big money' can play in suppressing the interests of a wider public whose views can be marginalised by both major parties.[4]

In the business world, strategies that undermine regulation, minimise competition and foster the exchange of executives between governments and companies constitute a further case of the corruption of influence. Defence companies – prestigious upholders of the national interest – have sustained close ties, particularly through 'revolving doors', with Ministries of Defence, ensuring that competition for large-scale contracts is minimal. Construction companies have long played and captured markets in alliance with organised crime and with the support of elected politicians.

In the banking sector, small- and large-scale private investors may find that major failures in corporate governance have written off a once-valued share. Nowhere has this become more apparent in the past decade than in the banking and finance sector, which has been engaged in both reckless lending in the mortgage market and criminal activity in ways that have led to charges in the courts from market-rigging to fraud. At the same time, banks have been successful in ensuring that the regulatory authorities do not develop the teeth to control them effectively. In the US after the financial crisis, the groundswell of support for regulation that would limit the ability of banks to engage in trading with their own capital (and so put depositors at risk) or to restrain executive bonuses has been systematically eroded by the lobbying power of Wall Street. In the UK, the appetite for regulating the City of London – the financial centre – had reached a high point by 2013, but effective lobbying has ensured that the Financial Conduct Authority, formed as one response to the crisis, would have no more leverage than its predecessor organisation, the Financial Services Authority.

Over at least the past 20 years, banks and companies have also taken every opportunity to reap the fiscal benefits offered by the authorities who control 'offshore centres' even when these are geographically inland and better described as 'secrecy jurisdictions'.[5] The authorities allowing this corporate and banking behaviour range from the state of Wyoming to the governments of Liechtenstein, Switzerland and Panama, and include 15 jurisdictions under the British Crown. The release of the 'Panama Papers' by the International Consortium of Investigative Journalists in April 2016 provided another shocking example of how these jurisdictions are used by national leaders and their networks to hide their assets, with the intention of disguising their origin in corruption. Estimates of the total funds held in this network vary widely and range from $7 trillion[6] to $20 trillion,[7] all of which is placed there to evade scrutiny and taxes. Either figure is very substantial in relation to the total assets of the US commercial banking system assessed at $16 trillion.[8] This offshore system has consequences for equality: as much as 8 per cent[9] of household wealth (quite apart from corporate income) may be held offshore in secrecy jurisdictions, thus enabling evasion on a huge scale. While many of these transactions are strictly speaking legal, they are viewed by a majority of the public as corrupt.

The judicial sector is undoubtedly key for fighting corruption but is, at the same time, susceptible to it. While judges' independence and integrity are generally high, there are countries that are an exception to this, where influence and wealth can buy judicial immunity. The US justice system straddles both the courage and thoroughness of its distinguished prosecutors such as Robert Morgenthau and Eliot Spitzer and the inadequacies of justice at the level of many states where judges must run for office and seek campaign finance. Doubts about the quality of justice inevitably impede the fight against corruption.

Differences between Europe and North America

How different from each other are the factors driving processes of influence-buying and power-selling in Europe and North America?

We argue that, in both cases, the main drivers of corruption are political finance and lobbying; opaque processes involving individuals, associations, corporations and banks; a weakened justice and police system; and failures of oversight, compliance and regulation (which extends to the governance of sport).

In Europe, political finance is for the most part more constrained because it is subject to more intensive regulation, although it is certainly a factor in electoral outcomes. In the financial sector, the situation is more complex because within Europe the position of the City of London is different to that of most continental banking sectors, which is different again to that of the US. In the US, sport remains an area much less affected by corruption than sport in Europe.

The corruption as described in this book has strong international linkages that come from external sources. These 'imported' factors include money from corrupt sources laundered from the rest of the world, including funds that are the fruit of organised crime and that are then held in 'shell companies' (with an untraceable owner) and subsequently invested in respectable assets such as high-end including investments in the 'junior' (and so less-well-regulated) financial markets in London and New York. Its impact is matched by the strength of organised crime networks that originate in Latin America and Asia but control human smuggling in the West, and cybercrime, which may originate in any part of the world, working jointly or separately from domestic cyber criminals.

Looking ahead

The message of the analysis and arguments presented here is not that the situation in its various manifestations cannot be reversed, but that specific and targeted effort will be required. This is discussed in our final chapter. The actions that are critical to this are re-establishing confidence that corruption is not undermining democracy. They extend to ensuring that banking and finance are seen to be rid of the fraud and corruption that characterised the financial crisis; they should include action by multinational companies to adopt more effective compliance systems that reject the use of corruption to increase market share. Separately, international action needs to be taken both on organised crime (including cybercrime), and in relation to the governance of sporting institutions, to address the triple threats of match-fixing, doping and failed governance. 'Secrecy jurisdictions' are themselves a theme that runs through this book and whose further regulation must be a part of action by both the EU and the US who together provide the umbrella that has protected them to date. In all of these areas, the objective will have to be to reduce the buying of influence and the selling of power. Most of these measures can only be successful in the context of international action, but are even more crucial at a time when corruption is increasingly recognised as a threat to global security. However, there is no substitute for a core group of Western countries addressing the challenging situation laid out in the following chapters.

2

The Rising Price of Power

The funding of political parties is at the heart of corruption in many countries, and Europe and North America are no exception to this pattern. Large-scale funders of political parties expect a return on their money if the party they are backing achieves power. The return may be either financial – because their party's victory generates contracts for them or their friends – or the buying of 'influence' through the adoption of policies that favour their narrow interest (such as a tax or a tariff or the protection of a business). Some donors have broader interests at heart but in all countries there are few major donors whose policy interests do not relate to them or their peer group – such as the industry they work in. Thus party funders are buying influence and elected politicians are selling power. As a consequence, the interests of the broader electorate, including those whose votes returned the politicians, may be overridden by large-scale party donors. In a range of countries this process is abetted by a 'lobbying' industry – pushing elected politicians for specific outcomes – which is sometimes closely linked to donors (as in the US) or may be largely separate from it (as in the UK and the European Parliament) but is nonetheless very effective. In the 'accession' countries of the EU, funds provided by 'oligarchs' and privatised enterprises that remain very close to the state play an increasing role in determining political outcomes. This chapter shows how powerful political finance has become in both Europe and the US and that its role is corrupting in the sense that public outcomes are too often determined by private interests.

USA: An end to limits

The effectiveness of legal barriers against corruption in the US has been a recurring challenge and the fight against it has never been more than partially effective, although various strands of corruption have often led to legislative reform. Concerns about corruption in political finance are part of this pattern and have triggered legislation designed to control it since the Tillman Act of 1907 when President Teddy Roosevelt sought to address the overbearing influence of corporations in politics.[1] Since the Watergate scandal of 1974 there has been heightened concern about campaign funding leading to new legislation in the form of the Federal Election Campaign Act amendments of 1974 and the Bipartisan Campaign Reform Act (BCRA) of 2002.

It was a film about Hillary Clinton that opened the way to the greatest challenge to this legislation governing political funding for 40 years. Financed in 2008 by a small not-for-profit entity, Citizens United, and funded largely by the energy magnates Charles and David Koch, it was intended to sabotage the prospects facing Hillary Clinton in her race with Barack Obama in the Democratic Party primary in that year, and was intended to be released on the cable channel DirecTV. However, the Federal Electoral Commission intervened to claim that it violated the BCRA, which banned political advertisements within 30 days of a presidential primary (and was intended to place a federal cap on 'indirect contributions' to federal campaigns by national party committees). The legal basis for BCRA was strongly challenged by Citizen United's lawyer, Ted Olson, who in hearings in 2008 and 2009 argued that its restriction cannot be justified in law because it placed limits on the ability of a company, which was ultimately a collection of individuals, to support a political viewpoint. Olson argued that only political donations that could be construed as seeking a very specific action by the candidate – and so could be described as a bribe – should be banned.

The argument ultimately fell on the responsive ears of five out of nine Supreme Court justices, and it fell to Judge Anthony Kennedy to write for the majority, which included Chief Justice John Roberts. Their finding in 2010 'struck down' all limits on corporate expenditure whether through political action committees (PACs), a means of providing indirect support to candidates, or directly to political parties (but maintained restrictions on the number of candidates one donor could support).

The impact of this decision was reinforced by a subsequent decision of the Supreme Court taken in April 2014 in response to a suit brought initially by an Alabama businessman, Shaun McCutcheon, against the Federal Electoral Commission, which lifted the cap on the number of contributions that an individual can give to both political parties and to candidates.[2] These limits had been fixed over a two-year cycle and were set at a total of $48,600 for candidates at the federal level, and $74,600 for political parties at the federal level. While calling these limits into question, the Supreme Court ruling did not abolish them, continuing to restrict contributions to individual candidates to $5,200 but set no limit on the number of candidates that could be supported. Consequently 'joint fundraising committees' that had been restricted to supporting not more than nine candidates could now support an indefinite number.

This ruling was as controversial as had been that of Citizens United. It split the nine justices of the Supreme Court 5:4, with

Chief Justice Roberts authoring the verdict on behalf of Justices Antonin Scalia, Samuel Alito and Anthony Kennedy with support from Justice Thomas Clarence (who issued his own even more vigorous rebuttal of limits on campaign expenditure). The four other justices issued a dissenting report. In his 'opinion', Chief Justice Roberts made it clear that he considered specific campaign limits to be a constraint on freedom of expression, as described in the First Amendment to the Constitution. He stated:

> There is no more basic right in our democracy than the right to participate in electing leaders... we have made it clear that Congress may not regulate contributions simply to reduce the amount in politics or to restrict the political participation of some in order to enhance the relative influence of others.[3]

Reaction against this came from all sides of the political spectrum. Senator John McCain, a former presidential candidate and co-author of BCRA, stated:

> I was disappointed by the Supreme Court's decision today. While I have advocated for increasing the aggregate limits on individual contributions to candidates and party committees, I am concerned that today's ruling may represent the latest step in an effort by a majority of the court to dismantle entirely the longstanding structure of campaign finance law erected to limit the undue influence of special interests on American politics. I predict that as a result of recent court decisions, there will be scandals involving corrupt public officials and unlimited, anonymous campaign contributions that will force the system to be reformed once again.[4]

These two legislative changes mean elected representatives can attract support without limit in scale or source through the intermediation of legally independent entities including PACs, Super PACs and tax-exempt independent expenditure committees (known as 501 c (4)s). Since reforms introduced after the political crisis of Watergate in 1974, which sought to limit aggregate contributions, PACs have been a crucial means to circumventing these limits, but have to operate by identifying with a cause rather than a candidate.[5] In the 2015/16 campaign, a pattern began to emerge of corporations with anonymous ownership (see Chapter 6) contributing to Super PACs to preserve the identity of the real donors.[6] Independent expenditure committees, legally devoted to 'social welfare', can use part of their budget to fund candidate-linked advertisements but cannot make direct contributions and do not have to declare their source of funds and consequently are often held to hold 'dark money'. The large-scale donations made through these mechanisms are obviously premised on the support by the elected representative for the policy agenda of the donor.

The scale of the increase in political donations triggered by these two pieces of legislation was very large, particularly in relation to campaigns for the House and the Senate, which increased from $2.3 billion in 2008 to $3.7 billion in 2012.[7] Total expenditure on both the presidential and House campaigns was $6.3 billion in the 2011–12 cycle[8] (although expenditure on the presidential campaign alone remained at about $2.7 billion). Of the total $6.3 billion expenditure, the relatively small number of 30,000 people provided $1.18 billion, and within this total only 4,000 contributed $400 million.[9]

The current situation is in direct contrast to the objectives of the framers of the Constitution, who intended that the Congress should be dependent 'on the people alone'.[10] The importance of this was stressed in correspondence between two of the founding fathers: Thomas Jefferson and John Adams.[11] Writing in August 1791, Jefferson expressed to Adams his worry that the Treasurer of the newly created United States, Alexander Hamilton, was attracting the support of Congress to the system of federal bonds he was engineering, of which lawmakers might be indirect beneficiaries. A recent biographer of Jefferson, Jon Meacham, summarised Jefferson's concern this way:

> He worried about the corruption of the legislature – that lawmakers were becoming financially enmeshed with the Hamiltonian system

of securities and bank shares. Such economic ties were not bribes in
the overt sense, Jefferson believed, but they did create a pernicious
climate of co-operation between the Congress and the Treasury.
This subtle form of 'corruption' troubled Jefferson, who saw it as the
means by which Hamilton and his allies could control the general
direction of government.[12]

Although Jefferson was primarily worried in this case about lawmakers' self-interest, he was also concerned about the type of congressional dependency Hamilton's measures would create and their
ability to co-opt support.

In the contemporary situation, political and legislative influence is achieved by a combination of contributions to campaign
finance (especially) at the congressional level and direct lobbying –
a process described in Chapter 3. It is the combination of expenditure on campaign finance and lobbying that obtains results in the
form not only of policy but also of tax and other concessions.
The Sunlight Foundation, which tracks the influence of money in
politics, conducted an in-depth study in 2014 of 200 large corporations who are active both as political donors and that have a substantial lobbying budget.[13] It found that between 2007 and 2012,
these companies spent a total of $5.8 billion on both activities, of
which $5.2 billion was accounted for by lobbying. The returns were
large: this expenditure earned $4.4 trillion in business support and
tax concessions, a figure that is further explored in Chapter 3. This
finance has bought not only influence but also policy outcomes,
which work to the direct advantage of the companies concerned at
the expense of policy designed only for the public good.

There are no more powerful exponents of the strategy of linking campaign contributions to lobbying than the brothers Charles
and David Koch – financiers of the Citizens United film – who
wield the additional weapon of the co-opted 'think tank' and advocacy group. Their huge resources stem from Koch Industries, a
company whose mainstream business is energy but which is now

a diversified conglomerate with a reported turnover of more than $100 billion per year. The Koch brothers have been committed to radical economic liberalisation and a reduced role for government since their youth.[14] David stood for vice-president in 1980 on behalf of the far-right Libertarian Party but collected only 1 per cent of the vote in the general election that brought Ronald Reagan to power. Vowing to work towards libertarian ends in more subtle ways, the brothers began to put together a strategy that came to dominate the right wing of the Republican Party.[15]

By 1998, their strategy was effectively in place: not only would the Kochs' PAC ('KochPAC') provide indirect support to a range of suitable candidates, but three foundations would reticulate funds through think tanks and pressure groups. The Charles Koch Foundation, the Claude R. Lambe Foundation and the David H. Koch Foundation embarked on a grant-making programme that between 2009 and 2013 totalled $214 million and by 2014 totalled $80 million per year,[16] channelled to at least 34 'not-for-profit' entities, ranging from the Heritage Foundation to the Cato Institute to George Mason University. Alongside these policy-oriented and advocacy institutes were more obviously political vehicles such as the Americans for Prosperity Foundation, which became a key (although indirect) supporter of Tea Party candidates from 2005 onwards, creating a membership base of 330,000 and eventually having a crucial impact in the congressional elections of 2014, in which the Republican Party gained control of both Houses.

However, the congressmen and senators who were elected in this landslide were not necessarily of one mind: by November 2015, a large faction of the Republican Party, opposed to the budget negotiations led by the speaker of the House, John Boehner, forced his resignation, further increasing the tension between the Obama presidency and Congress. This dogmatic position brought effective government on a range of issues – from climate change to corporate governance – to a halt. The response of the Koch brothers and their network was both to adjust their strategy to show more concern for the poor and disadvantaged,[17] and to increase their efforts and fore-see total expenditure in the 2015/16 electoral cycle of no less than $889 million between candidates, think tanks and advocacy organi-sations.[18] What they had not foreseen was the emergence of Donald Trump as a front-running Republican candidate, able to largely self-fund his campaign up to the convention stage and capture many of the parts of the system that the Kochs' network had prepared.

It is not surprising that there was to be a strong public reac-tion against the intrusion of billionaire finance into mainstream congressional politics. The candidature of Bernie Sanders in the primaries for the 2016 election was largely based on a campaign attacking the corruption involved in party finance. As a sena-tor for Vermont, elected in 2007, he had witnessed the impact of campaign finance on daily politics first-hand. But it was Elizabeth Warren, elected senator for Massachusetts in 2012, who put this most succinctly in 2015:

> And now that I have been in the United States Senate for two years, I've had a chance to see it up close and personal. More than ever, I am convinced that the game is rigged... For all the talk about rein-ing in government, what's really going on is a concerted effort by lobbyists and lawmakers to keep bending the levers of Government so they work for the favoured few.[19]

How corrupt are states?

The pattern and characteristics of corruption at the level of states is very varied, reflecting not only cultural and social traditions of states but also the different legislative and executive traditions that have arisen from them. Recent surveys of both the levels of corrup-tion state by state and the institutional capacity of states to address the issues have shown how different these outcomes can be.

Columbia University's Center for the Advancement of Public Integrity (CAPI) has ranked states by the strength of their institutions to address corruption. The study ranked them on a scale of A–F.[20] Key criteria included control of political finance, electoral oversight and judicial accountability. No state achieved an 'A' rating averaged across all criteria, although Massachusetts achieved it in relation to the control of political finance. The highest overall grade achieved of 'C' was achieved only by Alaska, California and Connecticut. The lowest ranking of 'F' was achieved by (among others) Louisiana, Maine, Pennsylvania, Wyoming and Michigan.

Three states show how different the situation can be: New York, Illinois and Massachusetts – although on the CAPI rating, both New York and Illinois scored a 'D' and Massachusetts a 'D+'. In fact New York state and the City of New York have been dramatic centres for the theatre of corruption for at least two centuries, epitomised by the Tweed Ring that 'captured' the City government in the 1860s.[21] Corruption has continued to be a highly contentious issue. Andrew Cuomo, the governor of New York state and the son of former governor Mario Cuomo, was elected to office in 2010 vowing to clean up politics in Albany, the state's capital. He had to contend with an Assembly and Senate that in the previous ten years had seen 28 legislators leaving office in disgrace.

The legislators had either been fined or jailed on a wide range of corruption charges that included bribery, perjury, sexual harassment, theft of state grants, the extortion of money to secure judicial outcomes and a sham marriage to subvert immigration laws. In order to initiate his proposed clean-up, Cuomo persuaded the State Assembly to pass an anti-corruption bill and a new ethics code. Public dissatisfaction with this relatively feeble strategy led Cuomo to appoint the 'Moreland Commission'[22] in 2013, which was sufficiently abrasive (including leads to the governor's office) to cause him to disband it in 2014.

One supporter of this abrupt end to the Commission was Sheldon Silver, who had been a member of the State Assembly since 1977 and was elected speaker in 1994. As speaker, he had become the dominant force in the Assembly, determining legislation with a small cross-party cabal, a very powerful position in a state with a population of 20 million and an annual budget of $150 billion. But his support for the abolition of the Moreland Commission did not allow him to escape arrest by the FBI on five charges of corruption in January 2015, each with a potential sentence of 20 years. Central to the FBI's case was that Silver had received $6 million in payments from two law firms in return for steering cases to them (both directly and indirectly).[23] In November 2015, Silver was found guilty on charges including fraud, extortion and money-laundering.[24] Strangely enough his ex-counterpart as Senate majority leader, Dean G. Skelos (together with his son), was also found guilty less than two weeks later by the Federal Courts on corruption charges.[25] Both these cases were successfully prosecuted by US Attorney Preet Bharara, who took up the mantle of cases considered but abandoned by the Moreland Commission. After the Skelos trial, Bharara is reputed to have tweeted:

> How many prosecutions will it take before Albany gives the people of New York the honest government they deserve?[26]

The state of Illinois and the city of Chicago have struggled with their reputation for corruption for more than a century. The reputation lives on: four of the last nine governors of the state were jailed.[27] In the past 40 years, 33 aldermen (elected councillors) have been found guilty of crimes such as bribery, extortion, embezzlement conspiracy and tax evasion. The kernel of the corrupt rackets that underlie these cases is the interface that has existed between the two main political parties at City Hall, the ability of local party machines to return selected candidates and the award of contracts to corporate supporters. Contractors are expected to 'pay to play'. A 1990 investigation by journalists at the *Springfield State Journal-Register* quoted then Illinois auditor general Robert Cronson as saying:

> The general feeling among state contractors is that you are infinitely better off if you contribute. And the feeling in government is that you've got to reward your friends or you don't get re-elected.[28]

A recent and dramatic demonstration of the enduring strength of this tradition is the career of former state governor Rod Blagojevich, who, when serving his term of office, was arrested by the FBI in December 2008 and charged with several crimes of corruption, including the 'sale' of President-elect Obama's Senate seat. Blagojevich was a product of the Chicago system, born in the city, graduating from law school in California, joining the office of Alderman Eddie Vrdolyak – himself later convicted on corruption charges – and successfully running for office in the state legislature in 1992. This was a first step on the electoral ladder: he ran for a seat in the 5th congressional district of Illinois in 1996 and for governor in 2002. Few doubted that he intended to reach even higher and contemplated the presidency. The campaigns for each of these offices required ever-larger sums and Blagojevich mastered a system of unrivalled effectiveness, linking elected representatives to the procurement process in the state legislature in return for campaign contributions graduated by the scale of the contract.

The appointment of a senator when a seat falls vacant between elections is in the hands of the state governor, and the election of Barack Obama to the presidency created such a vacancy. More than one Illinois politician sought the seat, including US congressman Jesse Jackson Jr and former Illinois attorney general Roland Burris. The teams of both men actively lobbied Blagojevich for the seat, which the governor saw as an opportunity to raise his campaign chest by as much as $1.5 million. Jackson overstepped the mark in relation to a separate case involving the misuse of campaign funds and faced criminal charges by the FBI, leading to a prison sentence. Burris was awarded the job, but faced enquiries from the Senate Ethics Committee, who found a phone conversation between Burris and Blagojevich 'while not rising to the level of an explicit quid pro quo... was inappropriate'. Unfortunately for Blagojevich, the FBI had been wiretapping his phone during the weeks when the 'sale' of the seat was under discussion and his insistence that he wanted to raise money from the seat allocation could not be denied.

In a recent analysis of the origins and continuing prevalence of corruption in Illinois, Thomas Gradel and Dick Simpson, veteran observers of the issue, conclude:

> Illinois is among the most corrupt states [in the US] and Chicago is undoubtedly the most corrupt city in our nation. There is a severe cost to this corruption at many levels. We can no longer afford to sustain these moral, political and monetary costs. Change is both possible and desirable.[29]

Massachusetts is a contrasting case where a long history of the 'gerrymandering' of congressional districts has created recurrent campaigns to clean up state politics, which have had a significant impact. The most recent campaign followed the prosecution and imprisonment of three recent Speakers of the State House of Representatives, in office between 1991 and 2009,[30] who were found guilty of federal criminal charges. The consequent ethics reform package of 2009 dealt with a range of issues and led to a strong campaign finance reform law that has earned wide respect but still contains anomalies such as a failure to ban campaign donations from lobbyists. Nonetheless it was strong enough to lead to the resignation of the state Lieutenant Governor in 2013 as a result of his acceptance of a donation from a donor under federal indictment. Pressure from within the state from civil society groups is likely to tighten rules further, especially in relation to strengthening the hand of the state, as opposed to federal, corruption prosecutors.[31]

These cases show how lawmakers and even groups of lawmakers in state legislatures can be seriously corrupt.

* * *

The 2015/16 election campaigns saw a major revival of the longstanding resentment of the role of both private and corporate money in campaign finance and discussion of 'corruption' in politics on a scale not seen since Watergate in 1974. Bernie Sanders argued strongly for the repeal of Citizens United legislation although his campaign did benefit from a PAC; Hillary Clinton benefited from a range of PACs and Super PACs; Donald Trump railed against 'dark money' but was able to fund a majority of his campaign costs up to the Republican Convention from his own pocket (although much of it classified as a 'loan'). Other running candidates such as Jeb Bush, Ted Cruz and Marco Rubio all raised funds through the PAC system, delaying their announcement to run in order to maximise PAC-based support. Nearly all Congressional candidates maximised the support they could raise through PACs and other 'independent expenditure committees'. The question of whether this system could be unravelled was complex. Thomas Edsall, writing in the *New York Times* in September 2015 asked: 'Can anything be done about all the money in politics?' and commented: Nearly everyone in America agrees that there is too much influence seeking money in politics, except for the people who benefit from it.[32]

Integral to this system of influence is the process of lobbying in which registered lobbyists are able not only to fight for the cause they are employed to promote, but also to raise funds for the congressmen and senators whose work in committees and votes they intend to secure. This is indeed the buying of influence by fundraisers and lobbyists and the selling of power by elected representatives. The dangers of corruption that this posed were recognised by as disparate a pair of politicians as Senator McCain and President Obama (then senator). But their reformist efforts were not enough, as Chapter 3 will show.

Europe

Nearly all member states of the European Union (EU), except for Sweden and Germany, have some limits on either donations or expenditures – and often both – which in many cases are much stricter than the few limits remaining in the US. However, corruption is a recurrent element in European party finance in spite of the prevalence of such limits. The patterns of corruption are different in the countries of Western Europe (those that had become members of the EU by 2003) and those of Eastern Europe, particularly those who joined between 2004 and 2007. In Western Europe, the issues have centred on the origin of funds, the manipulation of the regulations (including subverting spending limits) and the misuse of public funding for campaigns. After the fall of the Soviet Union, Central and Eastern Europe adopted a raft of regulatory measures that represented international best practices. These measures are now under challenge as parties in power seek to co-opt both state resources and those of private companies who benefit from their association with the state. We will discuss these two regions separately.

The present, relatively sound, state of Germany's party finance regulation is a result of the dramatic corruption cases that characterised the late 1990s involving both the CDU and the SPD parties. Helmut Kohl – chancellor from 1982 to 1998 – was applauded both inside and outside Germany for his triumph in integrating West and East Germany. François Mitterrand, president of France, became a key supporter of this project within Europe. One of the means of cementing this strengthened alliance was a sale of the Leuna oil refinery, in the former East Germany, to the French flagship company Elf Aquitaine, which was later found by a Parliamentary Committee to have facilitated a major commission paid to Kohl's CDU Party. However, more dangerous for Kohl at the time was an arms deal with Saudi Arabia involving the sale of 46 Thyssen tanks facilitated by Karlheinz Schreiber, a middleman. In this case, the prosecution service in Bavaria established that the CDU party treasurer had received a cash donation from Thyssen to arrange the government's support for the suspension of export control limitations on sales to zones of potential conflict. It later became clear that Schreiber had handed over DM 1 million in cash to the CDU Party treasurer, which was ultimately paid into secret accounts maintained by the CDU.[33] These accounts were revealed to be substantial and were DM 17 million by 2000. In 2000, the CDU was fined DM 41 million. By the time these events were exposed, Kohl had already left government and fought his case from the side-lines. The Committee of the Bundestag that investigated these cases in 2000 concluded:

> The CDU, under the leadership of Dr Kohl in the 1980s and 1990s, maintained an existing illegal party financing system and took further steps to conceal it. The establishment of a wide network of escrow accounts in Germany, Switzerland and Luxembourg under the cover of trustees and foundations in Liechtenstein, over which huge cash sums transited, is similar to practices more commonly seen in organised crime and money laundering.[34]

Although the SPD took power in 1998, its own ability to confront the issues of corruption in party finance was restricted by a scandal in Cologne, revealed the following year, surrounding the construction of a waste disposal plant at a cost of DM 820 million but which was associated with a 'backhander' to SPD party funds of DM 800,000 and a number of payments to individuals.[35]

The impact of these scandals, affecting both major parties, was the passing of a new law – the Political Parties Act – in 2004. The legislation avoided placing limits on total donations or expenditure both on a recurrent basis and in an election period, and did not ban donations from either companies or trade unions. It proposed a judicious expansion of public funding as a part of parties' budgets, but limited this to one-third of a party's income in total – with the remainder being raised from private sources. Whether as a result of the law itself or in response to the dramatic corruption cases of the late 1990s, transgressions have been relatively minor. For example, the right-wing party Alternative für Deutschland (AfD) initiated in 2014 a process of selling gold bars on line, with €1.5 million raised – a tactic that was deemed acceptable by the President of the

Bundestag who is also the electoral supervisor. Aggregate expenditure by all parties was large at €1.8 billion from 2006 to 2009, or €450 million per year,[36] and it remains to be seen whether those contributing these sums will seek the reward of 'influence' and on what scale.

It is a remarkable fact that two ex-presidents of France have been arrested on charges related to corruption since 2007. The charges against Jacques Chirac related to his time as mayor of Paris from 1977 to 1995, which was followed by his period as president from 1995 to 2007.[37] Chirac was found guilty in 2011 of diverting public funds and abusing public confidence; he was given a suspended sentence. The guilty verdict was passed in relation to the payment of salaries to 28 party activists as if they were staff members of the Paris municipality at a time when they were actually working for Chirac's party. The charges against ex-president Nicolas Sarkozy, a possible candidate for the presidency again in 2017, are more complex and have two strands. The first concerns his electoral campaign in 2012 when he was accused of having taken a €50 million donation from President Gaddafi of Libya despite the fact that foreign donations are illegal in France. Sarkozy was indicted for the 'illegal funding of political campaigns'. In 2014, it was found that Sarkozy's UMP had a hidden debt of €79.1 million, which indicated the need for the Gaddafi donation. In the second case he was accused of accepting cash payments from Liliane Bettencourt, the formidable heiress to a large part of the equity in the cosmetics company, L'Oréal. In a case that attracted huge interest in France, it was reported that the treasurer of Sarkozy's UNP Party received cash payments at the Bettencourt residence of €150,000 at a time. Although the case was ultimately dismissed, it was of sufficient concern to Sarkozy for him to request confidential information from a magistrate, Gilbert Azibert, about a wiretap on him placed by the police. Azibert was to be rewarded with a comfortable post in Monaco.[38]

At the constituency level, French electoral legislation bans all anonymous donations and, in fact, limits donations to €7,500 per year from any one donor, with provision for an additional €4,500 to candidates in an election year. However, there is no limit to funding and expenditure at the national level. Neither companies nor trade unions are allowed to contribute. These cases have exposed continued disregard by political parties of the spirit of the fairly comprehensive legal regulation of the electoral finance system, which has led to a failure to control corruption. This has certainly contributed to the disillusionment with the established parties in France.

UK: Bending the rules

Party funding in the UK has been controversial since the growth of organised formal parties in the mid-nineteenth century and the first limits on campaign expenditure at the constituency level were introduced in 1883.[39] Recurrent scandals have turned particularly on 'cash for honours' or appointment to the House of Lords, an upper chamber that retains powers of both review and postponement. However, a series of financial scandals under the Conservative government of John Major from 1990 to 1997 helped New Labour, led by Tony Blair, sweep to victory in 1997 and the new government vowed to reform campaign finance for the indefinite future.

Indeed the Political Parties, Elections and Referendums Act of 2000 was both well-intentioned and well-crafted, drawing heavily on Canadian legislative practice, then considered to be the best in the English-speaking world. In essence, this revised limits not only on campaign expenditure at the constituency level but also at the national level during the campaign itself, officially designated at five weeks, and establishing an Electoral Commission to supervise the process. It did not, however, limit total contributions or the size of individual donations, thus keeping open Labour's potential to raise huge sums from the trade unions, its traditional supporters. The national expenditure limit was initially set at £20 million for each registered party, adjusted to £27 million in 2015. However, by 2006, New Labour itself had found ways to circumvent this figure by borrowing from wealthy supporters loans that carried 'commercial' interest rates. In the course of 2006, 12 such supporters made loans totalling nearly £14 million, with uncertain repayment dates, a very significant contribution to the Labour Party's budget and one that undermined the objectives of the legislation of 2000. The lenders included four individuals[40] who were recommended by Prime Minister Blair for seats in the House of Lords, although the relevant Appointments Commission rejected these recommendations when the media got wind of the story. In spite of the assertions of disinterest by the lenders, the public was largely unconvinced.

Indeed this scepticism was heightened by the fact that in the same year the Conservative Party had borrowed a similar sum of £13.4 million, which included loans of £3.6 million and £2.5 million respectively from Lord Michael Ashcroft and Michael Hintze. Ashcroft was an entrepreneur with a financial empire based in Belize, where he was also a citizen and had been the ambassador of Belize to the UN from 1998 to 2000, the year in which he was made a member of the House of Lords.[41] Michael Hintze is a very successful financier who founded the CQS hedge fund and also sits on the board of the Vatican Bank. Not long after these borrowing arrangements for the Conservative Party became public, the UK's then third most significant party, the Liberal Democrats (winning 60 seats in the 2007 election) suffered a similarly ignominious revelation when it became clear that the party had accepted a donation of £2.4 million from Michael Brown, a businessman based in Malta who was shortly to be prosecuted for fraud. Although Brown was found guilty in 2008,[42] the party did not repay the donation. Thus, the decade after 2000 did nothing to reassure the British public that political finance was becoming cleaner, in spite of the new legislation.

These controversies attached to major contributions to any of the parties were probably a disincentive to many more modest potential contributors. As a consequence, the parties became increasingly dependent on a very small number of donors, originating for the Conservatives in the financial sector and for the Labour Party in the unions. Total expenditure by all parties in the formal five-week period of a UK election is roughly £80 million, with £50 million being spent by parties at the national level.[43] From 2005 to 2010, the biggest three donors to the Labour Party were the four unions (Unite, Unison, USDAW and the GMB) who collectively contributed £38 million; in the period from 2010 to 2015, the same four contributed £31.7 million.[44] In the case of the Conservatives, the top four donors contributed £14 million from 2005 to 2010 and £11.7 million from 2010 to 2015. Of the top 15 donations – worth a cumulative £23.7 million – 52 per cent came from individuals in the financial sector,[45] about twice the level for the 2005–10 period. None of the financial backers of the two parties did so without the intention of supporting a particular slate of policies. Donors from the City of London and the hedge fund industry clearly wanted the status of the City to be protected at a time when the regulatory framework for all financial institutions was being intensified both from the government of the UK and from the European Commission. The unions wanted to reverse the steady erosion of the strength of labour contracts, the reduced availability of pensions and to increase the level of the minimum wage. Reliance on an extremely small number of donors by each of the principal parties went along with parallel demands on policy outcomes.

This pattern of financial contributions confirmed the age-old practice of selling seats in the House of Lords in return for financial support. Public opinion has become increasingly hostile to appointments in the House of Lords that reflect financial support for any of the parties.

Italy: A web of favours

In the course of December 2014, the Italian police struck against mafia-type organisations in Calabria, Umbria and Rome. The first two of these were focused on the 'Ndrangheta and the third on a little-known group, 'June 29th', which had carved out a significant mafia-type role in Rome (including contracts for the management of camps for migrants). In Umbria, 62 suspects were arrested; in Calabria, the police mounted a 'dragnet' to catch associates of Giovanni Tegano, who four years earlier had been considered to be one of the most wanted mafia leaders in Italy; in Rome, the police arrested 46 suspects and placed 100 others under investigation. These included Gianni Alemanno, who had been mayor of Rome from 2008 to 2013 and was a political ally of Silvio Berlusconi and his Freedom Party. In Umbria, the police confiscated assets worth more than €30 million, apparently largely derived from the construction business. In Rome, 'June 29th' had been run by Massimo Carminati whose home was found to hold a stock €204 million in cash.

The Italian press laid bare the links between Mayor Alemanno, Carminati and his right-hand man, Salvatore Buzzi. Prime Minister Matteo Renzi (a former mayor of Florence) promised much tougher criminal measures against 'the corrupt' who would be 'forced to repay everything, right to the last cent'. In his photogenic style, and in rolled-up shirt sleeves, he commented 'The wind has changed'.[46] But the change he envisages may not be so dramatic and in fact Renzi's comments confirmed that one of Italy's longest standing problems – the links between various mafia groups, political fundraising and political power had not been severed.

The longstanding nature of these links is remarkable. Three of Italy's best-known post-World War II leaders have found themselves in court. Giulio Andreotti, seven times prime minister between 1972 and 1992, was charged not only with an 'association' with the Sicilian mafia but also with being an accomplice to the murder of the investigative journalist Carmine Pecorelli. His links with Sicily were born out of his need to strengthen his faction of the Christian Democrat Party following the election of 1989. He chose as an ally Salvo Lima, a former mayor of Palermo who was a fully-fledged

'man of honour' and who could deliver most of Sicily's 60 deputies[47] to support his faction of the Christian Democrats in Rome.
The dapper Lima continued to be a key supporter of Andreotti,
eventually becoming a member of the European Parliament. But
for Andreotti it was ultimately a dangerous link: Lima was shot
dead from a motorbike in March 1992, 12 days before Andreotti
himself was due to visit Palermo. Bettino Craxi, prime minister
from 1983 to 1987, was charged with raising funds for the Socialist
Party illegally (and in 1992 fled to Tunisia before a court sitting
could reach a verdict); and Silvio Berlusconi (three times prime
minister between 1994 and 2011) was represented in court more
than 30 times during these years on charges that included fraud,
bribery of senators and a relationship with the mafia.

One of the more remarkable ironies of the rise and fall of
Silvio Berlusconi is that his first and successful bid for the office of
prime minister in 1994 rested on a campaign to 'modernise' Italy
in the spirit of efficient business and in reaction to the corruption
uncovered in the '*manu polite*' campaign. Berlusconi could claim
that his experience in building a successful construction and media
business empire gave him and his Forza Italia party the credibility to clean up government. But in reality his strategy has been as
much to preserve his vast financial empire, already under pressure
in the early 1990s, as to dramatically increase its size. For much of
his time in national politics he remained chairman of Fininvest – a
sprawling holding company with ultimate control over three television channels – and was the owner of the AC Milan football
club. In fact his entry into national politics was to drag them to a
new low, but he remained either an elected deputy or senator for
19 years until 2013. In 2013, the national Court of Auditors was to
conclude that during Berlusconi's time in office, all political parties had raised a total of €2.2 billion from general taxation – or
€160 million per year – but that only €579 million could be verified, implying a net surplus to the parties that was not accounted
for of €1.67 billion.

During these years, the need to be regularly represented in court, whether as an elected deputy, senator or prime minister, became a one day per week assignment for Berlusconi. The more dramatic cases included those in which he was accused of bribing elected deputies in 1995 to wean them away from support of Romano Prodi and to bring down the government; of having a 'partnership' with the Cosa Nostra in Sicily; and of committing tax fraud. In relation to links with the mafia, the High Court of Palermo heard the case against Berlusconi and his close political associate Marcello Dell'Utri in 2004. Dell'Utri was awarded nine years in jail, sentences that were upheld in retrials culminating in the Supreme Court in 2014, but Berlusconi was acquitted. The Statute of Limitations (which defines a cut-off period for any court proceedings) also saved Berlusconi in most of the 30 cases that have dogged his premierships. But this successful and careful management of cases came to an end in 2013. In the tax fraud case of that year he was awarded a four-year jail sentence and required to pay €7.3 million in back taxes – a small sum for a multibillionaire. The jail sentence was soon modified by the courts to a one-day-a-week assignment to work with dementia patients in a care home near Berlusconi's palatial country residence. But he was nonetheless expelled from the Senate and for the first time since 1994 left without an elected position.

It is easy to think of Berlusconi's system as a unique conjunction of financial and political power enabling him in three administrations to run well ahead of his political opponents. This was true in the sense that his business empire was huge in relation to Italy's economy, and its dominance of the media gave it unique control over the public agenda. However, his rise was closely bound up with the other party leaders whose careers intertwined with his. For example, in the early 1980s, both Craxi and Giorgio Napolitano, Italy's president from 2006 to 2015, were politicians of the left, but the newspaper they founded – *Il Moderno* – was subsidised by the up-and-coming property magnate, Berlusconi. Craxi was prosecuted for acquiring political finance illegally as a result of the '*manu polite*' campaign – a condition for Berlusconi's success in 1994 – but had been the best man at Berlusconi's second marriage ceremony in 1990. Napolitano, ascending to the presidency of the Republic in 2006 granted both himself and Berlusconi immunity from prosecution in all cases while in office in 2008. Although this immunity was twice challenged in the courts and ultimately voided, it bought the old associates time to avoid any effective court action and ultimately to be saved by the Statute of Limitations.

Has this nexus of finance, politics and power been broken by the arrival of Beppe Grillo's Five Star Movement, sweeping up 25 per cent of the vote in 2013, or by the governments of Enrico Letta, elected in the same year, or Matteo Renzi, elected in 2014 with a technocratic edge? Renzi was mayor of Florence before being elected prime minister in 2013. His commitment to a new kind of politics – indicated in his response to the arrest of the 'June 29th' group in December 2014 – did not prevent him earlier in the year from entering a four-man conclave with Berlusconi[48] to develop a new electoral regime that was embodied in a new constitutional arrangement in 2015.

In Italy, the pattern of political funding has been geared particularly to the financial interests of the big donors but in different ways to, for example, the US and the UK. Mafia groups such as June 29th and the 'Ndrangheta have backed political parties who were willing to kickback contracts to them, especially in the construction sector. At the same time, Berlusconi's most consistent objective in politics has been to preserve his media empire and ensure that the numerous lawsuits it has faced are unsuccessful. But a constant thread in Italy's governments since the 1950s has been the reality of the continued effectiveness of organised crime and the need for the government in power to deal with it directly or indirectly. This is not 'machine politics' but the politics of two different kinds of business empires: in the case of the mafia, this represents blatant corruption; in the case of the Berlusconi empire, it represents the politics of private interest.

Spain: The 'Geneva connection'

In November 2014, Ana Mato, minister for health in the People's Party government of Mariano Rajoy, was forced to resign. She had been a star of the party, having first worked for Spain's future prime minister, José María Aznar, in 1987. Her ex-husband, Jesús Sepúlveda, had been the mayor of a suburb of Madrid, and was also an elected MP, but had become entangled in a construction industry scandal. In 2014, Mato had protested her innocence of the scandal for many months, even saying she was not aware that her ex-husband had been given a Jaguar car as a gift.[49] Their involvement in a major construction scandal was the tip of an iceberg.

The underlying reality was dramatic. The treasurer of the People's Party, Luis Bárcenas, had arranged to hold at least €22 million in foreign bank accounts, mainly in Switzerland.[50] These funds were in part derived from a continuous strategy of extracting money from construction projects in linked deals collectively known as 'Gürtel', and involving the regional governments of Madrid, Valencia and Castilla-La Mancha. It took the commitment of Judge Baltasar Garzón (whose crusading prosecutions led to his forced resignation in 2010) to begin to crack the Gürtel story, leading to a prosecution pursued by High Court Judge Pablo Ruiz and brought to trial in 2009. Over more than ten years, a wealthy construction entrepreneur, Francisco Correa, had initiated deals that ensured a pay-off for the People's Party, sometimes completely changing the rationale for the project and switching subsidised housing schemes into projects designed for the wealthy middle class. A significant part of the funds that had been skimmed were also held in Switzerland. The prosecution found that Correa's network included six regional governments and 200 official suspects. In January 2015, the Anti-Corruption Attorney General's Office sought a prison sentence of 123 years for Correa and 42 years for Bárcenas. A total of 41 defendants faced up to a possible 800 years in prison.

In 2014 the Spanish public had come to grips with the fact that the democracy launched in 1978 was riddled with corruption and that all parties had used corrupt funds to finance their quest for power. A report issued in January 2015 by Olayo González Soler, chief prosecutor of Spain's Court of Auditors, found that in 2012 all parties had 'committed tax fraud and other financial crimes'.[51] The conservative People's Party had €1.3 million undeclared and, according to the chief prosecutor, 'may have received' €8 million in illegal donations since 1995. The Socialist Workers' Party had loaned €4.4 million to its associated foundations, which would otherwise be bankrupt. The Democratic Convergence of Catalonia had shown an income of €1.7 million for services that it had not provided, and the Basque National Party failed to report €4.9 million in income.

The political consequences of this were real. In the general election of 2015, Podemos, frequently described as an 'anti-corruption' party, won 20 per cent of the vote, capitalising on a full-scale reaction against the corruption of Spanish politics. One of its more remarkable recruits was the 88-year-old former national anti-corruption public prosecutor, Carlos Jiménez Villarejo, who was successfully elected together with four other Podemos candidates to the European Parliament in May 2014. He focused his campaign on disgust with the failure of the judiciary to bring to court more than 500 of a total 2,000 judicial investigations of corruption-related cases, pointing out that only 15 of these had led to a jail sentence. However, by late 2015, the public prosecutor had initiated cases against 40 members of the People's Party on charges of fraud and corruption, armed with strong evidence.

By 2014 the country's new found penchant for addressing corruption had reached two other leading lights in Spanish life. First, the husband of Princess Cristina (sister of King Felipe VI) was charged in 2014 with responsibility for corruptly gaining contracts at a sports foundation that he managed. Second, Rodrigo Rato, once a highflying minister of finance for the People's Party, later managing director of the International Monetary Fund and finally CEO of a leading Spanish bank, Bankia, was charged with 'alleged fraud, concealment of assets and money laundering'. Bankia, which was a recent amalgam of six regional savings banks, had close links to the People's Party and had to be bailed out in 2012 within two years of its formation.

In Spain the intermingling of political goals and private financial gain were laid bare, and the public had grown increasingly disillusioned with this toxic mix. However, in the general election of December 2015, in a close-fought election, the People's Party attracted more votes than any other party, but not enough to form a government, suggesting that the Spanish public could decry corruption and yet vote for the party that appeared to have reversed the country's ailing economy.

The characteristic of political finance in Western Europe is now one of a system under threat and one where both subtle and unsubtle forms of corruption are pervasive. The spectrum is wide, ranging from the dominance of narrow interest groups in the UK, to the criminal infringement of electoral regulations in France, to the use of foreign bank accounts in Spain, to the continued proximity between politics and mafia groups in Italy. Of the larger countries, only Germany, scarred by the corruption scandals of the late 1990s, has succeeded in building what for the time being appears to be a political finance system free of corruption, which is nonetheless exposed to the US-style dangers of avoiding limits on total expenditure.

Central and Eastern Europe

The withdrawal of the Soviet umbrella from Eastern Europe in 1989 generated the highest of hopes yet held for the future of 'liberal democracy' as developed in Western Europe and the US. The distinguished historian Francis Fukuyama in his book *The End of History and the Last Man* argued that humanity had reached 'the end point of mankind's ideological evolution and the universalization of Western liberal democracy as the final form of human government'.[52] Not only did this view have wide support but it also galvanised activity from the 'West' to promote liberal democracy wherever the one-party state dissolved in the post-Soviet world. As a consequence, the nature of electoral systems and the rules and mechanisms that underpinned them became the subject of both debate and experiment in Central and Eastern Europe.

The bodies active in this process included the Organization for Security and Co-operation in Europe (OSCE), the Council of Europe and the European Union. Meeting in Copenhagen in 1990, the OSCE issued the 'Copenhagen Document', which stated 'there must be a clear separation between the state and political parties; in particular, political parties will not be merged with the state'.[53] On paper, the stage was set for electoral regimes that would enable both small and large parties to compete on a fair basis. By 1993, the Council of Europe stepped in with detailed recommendations on how to avoid corruption in the electoral process including proposed rules on caps on expenditure, and limits to corporate financing.[54] Versions of these rules were widely adopted in Central and Eastern Europe and at a minimum banned both foreign and anonymous contributions, and in most cases introduced caps on campaign expenditure. In a world where mass membership of a party (other than the Communist Party) was not an established practice, the principle of public funding of campaigns by the state was widely accepted.

Routes to these ends differed. For instance, the Czech Republic never introduced caps on expenditure or contributions but provides public subsidies. Slovenia and Hungary have both public funding and unlimited contributions but limits on expenditure. There are few limits on the size of corporate donations except in Poland and Bulgaria. But overall the ex-Soviet group who joined the EU in 2004 and 2007 adopted a regulatory system that was advanced by world standards.

However, in the years of the new century – and especially since 2010 – the process of electoral politics has been undermined in several countries. This is the result either of the infusion of large sums of finance that escape regulation, or manipulation of the whole state system to sustain the interests of the regime in power. In relation to the funding issue: in an analysis of the 2014/15 election campaign, the not-for-profit Transparency International Hungary estimated that total expenditure by all four parties had been 11 billion florins (or $39 million), at a time when the limit per party was 995 million florins ($3.6 million) indicating a total permitted spend for the four principal parties of $14.6 million. Within this total, a number of smaller parties were awarded a total of 4.2 billion florins in state support but recorded a spend of only 320 million florins.[55] The difference was never explained, despite protests from civil society.

These figures do not capture the underlying forces that have shaped outcomes in, for example, Hungary, the Czech Republic and Poland, where forms of institutional corruption have undermined the promises of the 1990s. The most dramatic example of this is Hungary, where since his election to the presidency in 2010, Viktor Orbán and his party, Fidesz, have sought to move away from a liberal parliamentary system, reflected in the new constitution that was introduced in 2011, to an openly more authoritarian one. In a public speech in 2014, Orbán said:

> The new state that we are constructing in Hungary is an illiberal state, a non liberal state. It does not reject the fundamental principles of liberalism such as freedom… but it does not make this ideology the central element of state organisation, and instead includes a different, special, national approach.[56]

This has been reflected in a number of steps taken by the Fidesz government including the appointment to the courts of magistrates and judges who support the party. In 2011, the government cleared the way to sue no less than three former prime ministers who have been charged with 'criminal mismanagement of the economy'[57] (a tactic that failed). Alongside this went a shift in the control of the economy – particularly in relation to the media, the banks and telecoms – back towards either the state or handpicked oligarchs.

There are some similarities with the Czech Republic. At the time when the Czech Republic's second president, Václav Klaus, left office in 2013 he gave an amnesty to 6,000 prisoners in jail, a significant number of whom had been jailed on charges of embezzlement and fraud and some of whom were former MPs. The public's shocked response to this apparently high tolerance of corruption was reinforced under the newly elected government, which fell victim to indiscretions by its prime minister, Petr Nečas, in a saga involving his girlfriend and ex-wife. Nečas and some close associates were arrested but the charges were later withdrawn on grounds of parliamentary immunity.[58]

The public disillusionment underlying this story led to the election of Miloš Zeman as Czech president in 2013 and a regime in which the super-wealthy further strengthened their position. The most remarkable example of this was the rise to political power of the business magnate Andrej Babiš, reputed to be the second wealthiest individual in the country. Babiš has skilfully used control of the media group MAFRA to boost the party he founded in 2011 (ANO) and propel it to take nearly 20 per cent of the vote in the national elections of 2013. From this position of strength he was appointed finance minister and deputy prime minister in 2014, creating the sense of a regime in which wealth was very close to power and able to determine policy outcomes.

In 2016, the Hungarian 'model' is proving popular with the Law and Justice government in Poland. The party, whose effective leader is Jarosław Kaczyński, won power in the election of October 2015 and quickly asserted control over both the Constitutional Court and the publicly funded media. In spite of massive opposition on the streets, occurring within only three months of the election, it clearly intended to consolidate its power for the long term. In these national contexts, the electoral process will be skewed in favour of the incumbent party not only by its ability to access financial resources originating from the state but also by their control of media and the justice system. This is a different and potentially more complex kind of control than that which is manifested by political finance in the older established democracies of western Europe.

In each of the cases in America and Europe discussed here, there are powerful forces behind the electoral system that under-mine the extent to which they can be called 'democratic'. The fram-ers of the American Constitution were the most conscious of the danger of 'capture' of the system, the outcome of which some of them had observed in Britain or experienced from afar. Yet the controversy in the US about the extent of 'capture' by individual and corporate interest groups has never been more intense than it is today. In Italy the three constitutions that have been in place since World War II have failed to overcome the close links between apparently democratically elected governments and, on the one hand, business interests and, on the other, organised crime. In Spain, the most recent recruit to democracy in Western Europe, the power of corrupt money in party finance, has been exposed as a huge problem. In the UK, the extremely close links between the Conservative Party and financial interests in the City of London and the Labour Party and only four trade unions are occasionally publicly recognised, but are very far from the spirit of the last major change in electoral legislation in 2000. These types of party financ-ing may be characterised as the 'buying of influence and the selling of power', and pave the way for a hyperactive lobbying industry on both sides of the Atlantic, as Chapter 3 will discuss.

3

The Power of the Lobby

In the mid-1870s, President Ulysses S. Grant, hero and successful commander of the Unionist army in the Civil War, sat most afternoons in the lobby of the Willard Hotel in Washington, DC, and received citizens acting for themselves or others who wished to gain his support for their cause. Grant's dark beard and continuous cigar chomping made it difficult for citizens with a mission to establish whether their case had been recognised or rejected. Either way, the location of the interviews meant that citizens of any description seeking to influence government were to be described as 'lobbyists', a description that has survived for more than 150 years.[1] Successful lobbying ensures that private interests obscure the public interest. While it is true that in a democracy any citizen has the right to try to influence policy, in practice lobbying in both the US and the EU often embodies the impact of a small interest group on overall public policy that subverts or excludes the interest of the broader public. One of the key framers of the US Constitution, James Madison, consistently argued that a functioning democracy must avoid being manipulated by 'factions' that were able to manipulate both legislature and executive into supporting the interests of a minority. However, the current lobbying system, in spite of serious attempts at reform, confirms that danger, both in the US and the EU. This is indeed the corruption of influence.

In the US, lobbying is closely linked to campaign finance and the 12,000 lobbyists based in Washington, DC often combine the role of raising campaign finance with campaigning on policy; in the EU this link is much weaker but a similar number of lobbyists are kept busy pressurising the EU Commission (its executive), the powerful Council of Ministers and the European Parliament (with 751 elected members). In the case of the EU, lobbyists have undoubtedly had a major impact on policy outcomes. In the context of both the US and the EU, lobbyists have been particularly successful in resisting tougher regulation of aspects of banking, environmental measures related to climate change, and food safety.

United States

In Washington, since the 1970s, the scale of this industry has made it a byword for corruption. In addition to the registered lobbyists, in 2014 there were many engaged in political advocacy who were unregistered, suggesting a total figure of lobbyists and staff of 100,000. Lobbyists may work in-house for large corporations or for industry associations, or be hired by individual companies. This line of business is made profitable by the 90 per cent of public companies that rely on lobbyists, including industry associations, to pursue their interests. In 2009, the total recorded expenditure of registered lobbyists was $3.49 billion – a figure that excludes campaign contributions. The leading analyst of lobbying expenditure, Professor James A. Thurber of American University, estimates that the actual level of expenditure is closer to $9 billion – or about $12.5 million for each member of Congress. These figures include expenditure by citizen groups functioning as lobbyists such as the National Rifle Association, the Planned Parenthood Association and the Sierra Club.

The lobbying industry often makes use of the revolving door principle: the roll call of today's lobbyists often confirms their past experience as senators and congressmen. More than 50 per cent of those who leave elected office subsequently join or launch lobbying businesses, where they earn a huge premium over their congressional salaries, a fact that may even have become an incentive to run for Congress. The Center for Responsive Politics has identified 3,000 people whose careers have moved between Congress and the lobbying industry. Given the two-year term that members of Congress serve and the high electoral turnover, this tendency is not surprising.

The biggest 'investors' in lobbying, as shown in Chapter 2, are large companies who stand to benefit from the weakening of regulatory policies and the budgetary process. The biggest spenders by sector are the large pharmaceutical companies who collectively spent $228 million on lobbying in 2010, $8 million on campaign expenditure and $100 million on 'issue' advertising through PACs.

A detailed analysis by the Sunlight Foundation covering the years 2007–12 estimated the financial benefits that the biggest corporate investors in lobbying linked to campaign contributions had achieved. Table 1, on the next page, shows the result for the top ten companies. The right-hand column shows taxes paid net of contracts and concessions awarded to the company. The figures show that all of these ten companies (and in fact a further 190) have directly benefited from both their political contributions and from very low tax rates. Their funds have bought not only influence but also policy outcomes, which work to their direct advantage at the expense of policy designed only for the public good.

The benefits of effective lobbying go beyond these financial gains. An analysis of the factors that make lobbying a good corporate investment confirms that:[2]

Table 1   Top ten political contributions, lobbying costs and impact (2007–12)

	Political contributions ($M)[a]	Lobbying costs ($M)[b]	Total costs ($M)	Total federal contracts and support ($M)[c]	Effective tax
Goldman Sachs	16.5	21.4	38	229.4	23
Bank of America	12.6	32.6	45.2	476.2	n.a.
AT&T	12.4	99.4	111.9	3.8	6
Deloitte LLP	9.1	15.1	24.2	51.2	n.a.
Lockheed Martin	8.6	84.1	92.7	332	18
Boeing	8.2	95.5	103.7	355.6	2
Price Waterhouse Coopers	7.8	15.9	23.7	1279.7	n.a.
GE	7.6	151.5	159.1	43.1	9
Koch Industries	6.4	64.5	70.9	51.3	n.a.
Ernst & Young	6.2	13.6	19.9	682.5	n.a.

Source: Influence Explorer, Sunlight Foundation and Open Secrets, Washington DC, 2015
[a] to PACs and individual candidates
[b] disclosed spending on federal lobbying
[c] contracts awarded by or through Federal government and support to businees through loans and grants post financial crisis of 2007/8.

- The more firms lobby, the lower their effective tax rate.
- Compared to non-lobbying firms, companies that lobby are substantially less likely to be detected for fraud.
- Stock markets reward companies with politically connected board members when the party they are connected to is in power.
- Lobbying has a positive effect on the firm's equity returns relative to the market, and to a lesser degree relative to its industry.

The most powerful and public critic of the lobbying system in recent years has been President Obama himself. As a senator, paired with his later electoral rival John McCain, he introduced to

Congress in 2006 the Honest Leadership and Open Government Act (HLOGA), which was intended to curtail the lobbying industry by increasing transparency (through a register of activity) and to limit gifts to congressmen and senators. Apart from outlawing small gifts and lifestyle benefits – such as glitzy restaurant meals – the Act heightened requirements to record meetings between lobbyists and officials and elected congressmen. In addition, it lengthened the period to two years during which retiring senators could not be employed by a company and to one year for their retiring staff, the so-called 'cooling-off period'. The Act achieved a kind of success in that it led to the deregistration of a large number of lobbyists with recorded formal expenditure falling from $3.5 billion in 2010 to $3.2 billion in 2013.

President Obama sustained his commitment in his 2010 campaign, making an open promise:

> I intend to tell the corporate lobbyists that their days of setting the agendas in Washington are over, that they had not funded my campaigns, and from my first day as President, I will launch the most sweeping ethics reform in US history. We will make government more open, more accountable and more responsive to the problems of the American people.[3]

In practice, however, President Obama did not succeed in this objective in spite of making a strong start in 2008 when he issued a series of instructions designed to keep former lobbyists out of his administration. He appointed a well-known lobby reformer – Norm Eisen – to head this process, making him 'special counsel to the president for ethics and government'. This empowered the president to issue a series of executive orders with the unifying objective of both removing tools from lobbyists and increasing transparency in general. But these measures were ultimately undermined by a number of exceptions. First, Obama used a waiver on the employment of a specific ex-lobbyist – William

Lynn – as deputy secretary of defence. Second and more importantly, the president's heavy legislative agenda, of which the Medicare Bill was a crucial part, required the assembly of a large contingent of supporters in and out of Congress, of which lobbyists proved to be an integral part. The Sunlight Foundation found that the president and senior aides had worked particularly closely with lobbyists who were employed by the medical insurance and pharmaceutical industries, in support of what became known as 'Obamacare', and those employed by the banking and finance industry in shaping measures designed to regulate finance. In this way, the interests of the corporate sector were very well represented and Obama's enthusiasm for James Madison's determination that 'factions' should not dominate the political process proved to have a very short life.

The cases of several individuals in 2014 and 2015 show the resilience of the lobbying process and throw a light on the revolving door syndrome and its link to lobbying. Although in these cases there is not necessarily a proven link between their new work and their elected responsibilities, there is a clear infringement of the rules in relation to the cooling-off period and the individuals' move from regulating or policymaking to a (potential) lobbying position. This is a particularly acute issue when the law firms concerned become active drafters of legislation.

Kay Bailey Hutchison was a Republican senator for Texas from 1993 to 2013. She did not run in 2013 and her seat was taken by later presidential candidate Ted Cruz. When in the Senate, she had sat on committees that dealt with both defence and transportation and had been chairman of the Military Construction Appropriations Sub-Committee, a useful asset to future employers. Her 'cooling-off period' (in which she should not take lobbying employment) should have lasted until January 2015, but within a month of departure from the Senate she became a senior counsel at Bracewell & Giuliani, a powerful legal company with interests in the energy and defence sectors.

Republican Senator Jon Kyl (representing Arizona in the Senate from 1995 to 2013 and who was ultimately Senate minority whip) joined the law firm Covington & Burling within two months of leaving the Senate. In 2010, Kyl was listed by *Time* magazine as among the 100 most influential people in the world. While in the Senate, he had been a sponsor of the Unlawful Internet Gambling Enforcement Act in 2006, which banned internet-based gambling and was strongly supported by gambling interests in Nevada, particularly by Sheldon Adelson, a major contributor to Republican causes.

One of the key characteristics of the revolving door syndrome is the relationship between chiefs of staff and their congressmen or senators, since it may be the staff rather than the politicians who move on to lobbying companies. Robert Wittman, a Republican representative for Virginia, was a co-sponsor of the National Defense Authorization Act of 2013 and had been chairman of the Subcommittee on Readiness. Immediately after the Bill was passed, Wittman's chief of staff, Mary Springer, left to head the legislative affairs department at DRS Technologies (a subsidiary of Finmeccanica, the major Italian defence company), and registered as a lobbyist well within the proposed 'cooling-off period' of one year. She was quickly able to facilitate a modest contribution of $4,500 to Wittman's campaign chest from a PAC established by DRS. Ties between Wittman and the defence industry proved useful more broadly: in 2014 his campaign committee collected $221,000 from the defence sector, or about 20 per cent of his campaign fundraising. In this case, the links between the legislative process, the lobbying company and campaign finance are particularly clear.

The follow-up to the reforms to the lobbying process proposed by Obama and McCain in 2006 have been disappointing. Lobbying has proved to be so deeply ingrained in the system, and so well defended by lobbyists, their clients and many congressional representatives, that the prospects for change appear very limited. The current situation is one in which individual pieces of legislation have become increasingly complex, with some Acts running over 1,000 pages of legal text, partly because the political system has allowed lobbyists to insert an ever-larger number of clauses into individual bills. At the same time, partly because of congressional limits on the size of the Federal Civil Service, the ability of government departments to write very complex legislation is also limited. Thus lobbyists have secured steadily increasing influence, which even a president committed to reducing the power of the lobby proved unable to roll back. This is indeed the corruption of influence.

European Union

The key distinction between the lobbying industry in the US and the European Union is that in the EU, at the level of the EU Parliament, there is a much weaker link between lobbying and campaign finance, as most political campaigns are to a large extent funded by political parties with the support of public funding for this cause. However, the lobbying industry in Europe is very active and works through three modes: first, associations of small to medium-sized companies (who would find it expensive to lobby on their own); second, small groups of major companies (in, for example, aerospace or energy), or individual companies, who may be represented at CEO level; and third, think tanks that may in fact be funded to develop corporate-friendly policy. Any of these may lobby with in-house personnel or employ specialist lobbying companies. To be effective, the activity has to cascade through each of the EU's institutions, including the Parliament, and in many cases be followed up at the national level. The EU's current institutional structure (with the European Parliament as the lawmaking body that is directly elected by the EU's citizens, and the European Commission as the EU's executive that proposes and enforces legislation[4]) was finalised in the Lisbon Treaty of 2007. The lobbying industry has grown up in its present form since then, but for much of this time has been unregulated. In 2011, a 'voluntary' register of those lobbying the Commission and the Parliament was established. In 2015, the European Commission decreed that its staff could only meet with lobbyists already on the register, and Jean-Claude Juncker, president of the Commission, stated that he may propose making registration a legal requirement.

However, given the fact that national parliaments retain shared and exclusive powers, lobbying at the national level is of equal importance. Lobbying at the level of the 27 member countries takes many different forms. In cases such as the UK and Germany, it is a highly organised 'industry' in which most, but not all players are registered, and civil servants and elected politicians are obliged to record contact with its members. In other cases – ranging from Spain to Italy to Hungary – there is very little regulation. In the case of Hungary where the ruling Fidesz Party is in an extremely dominant position, the lobbying process is absorbed into the oligarchy close to the Prime Minister Viktor Orbán. In 2015, Transparency International undertook an assessment of the various controls on the lobbying industry within 19 countries of the EU and in Brussels and graded them according to the three criteria of transparency, integrity and equality of access. According to the research, the Commission and the Parliament were regarded as more transparent than equivalent institutions in the member states.

The current regulatory framework of the EU is inadequate to provide useful monitoring of the pressures that business and other interest groups can bring to bear to secure an outcome that meets private interests but is not necessarily in line with public interests. Many such business interest groups are well-funded: in 2012, the pharmaceutical industry spent €40 million on lobbying, and in 2013 the financial lobby spent a total of €120 million, deploying an impressive total of 1,700 lobbyists.

In 2014, the European Union set up a *Transparency Register*, which is designed to record all the lobbyists and to record meetings

Table 2   Breakdown of EU lobbyists by type

Professional consultancies	1,125
In-house lobbyists and trade associations	4,800
NGOs	2,430
Think tanks, academic institutions	677
Religious organisations	40
Local and regional governments	450
TOTAL	9,522

with all senior executives of the Commissions, and with all MEPs. This *Transparency Register* has made it much easier to measure the size of the industry. The participants in 2016 were categorised by the *Register* as shown in Table 2.[5]

The table shows that the largest number of lobbyists are in-house lobbyists within companies, as well as in companies' respective trade associations. Within this field, the largest number of companies are attributed to Germany, France and the UK (380, 294 and 292 respectively), although the fourth largest source was the US with 173.[6]

Success or failure in lobbying in Brussels is heavily influenced by the ability of interested parties (companies, trade associations and NGOs) to participate in the work of the 'public consultation groups' and 'expert committees' that determine the formative phase of new policies and initiatives. In the following section, we discuss how this manifested itself in banking, tobacco, food safety and health, red tape and deregulation, and climate change and the environment.

Banking

The consequences of the banking crisis of 2007/8 hit Europe in full about a year after it hit the US, but with equally grave results from which the economies of the EU have taken even longer to recover. The push for tougher legislation and regulation that arose from the financial crisis created an intense round of debate and lobbying in both the US and Europe. In response, the banks on both side of the Atlantic have been very active in lobbying to restrict regulation to a minimal level or to be less demanding (for example, in increasing capital requirements) than those recommended for all banks by the Basel Committee on Banking Supervision and known as Basel I, II and III. Steps taken to reduce the effectiveness of the UK's regulatory regime by the UK's then chancellor of the exchequer, George Osborne, in late 2015 and early 2016 showed how successful this pressure could be (as discussed in Chapter 5).

The key to the financial sector's lobbying power is its successful dominance of public consultation groups. This dominance was not necessarily a new development: in fact pre-crisis EU banking legislation had been developed by similarly banking-dominated committees. So, as in the US, the banks (and in many cases the same banks) were writing their own regulations. These groups operated in parallel to formal and informal groups liaising with the Parliament, the most notable being the European Parliament Financial Services Forum, whose membership is published in the *Transparency Register*.

In a review of 17 public consultations dealing with the financial sector, the lobby analysts AlterEU found that of 906 participants, 55 per cent came from the financial industry, 12 per cent from other industries and 13 per cent from trade unions, NGOs and consumer associations. The detailed technical knowledge of the representatives from the banking industry was obviously huge. Not surprisingly it meant that out of a total 1,700 amendments to an EU directive on hedge funds, 900 were actually written by lobbyists who had been active in these committees.

Of course banks and finance houses based in London had to be equally effective in lobbying the UK government. A detailed analysis of the strength of the London financial lobby carried out by the Bureau of Investigative Journalism in 2013 estimated that total expenditure by in-house and external lobbyists was £93 million. The two largest spenders were the City of London Corporation and the aggregate of City law firms, each at £10 million; the Association for Financial Markets in Europe were close behind at £8.9 million and the British Bankers' Association (BBA) at £5.6 million. These are very large sums that are likely to go some way to explaining the marked softening of the UK government on the nature of financial regulation in 2015 as discussed in Chapter 5.

Tobacco

US experience confirms that the tobacco industry – anxious to deny any ill-effects from smoking – has been one of the most powerful lobby groups in recent history. Nonetheless it was obliged to pay out $200 billion in 1998 to victims of lung cancer and other smoking-related conditions. The industry's lobbyists, often representing the same companies, have been equally busy in Europe. A central issue, which the European Commission sought to promote in 2010, has been plain paper packaging for cigarette cartons and a ban on cigarette advertising in retail shops. In order to explore this strategy, the Commission employed the RAND Corporation, a well-respected American not-for-profit think tank with close ties to the military and the corporate world. The resulting RAND report concluded that 650,000 premature deaths in the EU can be attributed to smoking, and that a ban on all forms of tobacco promotion in shops would have an impact on reducing these numbers.

In response to the possibly disastrous effect on their sales of measures of this kind, the Confederation of European Community Cigarette Manufacturers (CECCM) proceeded to hire Professor John Klick from the University of Pennsylvania to review the RAND report. Amazingly, he recommended that it should be 'ignored in its entirety'. The trade body also argued that there was not enough space on cigarette packages to contain the relevant health warnings. Even the International Chamber of Commerce weighed in and argued that the reduced exposure of the manufacturer's name would be an incentive to counterfeit production. The CECCM campaign was partly successful: in 2012 the Commission introduced new proposals that abandoned plain packaging and recommended that branding could occupy 30 per cent of the package, finally increased to 35 per cent in a Directive issued in 2014.

Food safety and health

Issues that are scientifically complex, but with important commercial implications, provide a potential golden opportunity for sophisticated lobbying. One such area relates to a group of chemicals designated as 'endocrine disrupting', which can have a major impact on the human and animal hormone system. They are active in a wide range of consumer products ranging from food to containers for processed food to pesticides, and can be identified as playing a role in the origins of diseases such as prostrate, breast and testicular cancers, infertility, diabetes and obesity. In 2012, the Commission's Directorate for the Environment, which is effectively the EU's Department (or Ministry) for the Environment, received an expert report,[7] which concluded that it was not possible to define a level of use of endocrine disrupting chemicals (EDCs) that was safe. This finding would put the chemicals in the category of 'threshold drugs', implying they could only be used in restricted quantities. In 2013, this conclusion was supported by a joint report from the World Health Organization (WHO) and the United Nations Environment Programme (UNEP), which concluded that EDCs were a major threat to public health that needed to be resolved. The consequent proposal from the EU's Environment Directorate was that EDCs should be regulated on the basis that there was no 'safe threshold' below which EDCs could be used as food additives or in containers of processed food.

This potential conclusion incited a strong negative response from European agribusiness and food processing industries. Combined, the industry chose the sophisticated strategy of mobilising 56 scientists to write to the chief scientific adviser to the President of the Commission, and placing an editorial in July 2013 (with 18 signatures) in *Altex*, a scientific online journal devoted to toxicology. The editorial was later reproduced in 14 specialist journals. In both cases, the message was that it was perfectly possible to define an acceptable threshold for EDCs. This resistance was soon to be ratcheted up: it emerged as a 'trade barrier' in the talks leading the way to the proposed Transatlantic Trade and Investment Partnership (TTIP). The US Department of Trade specifically singled out the regulation of EDCs as a trade barrier to be removed through the TTIP negotiations. The Commission then fell into a stalemate caused by conflict between its relevant directorates, only to find itself sued by the Swedish government, which brought a case against it in March 2014 for 'failure to act' to ban EDCs, which – equally surprisingly – was supported by 21 member states. At the time of writing, it is clear that the lobby has succeeded in an indefinite postponement of any decision characterising a description of EDCs as threshold drugs – or at least until the TTIP negotiations are completed. This was a clear case in which corporate interests undermined a widely accepted definition of the public interest.

'Red tape' and 'deregulation'

One lobbying objective, initiated in 2013/14, has been a crusade to cut 'red tape' – EU regulations that may be described as impeding the free play of market forces. The push for this came from two ad hoc groups set up by the EU, firstly the High Level Group on Administrative Burdens chaired by Edmund Stoiber (a former minister president of Bavaria) and secondly, REFIT or the Commission's Regulatory Fitness and Performance Programme, which, according to then Commission President José Manuel Barroso, was intended to make EU law lighter, simpler and less costly.[8]

Stoiber's group was set up in 2007 and was given three terms that lasted until 2014. Its recommendations focused more on process than on content, identifying ways in which businesses could be more involved in consultative processes – implying that this is not already the case in 'expert groups'. Notably, the group suggested exempting small and medium-sized enterprises (SMEs) from all EU regulations. The latter recommendation is extraordinary since the EU's definition of SMEs excludes all companies with a turnover of less than €50 million or having less than 250 employees. The employment criterion would have excluded two-thirds of EU companies from relevant regulation but did not pass.

A close examination of the membership of the REFIT Stoiber group indicates that throughout its existence it was dominated by representatives of the agribusiness lobby Copa-Cogeca, Polish business lobby Lewiatan (particularly active in the corporate association Business Europe), executives from former technology giant Invensys, coffee conglomerate Illy and a clean coal lobby group, the Carbon Capture and Storage Association. More dramatically, it became clear that Edmund Stoiber himself was a paid consultant to audit and consulting group Deloitte, and had been chair of its German advisory committee at the same time as chairing the group. The work of REFIT received a boost at a meeting of the European Council[9] in October 2013. At the meeting, the UK's Prime Minister David Cameron produced a report entitled *Cut EU Red Tape*, which was not so much a recommendation to reduce red tape as to further roll back existing regulations emanating from the Commission. Remarkably enough, the measures that

Cameron proposed to roll back included soil protection, maternity leave and a regulatory approach on fracking (substituting voluntary corporate guidelines for compulsory ones). By June 2014, the Commission announced that 53 existing legislative initiatives would be scrapped (of which nine had been identified by REFIT). The distinguishing characteristic of these measures has been that the working groups behind them have been dominated by business representatives. In addition, the revisions have not been submitted to the European Parliament or to a wider category of stakeholders. In the course of this, the democratic process has been trumped by business-dominated edicts.

Climate change and the environment

There is no more important strategic issue for the EU than climate change. To resist initiatives designed to mitigate climate change, corporates with a big interest in fossil fuels have been very active in the EU, as in the US. In considering basic policy for the control of carbon emissions, the main corporate lobby – working particularly through the European Petroleum Industry Association (EUROPIA) – was successful in fighting the restriction of carbon emissions to levels prevailing in 2003. The alternative was a 'carbon trading emissions scheme' that enabled companies to increase their carbon output provided that they purchased additional 'rights to pollute' from a market to be established by the EU Commission itself. Any output that exceeded an allocated quota could be purchased at €40 per ton. There were a series of errors committed in setting up this market including a far too generous allocation of initial quotas, which led to a steady fall in the price. The errors included the Czech deal, discussed in Chapter 10, in which 70 per cent of permits were distributed outside the scheme. At the time of writing, the market price stands at €8 per ton, hardly a punitive charge on a wealthy corporate polluter.

Two key issues now on the policymaking agenda include the regulation of fuel quality (and the emissions it generates) and the 'fracking' of oil and gas.

The first issue is determined by the Fuel Quality Directive (FQD) the first of which was issued in 2009 with the objective of reducing the carbon intensity of transport fuels by 6 per cent between 2010 and 2020. By 2011, the more widespread availability of 'unconventional' fuels such as coal-to-liquid, tar sands (from Canada) or oil shale from fracking made these definitions more complex. The Commission then sought to categorise all fuels according to the source from which they were produced and assigned to each a particular greenhouse gas value. However, this approach has met very strong resistance from the major oil companies for whom alternatives to extracting oil, like coal-to-liquid, tar sands and fracking have become more important. Oil extracted from the tar sands of Alberta in Canada is the prime example, since its capacity to emit CO_2 is 23 per cent higher than most other oils. Its successful exploitation depends on its partial export to Europe. A consequence of this and the huge increase in the output from fracking is that the EU Commission has been under enormous corporate pressure, notably from the investors in the Gulf Coast facilities, to homogenise the FQD and abandon descriptions based on the origin of the fuel. This position has been heightened in the TTIP negotiations in which the US side has argued that there should be one 'intensity value' for all imported oil – a position that even members of the US Congress have resisted, expressing concern in July 2014 that 'trade and investment rules may be being used to undermine or threaten important climate policies of other nations'. In early 2016, the issue remains on the TTIP negotiating agenda and is unresolved.

The shale gas revolution in the US has transformed the cost of energy supplies contributing to a fall in the market price of traded oil from 80 cents per barrel in 2000 to 40 cents per barrel in early 2016, although in very volatile conditions. The technique underlying the shale gas revolution, known as fracking or the 'hydraulic fracturing of natural gas reserves', has developed amid major controversy in the US with stringent criticism from many groups concerned with the potential environmental impact of fracking on local communities, as well as contradictory messages from the national Environmental Protection Agency (EPA). By early 2016, the EPA still had to produce its first announced assessment of the environmental consequences of fracking.

Although the potential for fracking in Europe, measured by reserves, is not as widespread as in the US – and is further limited by population density – there has been a big push from the oil majors to legitimise the process in Europe, and considerable debate about whether this is a partial solution to Europe's energy deficit. A reasonable response from the EU would be the introduction of a regulatory framework that would include independent environmental impact assessments (EIAs) of any proposed drilling operation. Although under intense discussion in 2013/14, this has been resisted by the major energy companies working through several lobby groups – notably Shale Gas Europe, Business Europe (which has a wide range of concerns) and the Europe Energy Forum, which focuses on members of the European Parliament (MEPs). The American Chamber of Commerce in Brussels, which represents 160 US companies, is active in these circles. Shale Gas Europe, whose members include Total, Chevron, Shell, Statoil, Cuadrilla and Halliburton, is managed by the lobbying and consulting company FTI Consulting. Their campaign has been remarkably successful: in December 2013, in a vote on whether EIAs should be mandatory, no member state supported the proposition in relation to any gas project. The companies concerned were simply required to carry out their own impact assessments. Two member state governments played a major role in minimising regulation of fracking: Poland, which was very active in promoting the technology, and the UK, which behind a façade of 'cutting red tape' was actually very keen to see fracking initiated in the UK – and by implication elsewhere in the EU.

The EU's revolving door

The question of membership of advisory groups to the Commission and the Parliament is matched by the issue of active representation by MEPs of particular companies both when they are sitting as MEPs and after they have left Parliament (the 'revolving door'). This has been particularly controversial since 2011, when the UK's *Sunday Times* succeeded in recording the conversations in which three MEPs – Ernst Strasser from Austria, Adrian Severin from Romania and Zoran Thaler from Slovenia – agreed to table questions in the Parliament for a phoney company. When the story broke, the trio received surprisingly strong support from fellow MEPs, who called for the journalists to be prosecuted on charges of 'entrapment' and 'registering at the Parliament under a false identity'. The British MEP Sharon Bowles, at that time chairperson of the Economic and Monetary Affairs Committee, protested that they had been 'stitched up like a kipper'. In fact Strasser, Thaler and Severin were later jailed in their home countries with sentences of up to four years.[10]

Although this incident inspired the then president of the European Parliament, Jerzy Buzek, to introduce a code of conduct for MEPs, in fact the Parliament has remained very sensitive and even hostile to outside criticism of the ethics of its members and its willingness to consult on these issues. This is perhaps not surprising given that in 2016, 334 MEPs (45 per cent) have paid-for outside activities.[11] In addition, at the time of writing, the Parliament has still not issued guidelines for whistle-blowers from its own secretariat or the offices of MEPs, and its rules restricting ex-MEPs from taking jobs through a 'revolving door' based on their Parliamentary experience is often ineffective. Three cases show just how ineffective.

The issue of the 'revolving door' is as common to all of the EU as it is in the USA. In Japanese the practice is known as *amakudari* or 'dropping down from heaven' and, although criticised in that country for many years, is as strong in Japan as in Europe and America. In the case of the EU, the problem occurs in both the Commission and the Parliament. Two examples of the former are Neelie Kroes and Viviane Reding, both former European commissioners; an example of the latter is that of former MEP Sharon Bowles. The appointment of Neelie Kroes as commissioner for competition in 2003 was already controversial. In 1997 she had lobbied for Lockheed Martin, an American defence company that had close ties to the Italian company Finmeccanica, then under investigation for the sale of helicopters to Belgium. When the Commission reviewed her credentials for the appointment, they found that if she had been commissioner over the previous five years she would have had to recuse herself from 35 merger and anti-trust cases. Consequently, she had to promise never to engage in business activities once her term expired in 2009. In fact she became a special adviser to Merrill Lynch in 2015 which is active as a lobbyist in the International Swaps and Derivatives Association (ISDA).

Viviane Reding had been a commissioner for 15 years when she retired in November 2015, only to take up advisory posts in the Bertelsmann Foundation (an NGO close to the Bertelsmann group), Nyrstar and Agfa-Gevaert. Nyrstar is a controversial Belgian mining company with mines in Peru, Chile, Mexico and Honduras. In 2013 a wholly owned subsidiary of Nyrstar was fined in Peru for violating the environment. Nyrstar is a member of Eurometaux, a trade association focused on non-ferrous metals, which has an annual lobbying expenditure of €1.5–1.75 million.

Both these cases represent an extraordinary sale of expertise acquired in working in public positions to private interests – and from individuals who continue to draw between 40 and 65 per cent of the their public salary (as the Commission's 'retirement' package).

Sharon Bowles, who retired from the Parliament in 2014, had been chair of the Economic and Monetary Affairs Committee for the previous five years and was once voted the most influential British representative on EU policy.[12] Bowles had been a key figure in developing the most important new regulations governing the banking sector, and Committee records show that she had ten meetings with the London Stock Exchange between 2012 and 2014. Yet in August 2014 she joined the board of that Exchange. At the time, her former colleague in the Committee, Sven Giegold (representing Germany's Green Party) commented that this represented 'a swapping of sides that shamed democracy'.[13] The appointment was accepted in spite of the fact that all ex-MEPs receive a 'transitional allowance' equivalent to one month's salary for every year served as an MP, with a minimum pay-out of six months and a maximum of 24.

These examples are repeated in Brussels many times over, involving both Commission officials and outgoing members of Parliament, although often with a lower profile. While finding ways to make many years of experience of specific issues is a public benefit, the use of that knowledge for personal gain (following retirement or electoral defeat) discredits the democratic system, and certainly represents the corruption of influence.

*   *   *

In both the US and Europe, lobbying is a powerful industry whose impact cannot be overrated. While President Grant held court in the lobby at the Willard Hotel nearly 150 years ago, the legacy of those meetings lingers on. It is continuously reinvigorated by the exit from government and Parliaments of past officials and elected representatives who make a very good living by passing through the 'revolving door'. Canada has made greater strides than other countries discussed here in its control of the revolving door by insisting that the 'cooling-off period' after leaving a government or elected post is five years, monitored by a commissioner of lobbying. This is an important provision and one that could easily be adopted by other countries. But the lobby against change is very strong, as President Obama found and the painfully slow progress on the transparency of lobbying in the EU, confirms.

4

The Big Business of Corruption

Any competitive advantage gained through corruption is a mirage.
Robert Khuzami, director of enforcement, US Securities
and Exchange Commission 2009–2014[1]

Most big corporate corruption scandals have four things in common: the aim of the company was to win big government contracts; bribes were paid through intermediaries and agents; corruption was deeply engrained in the company's way of doing business, often with the knowledge and support of the company's leadership;[2] and the companies had weakly supervised anti-corruption and bribery compliance programmes. In addition to those 'traditional' cases of bribery, the corruption and buying of influence, particularly through political lobbying, as discussed in Chapters 2 and 3, is used.

The idea that doing business through bribery pays off in the long term is increasingly turning out to be a mirage. In the past decade, a growing number of companies have been investigated and prosecuted for corruption both in North

America and Europe. However, enforcement levels between the US and Europe, and within Europe, differ. With the Foreign Corrupt Practices Act (FCPA), enacted in 1977, the US set requirements for corporate accounting transparency, and make it unlawful to make payments to foreign officials to win business (now adopted in various forms by all OECD countries). As a consequence of this long experience and the expertise that goes with it, the US is the most active country in pursuit of transnational bribery. The highest-ranking fine on the top ten list of all FCPA settlements has been German engineering giant Siemens, which paid a watershed fine of $800 million in 2008, in addition to fines set by German authorities. In total, the bribery scandal regarding an alleged $1.4 billion through 4,300 bribery transactions to government officials (in Asia, Africa, Europe, the Middle East and the Americas) in 330 cases cost the company €2.9 billion in fines, fees for lawyers and accountants, and tax payments.[3] The Securities and Exchange Commission (SEC) alleged that between 2001 and 2006, Siemens made these payments mostly in cash from slush funds through a network of consultants and intermediaries, and with the knowledge of employees at all levels, including (now former) senior management. The SEC, which handed down the fine, remarked at the time: 'Seimens [*sic*] paid staggering amounts of money to circumvent the rules and gain business. Now, they will pay for it with the largest settlement in the history of the Foreign Corrupt Practices Act since it became law in 1977.'[4] The Siemens case is a showcase of large corporate corruption scandals: bribery was a part of the company's way of doing business to obtain large government contracts.

The reliance on government contracts for infrastructure, engineering and defence products, or medicines for public health systems, is a strong incentive to corruption. In 2014, the Organisation for Economic Co-operation and Development (OECD) looked at past bribery cases under the OECD Anti-Bribery Convention[5] and concluded that bribes were promised or paid most frequently to employees of public enterprises, followed by customs officials (see Chapter 8 on organised crime), health officials and defence officials.[6] This chapter will discuss corruption cases and vulnerabilities in the construction, defence and pharmaceutical sector and show how they reflect vulnerabilities of businesses more broadly.

Building with bribes: Corruption in the construction sector

The construction sector has long been vulnerable to influence peddling due to the closeness of local construction companies and local infrastructure or building departments. Most construction businesses depend on public contracts, and on public authorities for obtaining building licences and permits. These permits are, in turn, a lucrative way for public officials to solicit bribes in return for their favourable treatment and the granting of construction permits. A survey among UK construction companies confirms this: it found that 84 per cent of UK construction businesses believed planning permission processes to be corrupt.[7] After the planning stage, the tender processes for finding the best construction company can also be rigged. The sector's reliance on subcontractors and sub-subcontractors then makes it easier to conceal bribes and hide kickbacks around big construction projects. In the long chain of contractors and subcontractors, payments of bribes and kickbacks to officials can be made from any number of accounts and businesses, making them hard to trace. A well-known form of political entanglement with the construction industry is where construction firms win public tenders in return for political party funding.

The costs of doing business through bribery are high: one in ten UK construction companies estimates that the annual cost of corruption for them exceeds £1 million,[8] and many of the world's leading engineering and construction companies have been caught red-handed in Europe and the US, such as Balfour Beatty,

AMEC and perhaps most famously Bilfinger SE (formerly Bilfinger Berger), KBR and Halliburton.[9]

A classic pattern of corruption in the construction industry was unearthed in Canada in 2013–14 by the Charbonneau Commission, and kept Canadians in Ontario and Quebec both enthralled and shocked for many months at the corruption on their doorstep. The inquiry, named after its chairperson, Judge France Charbonneau, accused 102 individuals of being involved in the scheme. It heard some 300 witness and expert statements from the years 2011–14 and uncovered a vast network of corruption spanning construction companies to politicians, political parties and descendants of Sicily's Cosa Nostra. It found that construction contractors and consulting engineering firms had rigged competitive bidding processes through a system of collusion; that municipal officers accepted kickbacks to facilitate the award of contracts, and that some of the value of the construction contracts were paid to the political organisers and municipal elected officials and civil servants who had facilitated the deals. Of the 13 companies charged with corruption, ten donated a total of CAN\$ 2 million to federal parties between 1993 and 2006, when corporate donations to parties were banned. Most of the donations went to the Liberal Party that was in power from 1993 until 2006.[10]

A variety of actors were involved in the bribery scheme: construction companies and a construction cartel; public officials and political parties; and the mafia with links to the industry. Lino Zambito, for example, was a construction magnate in Quebec until 2010, when his company defaulted after he had been caught in an attempt to influence local elections in Quebec. When subpoenaed by the Charbonneau Commission, he gave a full account of the bribery and corruption around Quebec's construction sector. He described how the cartel of companies bid for construction contracts, and alleged that this was well-known by Montreal's then-Mayor Gérald Tremblay and other high-ranking officials. Zambito admitted that his company was part of a cartel, and reported that

2.5 per cent of the contract value went to the mafia, 3 per cent to the mayor's political party, and hundreds of thousands in cash, vacations and other expenses to Montreal's engineers and city employees.[11]

Another powerful illustration of how hidden contributions were channelled to political parties on the provincial level was given by Rosaire Sauriol, now former vice-president of engineering firm Dessau Inc., Canada's sixth-largest engineering and construction firm. 'You don't pay, you're done,'[12] Sauriol famously said during his hearing, describing corruption as a cancer that was everywhere. He explained how Dessau had employed an elaborate fake invoicing scheme to be able to raise cash donations to parties in Montreal and other cities in Quebec.[13] Other companies found other ways to donate illegally: the general manager of SNC-Lavalin, Canada's biggest engineering firm, explained that the company had employees write personal cheques to public officials and parties at the provincial level, reimbursing them at the end of the year through their bonuses. Similar techniques were used by other companies, along with straight cash-filled envelopes.[14] Companies claimed during the hearings that once they started donating to Quebec's ruling Union Montreal Party, construction contracts came rolling in, with the customary 3 per cent kickback to the party.[15]

In addition to the corruption scandal's links with political party finance, the Quebec construction case is also illustrative of the sector's unfortunate and long history with organised crime. Of the many figures involved in Quebec's construction scandals, Nicolo Milioto is one of the most powerful. Like Quebec's mafia don and 'Canadian Godfather' Vito Rizzuto and his sidekick Tony Accurso, Milioto was born in Cattolica Eraclea, Sicily.[16] In his hearings, he denied serving as a link to Rizzuto's Cosa Nostra family, Canada's most powerful crime family. A construction boss and middleman between construction companies and Montreal organised crime, he looks the part of a 'mafia type' in his mid-sixties. A video tape showed him handing bundles of cash to the Rizzutos. Milioto was dubbed 'Mr Sidewalk' – a nickname he disputes – after allegedly threatening a competitor to bury him in his 'deep sidewalks' if he did not withdraw a competing bid for a sidewalk contract. He also allegedly sent a sympathy card and flowers to the competitor's family, stating that it would be a shame if he had to do this for real. Despite Milioto's denial, there is overwhelming evidence that there were indeed strong links between Montreal's construction sector, Milioto and the Rizzuto crime gang. The Rizzuto family became one of Canada's biggest names in international crime under Vito Rizzuto, who was particularly infamous for his drug business in New York.[17] By the time of the Charbonneau Commission, the family's power was largely diminished after the death of Vito Rizzuto in 2013, and his son's assassination by a rival mafia family in 2010.

While mafia links have been proven in cities such as New York and Montreal, they tend to go beyond construction and fluidly move into organised crime more generally. However, the sector is, according to a research report by the Canadian government, at moderate to high risk from organised crime due to being a volatile market with numerous risks from weather to labour market fluctuations. This, in combination with a fragmented regulatory system, makes the sector vulnerable to 'both unscrupulous industry insiders and external criminal organizations'.[18] A company can, for example, rather easily be founded and used solely for the purpose of money-laundering; for example, by purchasing expensive heavy construction equipment. The report also notes that, of course, the construction section is 'not alone in being susceptible to these vulnerabilities'.[19] In Quebec, the strict language requirements for bidding companies and labour laws,[20] together with city officials' tempering with bids and bidders, led to 50 per cent of construction contracts going to only 16 of the 250 construction businesses in Montreal, and building costs that were more than 30 per cent higher than in other comparable projects outside Quebec.[21]

The Charbonneau Commission's final 1,741-page report concluded that 'corruption and collusion were far more widespread than originally believed'. The full extent of connections between the political parties and the Quebec construction industry will probably never come to light, as the Charbonneau Commission was explicitly tasked with looking only at Montreal and Quebec, and not at the federal level.[22]

Virtually every country is affected by corruption in the construction sector to some degree, and there is no doubt that corruption in building and infrastructure sectors has severe consequences, most notably overpaying for infrastructure and triggering lower quality.[23] Both in the US and in the UK there have been investigations against big construction and engineering companies in recent years. Half of UK construction companies still feel that more needs to be done to combat construction corruption within their industry, with 55 per cent expecting more action from their government.[24] Not-for-profit organisations such as the Global Infrastructure Anti-Corruption Centre (GIACC)[25] have done a great amount of work in identifying and preventing corruption in the construction and infrastructure sector by working closely with companies. The tools developed by GIACC range from general anti-corruption procedures such as a gifts and hospitality code and compliance to sector-specific tools such as contract clauses addressing corruption. On a policy level, the World Bank-supported Construction Sector Transparency Initiative (CoST) has been working with countries on disclosure of infrastructure data on infrastructure projects to increase transparency and oversight.[26]

Together with prosecution of high-stake construction cases under the FCPA in the US and the Bribery Act in the UK, both the pressure and the available solutions for the sector are increasing. Especially companies operating at an international level appear increasingly cautious and are setting up new (and better) compliance systems, a trend that can also be witnessed in the defence and pharmaceutical sectors. However, the success of these programmes will be judged not by their compliance on paper but by the absence of major construction corruption scandals not only at international level, but also at the national and municipal levels. To achieve this, the burden is not only on companies to reform, but also on government and public authorities to improve their own prevention and detection systems.

A bitter pill: Pharmaceutical corruption

In total, the global health system is valued at \$7 trillion. In many countries, it ranks among the biggest government budget items, making it a lucrative target for corruption.[27] Corruption in the health sector globally occurs at various levels of the health chain: patients are forced to pay bribes at public hospitals, national medicine procurement is being tampered with and corruption occurs within the pharmaceutical sector around the development, marketing and sale of drugs to consumers.

Despite its vulnerabilities it is usually not a sector that is associated with corruption in North America or Europe. However, in Europe, German pharmaceutical companies said otherwise and testified that corruption was indeed a problem: in a 2013 study by PricewaterhouseCoopers, one-fifth of German pharmaceutical companies stated that they lost out on a contract due to corruption-related reasons.[28] Three-quarters of companies said they believed medium to high levels of corruption surrounded post-marketing surveillance studies and consultant contracts, leasing of medical equipment, awarding of contracts for studies and sponsoring. And a quarter of companies stated that breaches of patent and marketing rights were a problem in the sector. The study also pointed out that despite all this, only one-third of pharmaceutical companies had an anti-corruption programme and 70 per cent of all companies thought that their broader programme regarding anti-corruption was sufficient.[29]

The results of mistrust in the health sector and health industry are tangible. During the measles outbreak in the US and Europe in 2015, a bitter clash of views between pro and contra vaccination reappeared. Doubts about the effectiveness of vaccination were voiced around theories alleging that the pharmaceutical industry suppressed data and studies that would hurt their business and sales, and that doctors were paid by the industry to speak for the effectiveness of vaccination.[30] When the effectiveness of drugs and vaccinations that are shown to save lives are being questioned out of a distrust for an industry or the belief that government regulation is being ineffective or corrupted, the consequences are enormous. News reports about pharmaceutical companies paying doctors as spokespeople, mislabelling of drugs, and bribery in medical service delivery and procurement have been frequent in both Europe and North America. The relationship between universities and academic research and the industry is also under scrutiny: pharmaceutical companies funding particular research or trials are both welcome donors for academia and a potential risk for the credibility of the research and the universities.

It is not uncommon for a medication to take ten to 15 years to develop and test, but monetary gains from a new drug can potentially be huge for investors and pharmaceutical companies alike.[31] The US pharmaceutical industry association Pharma claims that, on average, a drug costs $1.2 billion to develop. This raises the pressure for companies to ensure that their drugs are successful on the market.[32] The American pharma industry's self-reported revenue in 2012 was $286 billion.[33] For the same year, the European pharma industry association self-reported that their products' market value at retail prices were €238 billion (or $305 billion).[34] Looking at world pharmaceutical sales, North American companies dominate the market with 41 per cent compared with 27 per cent for European companies.[35]

Health systems and laws governing the pharmaceutical sector differ widely between the US and Europe, and indeed from country to country. But there are similarities: with high invest-ment, a competitive market and a relatively short lifespan of a branded drug, there are big incentives to undercut the regulatory system for higher profits. That the sector is vulnerable to corrup-tion is demonstrated by the large numbers of pharmaceutical companies that have been investigated for corruption charges ranging from illegal or off-label promotion, inflating prices and illegally passing on free samples and backhand deals, to brib-ery of foreign officials. Companies included AstraZeneca,[36] Bristol-Myers Squibb,[37] Pfizer, Eli Lilly & Co.,[38] Novartis[39] and GlaxoSmithKline,[40] plus numerous smaller companies.[41] This is a sign of both the sector's vulnerability, but also an indicator for weak compliance structures – at least up to the time of the com-panies being investigated.

In September 2012, the European Union introduced new safety rules, agreed between the European Parliament and health ministers of the EU member states, to enable EU safety evaluations and, if necessary, EU-wide withdrawal of drugs. At the same time, the EU required companies to become more transparent and state explicitly why they are taking drugs off the market if they decide to do so. The new rules were intended to prevent companies from masking safety concerns in order to protect their share price. These 'pharmacovigilance rules' that the EU agreed on – and stress-tested to close loopholes – were in response to one of Europe's biggest drug scandals in recent times, a French diabetes drug that was sold under the name of Mediator or Benfluorex from 1976 until 2009.

Benfluorex was sold in six European countries[42] to treat dia-betes and to suppress the appetite of non-diabetic people and, from 1999, was suspected of having heavy cardiovascular side-effects. The French National Institute of Health and Medical Research estimated in a 2012 report that, prior to the drug being taken off the market in France in 2009, it caused 1,300 deaths.[43] The delay of a decade in withdrawing the drug was unnecessary and swifter action could have arguably prevented these deaths. However, the manufacturer of Mediator, French pharmaceutical company Servier, is said to have pressured policymakers into not withdrawing it, for which individuals associated with the company went on trial in 2012.[44] Charges against individuals included the 90-year-old founder of the company, Jacques Servier.[45] Four doctors were indicted for allegedly accepting bribes from Servier while also serving on the marketing authorisation commission (Autorisation de Mise sur le Marché); Jean-Michel Alexandre, a pharmacologist and president of the French Medical Evaluation Commission from 1993 to 2000, was indicted on suspicion of having accepted more than €1 million between 2001 and 2009.[46]

Besides the judicial consequences, the scandal also led to the resignation of the head of France's public health agency and sparked an intensive debate about drugs regulation and the lobbying power of pharmaceutical companies both in France and within Europe.[47] Servier itself was found negligent in 2015 of having left a 'defective' drug on the market. This followed the trials of two patients who had sued the company for their health complications. However, the patients were only awarded €27,500 and €10,000 respectively.[48] The criminal proceedings against company employees were repeatedly put on hold and are not expected to continue before 2018, seven years after they started.[49]

The failure of Servier was that it did not take a drug with heavy side-effects off the market and allegedly used undue influence to ensure that it stayed on the market. But it also hints at a problem that can be found regularly in the sector: the misselling of drugs, i.e., selling it to cure a condition that it was not originally developed and authorised for. From the standpoint of the pharmaceutical companies, this makes sense: if the drugs help with more than one condition (in this case both diabetes and appetite suppression), this also increases the potential customer base and the drug thus generates more profit.

In one of the most spectacular misselling – or off-label marketing – cases, the British pharmaceutical giant GlaxoSmithKline (GSK) was fined a record-breaking $3 billion by the United States government in 2012 for promoting drugs for unapproved uses and failing to report safety data of drugs; persuading doctors to prescribe unsuitable anti-depressants to children; ignoring the failings of a diabetes drug; and paying kickbacks to doctors prescribing GSK's drugs.[50] It was the largest payment to resolve a fraud case ever made by a drug company.[51] To influence doctors to prescribe drugs, GSK paid for lavish trips to the Caribbean, tickets to sports events (to allegedly discuss the drug) and paid hundreds of thousands of dollars to a radio host who advertised an anti-depressant as a 'wonder drug' that helps 'you stop smoking, stay happy and lose weight'.[52] Legally, GSK was on safe ground when paying for doctors' trips to the Caribbean and similar 'incentives'. It is legal in many countries, including the US, for companies to incentivise doctors to prescribe certain medication. What was not legal, however, was misrepresenting the effectiveness or treatment options of any given drug.

In a plea bargain and a civil settlement, GSK admitted to promoting anti-depressants for unapproved use to children and adolescents, and pleaded guilty.[53] Andrew Witty, GlaxoSmithKline's chief executive, stated after the settlement that GSK had 'learned from the mistakes'.[54] The settlement with the US Department of Justice included a clause that obliged the company to execute a five-year 'Corporate Integrity Agreement' that required 'major changes to the way [GSK] does business, including changing the way its sales force is compensated to remove compensation based on sales goals for territories, one of the driving forces behind much of the conduct at issue in this matter'.[55] After the settlement, similar allegations against GSK were made for their sales practices in Iraq, Lebanon, Jordan and Poland, and most spectacularly in China where they were fined $489 million for paying bribes – this amounted to around 4 per cent of the company's 2013 operating profits.[56]

The GSK case is illustrative of a widespread phenomenon in the pharmaceutical industry: the engagement of key opinion leaders

(KOLs) such as academics and physicians both during the drug development and the drug marketing and sales stage. American pharmaceutical companies and most of their European counterparts set aside an average 15–25 per cent of their marketing budget for speaking events by KOLs. The combination of KOLs, funded research, lobbying, the ties to the financial market and political party funding all point to the same problem: the disproportionate influence of pharmaceutical companies on medical opinion, which can stand in the way of public health.[57] However, the prevalence of this practice as well as public pressure for more transparency have led to tightening transparency legislation for pharmaceutical companies, which need to state all their payments to KOLs on both sides of the Atlantic. What remains largely unregulated is the access of companies to policymakers through lobbying, as discussed in Chapter 3. In 2015, the pharmaceutical industry spent $238 million in lobbying in Washington[58] – an astronomical figure. Only the financial and insurance sector spent more, at $481 million.[59] In comparison, 2014 spending in the US on prescription drugs alone amounted to an estimated $275.9 billion:[60] health care is a huge and increasing budget item for the US and other governments, creating a sizeable market for the pharmaceutical industry.

When adding the donations made to political parties, candidates and PACs to the direct lobbying costs by the pharmaceutical sector, it is clear that the industry is wielding exceptional power. The reform measures encapsulated in codes of ethics of pharmaceutical companies and current anti-bribery legislation have not yet been sufficient to eliminate corruption in the sector. The scope for further changes is beyond the reach of this book, but is certainly a part of a necessary public agenda in both the US and Europe.

It would be easy but wrong to place the blame and responsibility for these failures on the pharmaceutical companies alone. It is the responsibility of governments to ensure that shortcomings of the market are addressed and that patients' safety is guaranteed by solid regulation. In the case of Mediator, Servier's failure to take a dangerous drug off the market has led to the French 'Sunshine Act'[61] – regulation that requires transparency of financial dealings of pharmaceutical companies and doctors. Together with transparency provisions, it is becoming easier for patients to understand the networks between companies and doctors. At the same time, legal deterrents are necessary to tilt the calculation of the trade-off between corporate profits and the risk of prosecution towards 'risk'. Corporate compliance structures, at least in leading pharmaceutical markets such as Germany, are not yet sufficient. Unfortunately, cases such as France's slow-moving trial of Servier do not induce hope, and neither does the continued political influence of the industry on both sides of the Atlantic. The fact that there are no mandated independent tests for the effectiveness of drugs, no databases not only for successful but also for failed trials, or databases that would let consumers track companies' payments to KOLs across all countries in Europe and North America means that attention on the sector needs to be more vigorous.

Initiatives such as the World Health Organization's Global Governance of Medicines Initiative as well as the work of civil society organisations on sectoral transparency and data transparency[62] have been crucial steps in addressing this issue and raising the bar for transparency both in the public and private sectors. It is in the interest of the whole public that they succeed.

The defence industry: Wired for corruption?

For many countries, the defence sector and spending on defence equipment and the armed forces makes up a sizeable portion of their national budget. While by no means the biggest budget item in any country – few countries spend more than 4 per cent on defence – it is easier to 'skim off' money from defence spending than from most other budget items for two reasons: it is highly lucrative and the complex design of procurement systems is often a facilitator. It is lucrative because defence contracts, as shown in the case of Greece outlined below, are often extraordinarily big contracts: buying new submarines is in a spending class of its own together with military aircraft and, of course, aircraft carriers. But even 'smaller' items become big budget lines when they are technically complex (such as military radars), or just bought in sheer numbers (e.g., uniforms for armed forces).Using corruption to influence defence policy towards a certain strategic objective, or influencing military personnel to decide on the specification for equipment or selling assets such as land, can lead to a financial windfall for a company or an individual.

In addition, there is a very limited number of defence suppliers to choose from: there are only about 20 top defence manufacturers, most of them located in the US and Europe. They have high-level technical expertise in defence, and an army of lobbyists to assist them. As a result, a small number of the manufacturers receive a large proportion of government contracts – and in turn spend a lot on lobbying ($126 million in 2015). The world's biggest defence manufacturer, the American company Lockheed Martin, is also one of the biggest recipients of US government contracts. In 2014, the company that produces the F-16 and the F-22 fighter aircrafts spent $14 million on lobbying activities in Washington, placing it among the 20 highest spenders.[63] Their rivals Northrop Grumman and Boeing are not far behind. In Europe, lobbying data is more elusive, but defence manufacturers such as BAE Systems (UK), Thales (France), EADS (Germany and France) and Finmeccanica (Italy) have traditionally had close links with their national governments.[64] Although the total value of arms contracts is generally on the decline in the US and Europe, with markets such as the Middle East on the rise, defence manufacturers nevertheless rely on good relations with their home government not only for contracts, but also for industrial policy and export licences. Home governments, in turn, are interested in selling their defence industry's products and increasing their exports, and are also responsible for issuing export licences for defence equipment. Besides checklists for export licences, there are surprisingly few oversight mechanisms for the defence sector. This is, partly, due to legitimate national security concerns, but where a sizeable budget is set aside for defence items, inadequate oversight leads to high risk. Where procurement and oversight systems are weak on the public sector side, compliance and procedures are weak on the private sector side.[65]

A case of the Greek Ministry of Defence buying submarines from a German defence company illustrates just how much money can be subverted in the process of defence procurement.

Apostolos 'Akis' Tsochatzopoulos is perhaps one of the best-known political figures in Greece. A white-haired, haggard and serious-looking man, he spent more than 20 years as a member of the Greek Parliament in various government and cabinet positions for the party he co-founded, the social democratic Panhellenic Socialist Movement (PASOK), one of Greece's major parties. While he was Greek defence minister, he ordered submarines for the Greek Navy from German engineering group Ferrostaal and in return received $26 million in bribes through various channels.[66]

After becoming defence minister in 1996, the Greek Ministry of Defence that he led signed a deal in 2000 with a consortium including Ferrostaal and the HDW shipyard in Kiel, Germany, for the delivery of type-214 submarines. The deal was worth €1.14 billion – more than the total budget for university education in Greece.[67] The contract was for the refurbishment of submarines, and for the manufacture of six brand new type-214 submarines. It was struck between Ferrostaal and the Greek Ministry of Defence and also included a consortium for the shipyard that was to build the submarines. The consortium ran under the name of HDW and included Germany's steel and military equipment manufacturer ThyssenKrupp.

Bribes were paid through a network of agents to Greek officials and Tsochatzopoulos, including coffers full of money handed to Tsochatzopoulos' cousin Nikos Zigras, who then handed them to the defence minister.[68] When cash became too dangerous, the bribery scheme changed to offshore accounts that Zigras had set up.[69] Tsochatzopoulos' arrest in 2012 took place at his most recently purchased neoclassical mansion on Dionysiou Areopagitou, the most prestigious – and expensive – address in Athens, located at the foot of the Acropolis.[70] The network was uncovered by prosecutors in Kiel, a coastal town in northern Germany that was home to the submarine building company HDW. The investigation at first stalled because German prosecutors received no help from their Greek counterparts for their investigation.[71] Eventually, however, other defence corruption cases came to light in the wake of the submarine case, such as €3.5 million paid in bribes to a Greek defence official by German arms manufacturer Krauss-Maffei Wegmann for helping to foster the procurement of 170 Leopard II tanks. This was brought to light because Krauss-Maffei Wegmann paid off the same official who also received around half a million euros in bribes for the submarine deal.[72]

In the trial looking into the submarine affair, Tsochatzopoulos and 15 others were convicted, including Ministry of Defence officials, Tsochatzopoulos' ex-wife, his daughter and his cousin Nikos Zigras, who was a key witness. While there is general agreement that the conviction of a high-ranking official for corruption was both overdue and welcome in Greece, the fact remains that Tsochatzopoulos was by no means the only person benefiting from a political system based on systemic corruption. In Germany, the CEO and the general manager of Ferrostaal were let off the hook with fines and suspended sentences. They admitted to knowing that €62 million was paid in bribes to secure deals in Greece and Portugal. Both stated that they were aware of the payments but did not ask or know who received the money. Fifty managers and private sector personnel were indicted but only two were convicted.

Of the six type-214 submarines that Tsochatzopoulos ordered in 2002, the first one was received by the Hellenic Navy in 2014. It needed further development until it was finally ready to operate. This was after a refusal by the Navy in 2006 to accept the first finished submarines into their service after tests had shown that the submarines had trouble staying afloat in rough waters, among other technical faults.[73]

The total amount of bribes Tsochatzopoulos received is estimated to be €55 million – money that 1,000 Greek demonstrators shouting in front of his home in 2011 demanded he pay back.[74] While some of the money was indeed recovered, Tsochatzopoulos' criminal career was far from over. Even in prison he allegedly was part of an organised crime gang run from his cell. Together with 36 suspects, the former minister was investigated by the Greek anti-terror unit. It was found that he had attempted to plan a bomb attack on a former Ministry of Defence colleague who owed him €2 million.[75]

The Greek submarine case pointed to two larger questions: first, how was it possible that not only a specific deal gets entangled in bribery but bribery got engraved in the system? And second, why did defence deals between an already-broke Greek government and German, French and Italian manufacturers come about while, at the same time, the leading European governments negotiated bailout deals and austerity measures for Greece?[76]

The country had long been Europe's largest importer of military equipment, partly due to historic tensions with Turkey over Cyprus that have led both countries to invest heavily in their militaries, and partly due to the vicious cycle resulting from these tensions: since Greece's large armed forces were established, a great deal of equipment was needed to make it effective. The country possesses more tanks than the armies of Germany, the United Kingdom and France combined.[77] Greece has thus long been a sought-after market for defence companies.[78] The US and Germany were the biggest suppliers of defence material to Greece: between 2005 and 2010, the Greek government spent $2.1 billion on German defence equipment alone, and another $4 billion for equipment from the US.[79] Defence expenditure contributed significantly to Greece's debts, which in turn became a source of controversy in the context of Greece's external borrowing in 2013/14. The German government was advising Greece to cut spending – but not defence spending. Meanwhile, Greek shipping magnates enjoyed tax-free status and military spending[80] remained the second highest of all NATO members, and unparalleled in Europe.

The broader context of this example of defence corruption is one in which defence spending and corruption remain closely entwined. In 2014, the world's defence spending was $1.8 trillion. If only one per cent of this amount was wasted on corruption every year – and that's a very conservative figure given that Russia has estimated that up to 20 per cent of its defence spending is lost on corruption – this would still equal $18 billion. Of the G20 countries (which make up 92 per cent of global arms exports), only seven have what Transparency International defined as 'meaningful oversight' over their defence budget, including public scrutiny and budget transparency. The G20 group has recognised that corruption, including the focus area of procurement, needs addressing.

The mixture of insufficient transparency of procurement systems and narrow oversight are the key to the problem in the defence sector: highly technical specifications are written by only a handful of people, and contract awards are decided by a similarly small group. In addition, national defence companies have always had strong links with their home governments, in whose interest it is to foster their exports. As in the construction and the pharmaceutical sector, the ability or willingness of defence companies to police their own ethics programmes is also a central part of the problem. Of 55 North American defence companies analysed in a

2015 study of corruption risks of defence companies in 2015, only four showed extensive evidence of meaningful ethics and compliance programmes.[81]

Some companies have increased their efforts to tackle bribery. For example, the International Forum on Business Ethical Conduct (IFBEC), embracing US and EU defence companies, has developed a set of 'Global Principles' but has so far shied away from either peer or independent review. Needless to say, the companies who are leading the industry's work on compliance and anti-corruption must face competition in markets that are ruthless, where geopolitics come into play and where there are still companies with little to no interest in serious compliance reforms. The defence sector has been and with some modifications will be for time one of the most difficult in which to suppress corruption.

The way forward

The cases of corruption in the pharmaceutical, defence and construction sectors are snapshots of the challenging nexus between the public and the private sectors. A growing number of global companies are starting to take the issue of corruption and compliance much more seriously compared with ten years ago. This is at least partly due to international initiatives, such as the OECD Anti-Bribery Convention of 1997. Although only a small number of countries – including the US, UK, Germany and Switzerland – are enforcing the follow-up legislation effectively, it remains an important beacon. At the same time, international scrutiny and national media coverage have been increasing, and citizens as consumers and investors are less and less willing to support companies who win business through illegal means.

In terms of prosecution, countries such as the United Kingdom have slowly begun to gear its system to so-called deferred prosecution agreements, modelled after already existing US judicial practice. There were 233 such agreements with the US Department of Justice between 2001 and 2012. In deferred prosecution agreements, companies can negotiate with prosecuting agencies to pay a fine and adopt a tougher ethical compliance programme. In reality, in many cases, this constitutes a route to enable companies to buy their way out of a guilty sentence. They do, however, also serve to reduce costs of lengthy trials (for the defendant and the state) and, in the best case, can serve as a vehicle for change for the companies. At the other end of the scale, prison is an option: in July 2015 four former executives (including the ex-CEO) of a Norwegian fertiliser company Yara International were jailed for two years for authorising bribes in Libya and India.

But enforcement, fines and public scrutiny only have a partial effect. Further regulation and oversight of each sector is necessary, requiring both commitment from companies (CEOs and their boards), and intelligent and consistent responses from governments. Voluntary commitments such as the UN Global Compact, which is based on the commitments of CEOs to implement a set of sustainability principles, and industry-specific initiatives such as the Extractive Industries Transparency Initiative (EITI) and IFBEC, have proven that sectors can self-subscribe to enhanced transparency.

However, for a transparency initiative to work, there will need to be commitment to change on both the side of the seller and the buyer, as well as transparency in the business deals themselves. In some cases, this has been achieved by independent oversight; for example, so-called Integrity Pacts[82] – voluntary but binding agreements between buyers and sellers to uphold transparency principles with the oversight of a third-party monitor or ombudsman. There is a strong case for companies and (importing and exporting) governments to use tools like this to control corruption in these sectors.

At another level, sanctions exercised by funders and tender boards can be effective. The World Bank, for example, has set up a Black List of companies that have been involved in corruption in World Bank projects. This database is public and used by other development finance institutions and UN agencies, governments and even some companies. Blacklisting is also exercised by the US Department of Defense. While not a perfect solution, blacklists certainly do ensure that companies listen when these organisations set out their anti-corruption benchmarks. Taken together, changes to the law that criminalise transnational bribery, much more explicit corporate codes and compliance systems, tougher procurement rules and the introduction of 'blacklisting' have created a different context for multinational companies than that which existed 20 years ago. However, ensuring that this impact is sustained will require constant pressure from both inside and outside companies.

5

The Bankers' Story: An End to Trust

> Pursue a straightforward, upright, legitimate banking business.
> Never be tempted by the prospect of large returns to do anything
> but what may be properly done under the National Currency Act.
> 'Splendid financiering' is not legitimate banking, and 'splendid
> financiers' in banking are generally rascals or humbugs.
>
> *Advice by the first US Comptroller of the currency,*
> *Hugh McCulloch, in 1863*

The reputation of executive bankers has suffered a dramatic
decline since the financial crisis of 2007/8. Widely seen as responsible for the collapse of the subprime mortgage market, for the
rigging of markets in interest rates and foreign exchange, for
sanctions busting and for facilitating tax evasion, 'bankers' have
come to be widely perceived as exploitative and corrupt. Is this
justified?

Chapter 1 explained that our definition of corruption embraces
actions that impoverish others for the sake of personal gain. The financial crisis of 2007/8 was triggered by high-risk 'reckless' lending in the

US subprime mortgage market compounded by trading in the complex products derived from that lending, which led to huge losses at the level of individuals. The manipulation of interest rates and the foreign exchange market, while technically the product of a cartel,[1] represented the misuse of entrusted power for personal gain at a cost to the public, and so was corrupt. The ever-expanding use of 'secrecy jurisdictions' (many of which are in 'offshore' centres such as the Caribbean) that assist in tax evasion and are hosts to enormous caches of corruptly gained funds, has further damaged the reputation of banks, which are critical pillars of this system of secrecy jurisdictions (as will be explored in Chapter 6).

This chapter will explore the background to these different forms of corruption in the banking sector. It will show that while individuals within the banks were the driving force in promoting dubious products and in market-rigging, senior management and executive boards failed to recognise or acknowledge the dangers of fraud and corruption, or were prepared to substitute the enforcement of ethical standards for ever higher profits. In the case of the practice of 'name stripping', which disguised the origin of funds originating in Iran and Sudan, senior managers were clearly the instigators of an illegal practice that represented a corruption of the ostensible values of their institution. The bonus system operated by the banks rewarded individuals extremely generously and was itself an incentive to the development of increasingly sophisticated products whose value ultimately unravelled. The chapter will also show how Wall Street ensured that the financial regulators who were supposed to ensure the stability of the system were in fact emasculated by political pressure from both Congress and the administration. These are the reverse of the principles that characterised the banks in the years before the financial crisis, as embodied, for example, in the words quoted above from the first-Comptroller of the US currency, Hugh McCulloch.

The crisis of 2007/8 had an important and recent predecessor: the near collapse in the late 1980s of the community-oriented banking institutions designated as 'savings and loan' (S&L) agencies. It is remarkable that this debacle, affecting the savings of millions, did not lead to significant regulatory reform and so set the context of the financial crisis of 2007/8. In this case, the banks and finance institutions, apparently shaped to meet the needs of small-scale borrowers (and especially of aspiring home-owners) blatantly failed to serve their purpose, and in fact worsened the condition of many borrowers. S&L institutions owed their origins to the community savings bank movement, established in the first part of the nineteenth century, but by the 1980s had become partly privately owned. However, they encountered a major crisis in the mid-1980s since they were partly dependent on wholesale borrowing at the national level and interest rates escalated to 14.5 per cent at the federal level,[2] forcing S&Ls to seek higher returns than those in the private housing market and invest in commercial property, the value of which eventually collapsed.

The failures of S&Ls that ensued were massive. Out of a total of 3,234 S&Ls, roughly one third were closed by regulators between 1986 and 1995 at a total cost of $160 billion, of which $132 billion was met by the taxpayer. The impact was contagious: more than 1,600 other small commercial banks also failed in the same period. Much of this pattern of credit constituted 'reckless lending', which endangered both the individual whose savings were with the S&L, and the borrower who leapt at the chance of accessing funds so easily, often with the intention of using them for consumption rather than the purchase of property. However, the S&L boom was also characterised by pervasive false accounting, which has been described by William Black, a member of the Federal Home Loan Board, as using 'a fraud mechanism that produced record profits and virtually no loan defaults, and had the ability to quickly transform any (real) loss found by an examiner into a (fictitious) gain that would be blessed by a Big 8 audit firm'.[3] The regulatory framework that failed to prevent the S&L collapse, and responded only after the crisis, remained largely in place in the build-up to the 2007/8 crisis.

As the drama of the crisis subsided and a restructured but smaller mortgage industry resumed viability, the political case for trying to ensure that low-income families could access mortgages on favourable terms persisted. Critical to this process were the mortgage companies Fannie Mae and Freddie Mac, which by the early 1990s were responsible as owner or guarantor for more than half the US mortgage market of $11 trillion. In 1999, under pressure from the Clinton administration, these two entities, in which the federal government had a stake, became active players in the 'subprime mortgage market', in which loans were extended to millions of low-income borrowers at initially low rates of interest and no collateral but the price of which increased after an initial waiver of repayment usually for two years. Fannie Mae and Freddie Mac expanded the 'securitisation' of these mortgages, which had commenced in the 1980s with Wall Street banks as partners. At that time they were looking for opportunities to deploy new and more sophisticated instruments that reduced their own exposure to risk and so would enable them to borrow more investment capital. Alongside these two giants were mortgage specialists such as Countrywide Financial Corporation, which by 2007 was lending $500 billion in a year and making 200,000 loans.[4]

Through 'securitisation', lenders saw an opportunity to spread their credit risk with others in the financial market. Packages of subprime loans were bundled together and sold on to investment and retail banks. The new investors then protected their asset through a series of relatively new products. One approach was through interest rate swaps that enabled one lender to trade a floating rate of interest for another party's fixed rate of interest; another was a credit default swap (CDS) in which the liability for a default was insured by a third party. Yet another was the 'synthetic subprime mortgage bond' whose value was measured by CDSs but had no underlying real assets. In a concept originated by J.P. Morgan, the insurance giant AIG was the first major company to take up the opportunity to insure mortgage packages (effectively a CDS). Entering this market in 1998, by 2001 the credit default swap business accounted for 15 per cent of AIG's annual profits of $300 million. Other big reinsurance companies were to follow rapidly including the European companies Zurich Insurance and Swiss Re.

By 2004, the content of the swaps had changed in such a way that the packages included bundles of up to 100 different types of mortgages from different parts of the US, a change that enabled high-quality, low-risk mortgages to be presented as low-risk or Triple AAA. Known as 'collateralised debt obligations' (CDOs) these instruments completely disguised the identity of the many thousands of borrowers covered by each package (more than 90 per cent of whom were in the 'subprime' category). Goldman Sachs were pioneers in this process, buying $50 billion of CDOs in 2004 and paying the credit rating agencies big fees to promote the packages as Triple AAA and arranging for AIG to insure them against default.

The availability of these instruments facilitated a phenomenal rate of growth of the underlying high-risk mortgages, which increased from a total of $125 billion in 2000 (12 per cent of all US bank loans) to a total of $1 trillion (or 24 per cent of total loans) in 2006.[5] The traditional criteria used by mortgage lenders were centred on the creditworthiness of the borrowers, although these had been undermined during the early growth of subprime lending. Now the volume and speed of transactions became the critical criterion by which loan officers in the field were judged; payment levels were higher for those with a portfolio of higher-risk loans. Between 2000 and 2003, the number of brokerage firms operating in the market rose from 30,000 to 50,000.[6]

This emphasis on speed went right up the banking column where, towards the top, players reformulated the underlying securities into packages that could be marketed on both the domestic and international market. In some cases, the investment banks, including Citigroup, Lehman Brothers and Morgan Stanley, themselves bought subprime lenders.[7] The attraction of this market for the big investment banks lay in the fact that investment in 'residential mortgage-based securities' (RMBS) required a lower capital requirement than other sectors. The banks concerned could sell on the bundled product for a large fee to other investors who in turn could insure their asset through credit default swaps. If they sold them on, they had in fact no capital requirement for this activity.

These packages were put together and their creditworthiness was signed off mechanically with a total absence of 'due diligence', the hallmark of good banking practice. Simon Head, a leading analyst of the impact of the digital economy, has described this process as follows:

> By the early 2000s, Goldman's derivatives trading could no longer be called banking in any meaningful sense of the term, but had become an industrial activity, turning out virtual products whose fortunes depended on the efficient management of processes: the accumulation of mortgages and other forms of debt from bankers and brokers, their transformation into financial derivatives, and their selling on to clients.[8]

This process eventually became the subject of major litigation against the banks by individual states on the basis that thousands of citizens and borrowers had been pressured into accepting subprime mortgages reflecting automated and completely irresponsible lending.

One of the apparent justifications for the banks' extraordinary enthusiasm for the bundles of subprime mortgages was the high value that the 'rating agencies' awarded them. The lead players were Moody's Investor Services, Standard & Poor's Financial Services (S&P) and Fitch Ratings, each of which was very active in the subprime market. Between 2002 and 2007, the total revenue from rating subprime mortgages multiplied four times over for both Moody's and Standard & Poor to a total, in both cases, of $265 million. In 2011, the CEO of Moody's told Senator Levin's committee on Wall Street and the Financial Crisis:

> What happened in '04 and '05 with respect to subordinated tranches is that our competition, Fitch and S&P, went nuts. Everything was investment grade.[9]

In fact by 2006/7, 90 per cent of AAA ratings awarded by these companies were awarded to subprime mortgages and it was these ratings that made the final securities so attractive to pension funds and other long-term investors in Europe as well as the US.[10]

But there was to be a reckoning. As default rates among borrowers escalated, reaching a crisis point in 2006/7, Moody's placed $105 billion on 'credit watch' in December and in January 2008 S&P downgraded $530 billion to junk status. Among the investment banks, Goldman Sachs was the first to change its behaviour dramatically by both continuing to sell bundled securities but 'shorting' the market at the same time, a strategy that earned the bank $1.1 billion.[11]

Some European banks had been particularly active in this market. Deutsche Bank in New York by 2007 had built up a large investment base in mortgage-related securities with a face value of $128 billion but a market value of only $25 billion. On the other hand it had a $5 billion dollar bet against the market in the form of a 'short position' on which in 2008 it eventually made a profit of $1.5 billion.[12] The Royal Bank of Scotland (RBS) was also an active investor in this market, and had a subsidiary, Citizens Bank, in Greenwich, Connecticut. Northern Rock in the UK, a traditional regional mortgage lender, expanded its mortgage lending and securitised some of it with the same buyers in the US as were buying domestic CDOs and related vehicles. In Germany, the seven 'Landesbanken', traditional regional lenders owned by local community banks but backed by state governments, were also active in the market, as was Rabobank, owned by Dutch agricultural cooperatives and the Spanish 'casas' or provincial banks.

RBS and Northern Rock incurred losses in 2007, which in the case of Northern Rock created the first run on a UK bank for 150 years, and both were taken into state ownership. In Germany, the largest of the Landesbanken, WestLB, totally failed, others had to be bailed out by state aid, and Landesbank Hessen-Thüringen was rescued by its component local savings banks. In neither the UK nor Germany had regulators proved more effective than in the US, although in Germany in the case of Landesbank Baden-Württemburg, the CEO went on trial for 'failing to disclose risk' and the whole former board of HSH Nordbank, in Schleswig-Holstein, went on trial on charges of inflating the balance sheet. In each of these cases, the banks, with a historic record as retail lenders based on their members' deposits, borrowed in the wholesale markets to finance their investment in this new class of asset. They had taken the credit rating agencies at their nominal value and now paid a heavy price.

How was this behaviour of the credit rating agencies allowed to occur? The agencies reported only to their own shareholders: the fourfold increase in fees that they earned from the subprime market was a boon. Furthermore, the fact that their fees were paid by the issuers of the securities they were grading was a perpetual incentive to give them a high rating. However they worked unchallenged by any authority and had long resisted being regulated themselves, and had successfully lobbied Congress for many years to achieve that status. This was reversed in 2006 when Congress passed the Credit Rating Agency Reform Act (which was mainly a response to the earlier Enron crisis). Senator Levin's Permanent Subcommittee of Investigation took the view that this legislation triggered the agencies' subsequent mass downgrade. The rating agencies were at the heart of the crisis and their wilful disguise of risk was corrupt.

The failure of the regulators went well beyond the rating agencies. The key regulators of the subprime lending business were the Office of Thrift Supervision (OTS) and the Office of the Comptroller of the Currency (OCC). The Seattle-based

Washington Mutual ('WaMu') was the largest of the 'thrifts', which the OTS supervised with $300 billion in assets, and the regulator had plenty of concerns. Between 2004 and 2008 it raised 500 deficiencies in WaMu's operations but the lender failed to act on most of them. The concerns were more than legitimate: when depositors finally became aware in 2007/8 of WaMu's weaknesses, they withdrew $26 billion in a few months. Eventually, in a move too late to save the bank, the OTS forced its closure, leading to an eventual sale to J.P. Morgan for a token $1.9 billion.[13]

A convenient peculiarity of the regulatory system was that, where activities of a financial agency were to some degree mixed and so did not necessarily fall under a particular regulator, the credit rating agency could select its own regulator, always selecting the one that would interfere least. As the subprime crisis mounted in 2007, Countrywide, a key and eventually notorious player in the subprime market converted to being an S&L from a bank-holding company so that its regulator became the OTS with its limited capacity for follow-up. AIG, the gigantic insurance company, with a huge derivatives business also registered as an S&L and similarly switched to OTS as the regulator for this part of its operations.

A 'light touch' approach was not the only limitation of the regulators in relation to the market. The most important of these was the Securities and Exchange Commission (SEC) whose Division of Trading and Markets nominally had wide responsibilities. However, the Commodities Futures Modernization Act of 2000 had ensured that the new sophisticated financial products would avoid regulation altogether and that they could not impose record-keeping on this market. Therefore, the SEC could not even ask the banks to report on their holdings of swap trades. As a result, the credit default swap market was 'ripe for fraud and manipulation'.[14] A different legal limitation was imposed on state level regulators, who were prevented by the federal Supreme Court from enforcing state consumer protection laws against banks chartered at the federal level.

Why was support for limiting regulation so strong? The situation was the outcome of a build-up of opinion in favour of near complete deregulation of financial markets on the grounds that they were self-correcting, so that institutions experiencing both frauds and loan failures would be swallowed up by stronger and more robust competitors. The powerful pressure for deregulation came from three sources: a renewed enthusiasm among influential economists for untrammelled market forces, politicians at state level (often moving to the federal level), and major players on Wall Street who were recycled to Washington in key positions in policymaking, the Treasury, 'regulatory' agencies and the Federal Reserve Bank.

The appointment by President Clinton of Robert Rubin, who had a background in risk arbitrage in Goldman Sachs, as director of the National Economic Council in 1993 and later in 1995 as secretary to the Treasury, ensured that a strong voice with experience in the new financial products would play a leading role in the development of policy. In close association with Alan Greenspan, chairman of the Federal Reserve, Rubin advised Clinton to reject the regulation of derivatives that was proposed in 1997 both by the Commodity Futures Trading Commission (CFTC)[15] and in several draft Bills in Congress.[16] Critical resistance to this came from the International Swaps and Derivatives Association (ISDA), a lobbying group financed by the banks, whose leverage in Congress was formidable. In 1998, Rubin and Greenspan shared public support for a moratorium on regulatory action, a precursor to subsequent legislation in 2001 that ruled out the subsequent regulation of derivatives.[17]

The succession of George W. Bush in that year ensured that there would be continuity in the influence of the big investment banks. Hank Paulson, who had also worked for Goldman Sachs from 1974 to 2006, became Bush's secretary of the Treasury and was an important enthusiast for the apparent risk-diminishing characteristics of the new financial products. At least a dozen senior ex-Goldman personnel joined government during the Clinton and Bush administrations, ensuring extraordinary continuity in the deregulation process.

A critical prize from this infiltration of policymakers from Wall Street was the repeal in 1999 of the Glass–Steagall Act of 1933, which separated commercial and investment banking. Although this division had been weakening for some years, it was only when Citicorp took over Travelers Insurance in 1998 that the separation was recognised as effectively redundant. Citicorp's lobbying prowess led to the subsequent introduction of the Gramm–Leach–Blilely Act of 1999, which created a new category of financial holding company with a very broad remit, enabling them to carry out almost any financial activity – to which several of the investment banks would eventually turn.

The mosaic that emerged from these forces is one in which campaign contributions (to anti-regulation senators and congressmen), funding for lobbyists, a 'revolving door' between Wall Street and Washington and well-articulated views from some key states created pressure for finance sector deregulation that ultimately proved overwhelming. However, the campaign, even with some powerful defenders in academic circles, disguised risk-taking on a promiscuous scale that in the short term was very harmful to millions of subprime borrowers, but also triggered an international financial crisis with an untold number of casualties, and with a huge impact on national economies. In this case, the interests of the banks had predominated at the expense of the public – a clear example of the corruption of influence.

This US mosaic is relatively subtle compared to the more blatant forms of corruption that characterised the extraordinary illegal acts of the European banks – or the European subsidiaries of American banks – in the first decade of the twenty-first century. A pattern of behaviour has emerged, focused particularly on the 'fixing' of interest rates determined by LIBOR (the London Interbank Offered Rate, which determines interest rates used in a range of markets) and parallel rate-fixing systems determining interest rates of the yen and the euro. These have been exposed in parallel with money-laundering cases involving major banks and the facilitation of tax evasion on a huge scale. The content of these cases has been revealed in a series of court cases that have unfolded from 2009 onwards and that by 2015 had led to fines totalling $235 billion being imposed by courts in the US and Europe. The US courts have been responsible for more than 90 per cent of these fines.

The rigging of LIBOR had been under investigation by the US Department of Justice from 2013. In 2014, Barclays Bank made an out-of-court settlement with various investors in which they paid $20 million to the investors and shared documents detailing relevant communications with other banks in relation to LIBOR.[18] In the same year, a UBS trader, Tom Hayes, had been charged by the US Department of Justice with the manipulation of LIBOR. His case was eventually taken over by the UK Serious Fraud Office (SFO), which brought a case against him in 2015. During the court case, the counsel for the prosecution described the trader as 'the ringmaster at the very centre' of the conspiracy. The SFO played tapes to the jury in which Hayes said:

> I probably deserve to be sitting here because, you know, I made concerted efforts to influence LIBOR. And, you know, although I was operating within a system, or participating within a system in which it was commonplace, you know, ultimately I was someone who was a serial offender within that.[19]

However, at the time of the court case in July 2015, Hayes said that:

> Everything I did my managers knew about... sometimes going up all the way to the CEO.[20]

This statement is at the heart of the question of where responsibility for the banks' actions lay and why no bank CEOs or chairmen have been charged in either Europe or the US (although the chairman of the executive board of Rabobank, Piet Moerland, resigned in 2013 citing responsibility for placing his bank in such an exposed position[21]). However in cases relating to LIBOR and other interest rate benchmarks in 2014 and 2015, the other banks participating in the network have been fined as institutions, implying a judicial acceptance that the banks' management was either fully informed about the practice or should take responsibility for failing to be informed.[22]

Manipulation by traders of the foreign exchange market had taken a similar pattern, causing the UK's Financial Conduct Authority (FCA) to carry out a major investigation in 2013. It found that the key London rate used to determine inter-currency rates (WM 4pm 'fix') was regularly being subverted by traders' manipulation of the rate. Drawing on colourful e-mail evidence of exchanges between traders ('there you go... go early, move it, hold it, push it'), the FCA concluded that:

> The traders formed tight knit groups or one to one relationships based upon mutual benefit... entry into some of these groups or relationship was controlled by the participants. These groups were given names, among them 'A Team' and the '3 Musketeers'.[23]

As a consequence of this investigation, and in an unprecedented move, four regulators in the US and Europe – the FCA in the UK, the CFTC and the OCC in the US, and FINMA in Switzerland – imposed fines totalling $4.3 billion on six of the world's largest banks. J.P. Morgan and Citigroup paid $1.01 billion and $1.02 billion respectively.[24] In 2015 Barclays, which was not one of the six, made a provision for a fine of $1.25 billion in relation to this market, although it was subsequently fined $2.32 billion for this offence. This case strengthened the public perception that rigging of markets in this way constituted corruption.[25] Andrea Leadsom, the then UK's economic secretary to the Treasury, stated in a BBC interview that: 'I think taxpayers will be horrified... I don't know if corruption is a strong enough word for it.'[26]

However, recognition by the courts of criminal wrongdoing by the banks has gone beyond the manipulation of interest rate and foreign exchange benchmarks. In the US, while fines for evading sanctions have been important, the highest-value fines have been for the exploitative selling or on-selling of mortgages in the subprime market, and in the UK for the gross overcharging of insurance products designed to guarantee repayment of mortgages and loans in the event of an unavoidable default. Between 2008 and 2014, total fines of $235 billion were led by Bank of America ($80 billion), J.P. Morgan ($38 billion) and Lloyds ($20 billion). Table 3 captures the weight of different offences and the leading offending bank.

The fact that recognition of criminal activity is indicated by these figures is at one level impressive. However, it is important to recognise that more than 90 per cent of the total of $235 billion has been levied in US courts and that there has been no trial of a CEO or other key executive in any of these cases. This is in stark contrast to the trials involving criminal activity in the S&L sector in the 1980s, when 800 S&L executives or chairmen were prosecuted. The reasons for this are not hard to see: the power of influence by the big banks in Washington is paramount and emanates from their strategic support to key chairmen and members of congressional committees.

In the UK, the influence of HSBC, Barclays, RBS and Lloyds in both the Treasury and Parliament has been irresistible. By 2016, it was clear that the UK Treasury was determined to relax moves to tighter regulation that had been heralded by Mark Carney, governor of the Bank of England. Martin Wheatley, appointed to be the first CEO of the Financial Conduct Authority in 2012, who had vowed to 'shoot from the hip and ask questions later', was to be replaced by a 'safer pair of hands'. The banks themselves, in reformist mode for five years or so, changed tack, as indicated in the resignation required from the CEO of Barclays, Antony Jenkins, who had sought to engage the majority of bank staff in a far-reaching

Table 3　Total bank fines by offence and largest payment (2008–15)

Offence	Total fines (in billion $)	Highest fine by bank	Total fine (in billion $)
Misselling mortgages (US)	140	Bank of America	80.0
Misselling insurance (UK)	43.5	HSBC	5.3
Sanctions and money-laundering	23.6	BNP	8.9
Forex manipulation	9.9	Barclays	2.3
LIBOR and interest rate manipulation	7.7	Deutsche	3.5
Facilitation for tax avoidance	3.4	Credit Suisse	2.6

Source: Taku Dzimwasha, '20 global banks have paid $235 billion in fines since 2008', *International Business Times* and Reuters Graphics, 24 May 2015.

ethics programme. The composition of the new Banking Standards Board, partly set up to address 'banking culture' was full of good intentions but was designed to seek influence by argument and had no teeth.

Questions surrounding the banking crisis continue to reverberate through the media and in political circles. The consequences of the crisis remain with society as a whole. The 'technical' origins of the crisis – from an imbalance in global liquidity to the accelerated growth of a plethora of new financial mechanisms – have been discussed in a range of books.[27] But the moral issues underlying it have received less attention. Doubts about whether 'rate-fixing' is really a form of corruption have shaped the debate and moderated the analysis. In fact, each facet of the crisis can be safely described as corrupt.

Some of the controversy centres on whether it was the banks as institutions that had become corrupt or if it was the individuals within them? Each case is different. In 'subprime', the individual agents, many of whom were registered brokers, who persuaded low-income borrowers to accept 'risky' mortgages can be safely categorised as 'loan sharks'. The mortgage providers and banks that employed the agents saddled their institutions with faulty assets at the expense of their shareholders and depositors – an institutional question. The investment banks that hoovered up the mortgages and securitised them, often only mechanically, came close to deliberately misleading the finance houses, including those in Europe, which bought them. This too was an institutional question. The reliance of all parties on credit rating agencies who distributed Triple AAAs in response to fees from those they were rating was also an institutional question. In the 'subprime' drama, the argument that corruption was restricted to individuals or teams of individuals cannot be upheld.

In the case of market-rigging, the case for individuals rather than the banks to be held responsible is a more open question, which turns on whether senior managers knew what was happening in these very fast-moving markets. As we have shown, it was a defence of Tom Hayes, the UBS trader, to say that his managers knew all about his activities in the market. Other cases, notably where traders have lost huge sums, suggest that traders can easily evade the eye of management. The networks explored in the several relevant trials show how few players are needed to achieve a successful rigging of the market. But the evidence presented to Senator Levin's committee on the financial crisis – notably in its investigation of decision making within Goldman Sachs[28] – suggests that boards understood what their traders were doing, and so should be held responsible both for the actions of the traders and the culture that had enabled it. It is clear that the advice given by Andrew McCulloch, as first Comptroller of the US Treasury to 'pursue a straightforward, upright, legitimate banking business' has suffered a fundamental shock from which it has yet to recover.

6

On- and Offshore Secrets

In 2012–13, the International Consortium of Investigative Journalists (ICIJ) conducted an unprecedented investigation into accounts held in many of the world's 'offshore centres', which may be better defined as secrecy jurisdictions. Mobilising 86 journalists in 46 countries, it examined 2.5 million accounts attributed to 130,000 people leading to reports published in five of the world's most serious newspapers. The director of the project for ICIJ, Gerard Ryle, commented in March 2013 that the investigation had revealed:

> A well-paid industry of accountants, middlemen and other operatives [that] has helped offshore patrons shroud their identities and business interests, providing shelter in many cases to money laundering or other misconduct. This involves many of the world's top banks – including UBS, Clariden and Deutsche Bank.[1]

The ICIJ accused these banks of having 'aggressively worked to provide their customers with secrecy-cloaked companies in the British Virgin Islands and other offshore hideaways'.[2]

The list of alleged tax evaders was as long as it was diverse, including government officials and their families in places as varied as Pakistan, Azerbaijan, Thailand and Canada. The ICIJ also commented that the list also includes, 'American doctors and dentists and middle-class Greek villagers as well as families and associates of long-time despots, Wall Street swindlers, Eastern European and Indonesian billionaires, Russian corporate executives, international arms dealers and a sham-director-fronted company that the European Union has labelled as a cog in Iran's nuclear-development program.'[3]

The ICIJ reinforced this coup in April 2016 when it acquired a huge set of files from the legal company Mossack Fonseca, based in Panama, which were immediately dubbed the Panama Papers.[4] This cache of data included 11.5 million documents and, among many other findings, identified 113,300 shell companies that had been established by the company in the British Virgin Isles on behalf of a wide range of clients including 14 current and former heads of state or national leaders.

The continued existence of 'secrecy jurisdictions' – or places where the identity of the owner of financial assets can be disguised[5] – is one of the greatest incentives to forms of corruption that may take place thousands of miles from their location. It is the secretive element of this system that defines it. And so countries such as Luxembourg, which are members of the EU, or its closely associated neighbours such as Monaco, or Montana in the US, can offer a service in opacity that is competitive with centres with a higher profile, such as Jersey or the Cayman Islands. Switzerland, with its long history of banking secrecy, in spite of recent reforms, retains one of the world's most secretive banking sectors. The City of London, assessed on its own account, has an intermediate degree of opacity but if assessed with its affiliated network of genuinely 'offshore' centres, is highly secretive. Several US states have secrecy regimes that compete with higher-profile 'offshore' centres.

Although now under pressure from international bodies – most notably the OECD – secrecy jurisdictions provide a key haven for 'illicit flows'[6] and corruptly gained funds channelled from a wide range of countries and activities. The principal sources of these funds are:

- The evasion of tax in their country of residence by individual citizens.
- Income from 'mispricing' or the manipulation of invoicing of exports or imports to defraud exporting countries of tax revenues.
- Income from organised crime originating from both within and outside America and Europe.
- Commission and bribes from large-scale corruption taking place in a range of countries.
- Income derived from international trade in products such as coltan, illegally cut timber and 'bunkered' oil (syphoned from pipelines), which have been sold into formal markets.
- Trade in small arms that have been sold into small and large-scale wars.

Although there is no totally reliable estimate for the aggregate value of these flows, the annual total is assessed by several competent analysts at about $1 trillion per year. The total value of the 'stock' of these flows is more open to dispute but is often placed at a minimum of $10 trillion,[7] equal to about half the assets in the US banking system.

However, this widely disbursed cluster of secrecy jurisdictions is largely managed by the same banks who manage the markets of formal financial centres such as New York, London and Frankfurt. No international investment bank is without a subsidiary in one or more of these centres. For example, Barclays Bank confirmed to the UK House of Commons Committee in 2009 that it had 315 subsidiaries in various secrecy jurisdictions.[8] While local and state governments may set broad incentives and determine whether taxation is zero or nominal, the real players are the banks domiciled there. Whether or not they are the subsidiaries of large international banks they are also the 'correspondent' banks of a range of banks throughout the world and have funds transferred to them on an automatic and overnight basis. One of the advantages of this for the banks is that funds can then be transferred to the larger financial centres and so increase their liquidity.

The Tax Justice Network is a leading analyst of these networks and its *Financial Secrecy Index* ranks centres in terms of their degree of secrecy, principally in relation to both governments and international investigators with a valid rationale for investigation. The 'most secretive' states include the ten that are British 'Overseas Territories' in the Caribbean and Gibraltar. However, in the same category are Switzerland, San Marino (linked to Italy) and Liechtenstein (geographically close to Germany). There is a second category of secrecy that includes the Channel Islands and the Isle of Man (close to the UK) and Monaco (close to France). The US states with comparable jurisdictions fall somewhere between these two, as discussed below.

This is a system that is very well established and very useful as a means of disguising activity that would be considered to be unacceptable by public opinion in most of the EU and the US, as the initial reactions to the ICIJ exposures confirmed. The attractions of those centres under UK jurisdiction lie primarily in three factors: first a legal acceptance since the nineteenth century of the principle that there is a legal distinction between where a company is registered and from where it is controlled; second, the use of 'trusts', which enable the real ('beneficial') owners of assets to appoint trustees who become the real managers of the assets (and often neither of whom can be identified in an accessible register); and third, a deliberate strategy agreed between the governments of both the UK and the centres concerned to promote them as safe financial havens within a broadly attractive legal framework. The first two of these factors also apply within the US states that have comparable rules for facilitating financial secrecy.

The attractions of Switzerland lie in its longstanding tradition of anonymous banking fully recognised in its legalisation of secret accounts in 1934. This has been severely challenged in recent years, particularly as a result of successful legal pressure from the US government to provide data on the accounts of thousands of US citizens who were sheltering their income and capital from tax. This ran in parallel with pressure from the government of Germany on Liechtenstein, which was unsuccessful until a whistle-blower provided data – for a price – on 1,000 German citizens with accounts held there in the LGT Bank in 2005.

An even more dramatic case of private tax evasion was generated by an exposé of HSBC in 2015 (which post-dated the ICIJ exposures of 2013).[9] The giant international bank had been criticised for hosting the accounts of 7,000 UK citizens, primarily high-net-worth individuals including a number of celebrities, in a private bank owned by HSBC in Geneva. The content of thousands of these accounts was collected on disc and conveyed to the tax authorities in France by Hervé Falciani, a part-time IT specialist at the bank in 2010. It revealed a representative cross-section of accounts typical of banks in such jurisdictions. Among clients of HSBC later identified in leaks to a consortium of media outlets were Rami Makhlouf, the cousin of President Assad and said to be the richest man in Syria. He held $15 million in multiple accounts and some of his assets were vested in Drex Technologies, a shell company registered in the British Virgin Isles which was on US sanctions lists from 2008. Clients from Africa included Shailesh Vithlani, a key player in a 2005 deal involving the sale by BAE Systems of a radar surveillance system to Tanzania earning him a $10 million commission. In South Africa, an agent close to the African National Congress, Fana Hlongwane, acted for at least four international arms companies and maintained accounts that also held more than $10 million in 2006. In the same year, Kenya was shaken by the 'Anglo Leasing' scandal in which more than $600 million was diverted to shell companies nominally domiciled in the UK. Two of the architects of the deal on the Kenyan side were Deepak Kamani and Anura Perera whose commissions were held by HSBC before being channelled to other offshore entities under their control.

As EU governments have moved to curtail their citizens' tax-evading strategies, the banks and finance houses have developed countervailing offers to their clients. In 2003, Switzerland signed an agreement with the EU that would allow deposits in Swiss banks to maintain their secret status, in return for the banks handing over an initial 15 per cent of income from savings accounts to tax authorities in other EU states. In order to assist clients to avoid even this light level of taxation, HSBC offered to establish a shell company for a specific client in an offshore jurisdiction such as Panama or the British Virgin Islands. This vehicle in turn could be owned by an offshore trust in, for example, Liechtenstein, where the content of the trust deed would remain secret and the crucial separation of ownership (the original beneficiaries) and control (appointed but anonymous trustees) can be maintained. When the pirated information from HSBC reached the UK tax authority, it found that at least 1,000 of the 7,000 UK clients of the bank had been evading tax through such vehicles. These figures come from the case of one bank, although a very large one.

However, funds on a huge scale derived from corrupt sources, including 'illegal' capital fight, may be laundered through London and New York as well as through dedicated 'secrecy jurisdictions'.

The international property market is awash with funds that have first been deposited in these jurisdictions and that have been expatriated from a range of countries. Within the property market, both New York and London are prime magnets. An investigation into this by Transparency International UK in 2015 found that 10,000 properties had been bought in the UK by an offshore entity in 2014 and that the total number of such properties in 2012 was 95,000.[10] An earlier study by the *Financial Times* found that a total of a minimum $140 billion[11] was invested in UK property from an offshore jurisdiction. In the prime section of this market (with a value of $11 billion), China accounted for 16 per cent, Russia for 11 per cent and the Middle East and Africa for 12 per cent. Within this prime market group, 36,000 properties (both residential and commercial) were registered to shell companies in secrecy juris-dictions, of which 60 per cent were in the UK's 'offshore network'. Clearly, the scale of the investment and the standard use of shell companies suggests at a minimum an objective of evading taxes on a huge scale and often represents the laundering of corruptly gained funds into this market.

The scale and impact of this kind of money-laundering is assessed globally by the IMF at between $2.5 and $3.8 trillion per year. These figures are equivalent to between 3 and 5 per cent of global GDP and represent a much broader range of funds than those that are channelled directly into specific 'secrecy jurisdic-tions'. While the overall figure is contested[12] there is also a lack of a reliable analysis of the division of the total by country. In the case of the UK, the Financial Services Authority estimated total funds laundered at between $40 billion and $85 billion in 2014, repre-senting between 1 and 2 per cent of the world total. The compar-able estimated figure for the US in 2014 was $300 billion,[13] mainly attributed to fraud and drug trafficking.

A parallel situation exists in New York, where the annual investment in properties with a value of over $5 million is $8 billion, about half of which is bought by shell companies with anonymous owners registered either in US states where ownership can remain secret, or in offshore jurisdictions in the Caribbean.[14] In both these cases, money with a dubious origin has been invested in very high-value property, yet its ownership has been obscured. While the proportion of these property investments that can be attributed to funds laundered from criminal activities is not clear,

the scale of the investment and the standard use of shell companies suggests at a minimum an objective of evading taxes on a huge
scale and often represents the laundering of corruptly gained funds
into the formal property market.

A more direct destination of laundered funds are commercial banks and other financial institutions, each of whom
are required to report attempted deposits of more than $10,000.
Among other checks, the banks are supposed to determine
whether these funds have been placed by 'politically exposed
persons' (PEPs) who appear on a shared international list. This
includes both elected politicians and civil servants of regimes
considered dubious, and numbered 46,888 in 2014. Under anti-
money-laundering regulations, the banks are supposed to make
a 'Suspicious Activity Report' (SAR), which may relate to PEPs or
simply to an individual attempting to make multiple deposits. In
2014, the UK National Crime Agency (NCA) made reports covering only £230 million and put a stop to only half of the transactions involved. This figure represents about 0.4 per cent of the total
flow of laundered funds estimated by the then Financial Services
Authority. However, within the EU, the NCA delivers a higher
number of reported SARs to Europol (the principal coordinator
of police investigatory work) than any other member country,
implying that the SARs regime is generally extremely ineffective
across Europe. Clearly, these checks are completely inadequate
as a means of ensuring that corrupt funds are excluded from the
banking system in London and New York. There is also no reason
to suspect that total flows of laundered funds will diminish over
the next decade, since the underlying conditions in Russia, China
and the Middle East make a reduced drive to externalise funds
unlikely, and the attractions of the US and parts of the EU as 'safe
havens' are likely to be sustained. Consequently the 'stock' of laundered funds is likely to increase.

The question of the identity of corporate ownership is also
a critical touchstone of the extent to which forms of corruption

are tolerated. While on the one hand the G8 and G20 in 2016 are addressing the question of 'beneficial ownership' the number of shell – and therefore secretive – companies holding assets in Switzerland has dramatically increased in recent years. In 1982 they accounted for just 30 per cent of accounts and in 2014 for 60 per cent of them.[15] The UK has made a commitment to making beneficial ownership fully transparent in company registers. However, the legislation passed in 2014 did not extend to foreign companies operating in the country, or to companies in secrecy jurisdictions holding UK assets. In relation to companies from the rest of the EU, this gap will be partly addressed by a requirement that all countries have a beneficial ownership registry in place by 2017. It remains to be seen how effective these measures will be and whether they will be riddled by exceptions.

States' rights and opacity

The US is both an international campaigner for maximum transparency in banking and a combatant of 'illicit financial flows' while living with a corporate registration regime that at the level of some states is very contradictory. This fits into a broader framework at the federal level where for many decades US government policy has sought to make the country an attractive haven for international capital, creating a generous regulatory and low tax environment for footloose capital. This has extended to a legal regime that has allowed financial institutions to handle the proceeds of crime, provided that the crime was committed outside the US. The International Banking Facility Act of 1981 allowed US banks to maintain separate books of account that allowed them to be exempted from the banking regulations that were then driving many of them abroad. In recognition of the contradiction this posed to US international policy, in 2010 Congress passed the Foreign Account Tax Compliance Act (FATCA), which required all US citizens living abroad to report their overseas income and pay tax upon it.

The key states in the game of opacity are Delaware, Wyoming and Nevada, with Colorado and Montana not far behind. Each of these provides a suite of facilities to companies seeking secrecy. This process originated from roots without an international dimension but came to be seen by the states as a very valuable source of revenue. By 1986, Delaware was advertising its non-transparent services on the basis that 'we protect you from politics (of your own country)'. This stand was strongly supported by the state-level service providers who stood to gain most from it. The consequence has been far-reaching: two million companies are formed in the US every year, many of them anonymously, without state-level regulators asking for the identity of their owners.

Senator Carl Levin (D-Michigan), who retired from the Senate in 2015, has been a consistent critic of this system. As ranking minority member and later chairman of the Permanent Subcommittee on Investigations, Levin commented that of companies formed 'a minority function as a conduit for organised crime, money-laundering, security fraud, tax evasion and other misconduct'.[16] In a hearing in 2006, he told the Committee that Colorado incorporates 5,000 companies each month, nearly all of them set up by computer with no human intervention or review of the identity of the shareholders.[17] The cost of establishing such a company is less than $100. The same Committee heard that the FBI estimated that $36 billion had been laundered into the US from the former Soviet Union through these vehicles. The Department of Justice reported to the Committee that $15 million of federal government funds intended to upgrade the safety of nuclear plants in the ex-Soviet Union had been diverted by Russian officials into shell companies in Pennsylvania and Delaware. The chairman of the Committee at the time, Senator Coleman, commented, 'these financial and support services rival those offered in some of the most notorious offshore havens'.[18]

An assessment of the lack of transparency in nearly all secrecy jurisdictions is made by the Financial Action Task Force (FATF), an international watchdog originally set up by the G8 in 1995, but now with a wide membership of 36 countries. In assessing its members one of its criteria is whether the 'beneficial ownership' of a company is clear. Of the 12 countries evaluated in 2012, only two were completely non-compliant: Switzerland and the US.

It is clear that both banks and the governments of secrecy jurisdictions are crucial to sustaining the system. But there is a crucial intermediary: the audit and accounting profession. The 'big 4' auditors (PwC, Deloitte, KPMG and Ernst & Young), the majority of whose business is derived from forms of consultancy, have been very active in formulating and marketing tax evasion mechanisms for individuals and companies. In 2013 the UK House of Commons Public Accounts Committee recorded that according to HMRC in 2005 'half of all known tax evasion schemes had been marketed by the Big Four'.

How did these schemes work? Deloitte had designed a scheme for Deutsche Bank that used a vehicle registered in the Cayman Islands to enable 300 of its staff to avoid both income tax and national insurance payments on their bonuses. In 2005, Ernst & Young established an 'employment benefit trust' in Jersey for the same purpose of avoiding tax – a vehicle that was, however, declared unlawful by the House of Lords in July 2005. In May 2012, the BBC documentary programme, *Panorama*, showed how PwC had designed schemes to enable the pharmaceutical giant GSK, and the UK newspaper publishing group Northern and Shell to shift profits to Luxembourg through transfer pricing and a complex intra-company loan system (in a context where income from interest payments attract no tax).

There has been a high degree of public interest in both Europe and the US in the very low levels of tax paid by software giants such as Google, Microsoft and Apple, heavily challenged in 2016. In each of these cases, tax advisers have set up systems that have been possible only because of the 'secrecy jurisdictions'. Between 2006 and 2011, Google UK generated revenues of $18 billion but paid only $16 million in tax, achieved by routing revenue from the UK and elsewhere through both Ireland and Bermuda. In 2013, Google argued to the House of Commons Public Accounts Committee that because its advertising sales take place in Ireland, the tax arrangements are lawful. The chair of the Committee, MP Margaret Hodge, stated that:

> This argument is deeply unconvincing and has been undermined by information from whistleblowers, including ex-employees of Google, who told us that UK based staff are engaged in selling. The staff in Ireland simply process the bills. The company's highly contrived tax arrangement has no purpose other than to enable the company to avoid UK corporation tax.[19]

But the UK is far from the only 'victim' of the tax strategies of the current digital corporate giants. The US, as their original domicile and source of their technical brilliance, has also been deprived of revenue it could very well use. Of total US corporate profits of $2.1 trillion in 2013, about $650 billion came from foreign sources. However, 55 per cent of this figure ($360 billion) is sourced from tax havens or countries with extremely compliant tax regimes – Bermuda, Luxembourg, Ireland, Singapore, Switzerland and the Netherlands – indicating that about 20 per cent of US corporate profits accrue in tax havens. They are liable to a 35 per cent tax if and when repatriated and so tend to be held offshore or reticulated to the US only over several years.

* * *

The existence of 'secrecy jurisdictions' and the ease with which illicit funds can be laundered through financial centres is not accidental. It is a phenomenon that has grown over time because it has satisfied different interlocking interest groups. These include the major international banks, able to increase their total deposits through 'offshore' subsidiaries; the governments of the US and the UK, keen to see increased deposits in dollar and sterling accounts; wealthy individuals keen to avoid domestic taxation and multinational companies eager to 'park' funds in low- or zero-tax regimes before channelling them (if at all) to their national domicile. The companies concerned have in many cases a stock of funds gained through 'mispricing' that form a part of the corporate funds held in these jurisdictions.

The network that has been generated by these converging interest groups has also proved a boon to organised crime and the perpetrators of large-scale corruption who have been able to hide their assets in various parts of the system. Although there have been challenges to the system since the 1990s, it has only been since 2012 that there has been a serious attempt to reduce the attractions of these jurisdictions to companies and individuals. For the time being, as the Swiss experience shows, the number of shell companies registered within them is growing rather than falling, and the overall picture is still one in which the jurisdictions are a boon to those seeking to evade taxes, hoard corruptly gained funds and disguise the fruits of organised crime.

7

Justice for Sale?

> Given the nature of police work, it is no shame to find corruption within the service: the shame is not doing anything about it.[1]
>
> *Association of Chief Police Officers, UK*

Police corruption: Transforming blue walls of silence

The suburbs of Marseille are a tough place. Although famous for the footballers who grew up there, Zinedine Zidane and Eric Cantona, the citizens of France's poorest big city seldom have glorious careers. In 2012, a third of all murders in France took place in the Marseille region, with almost all victims under the age of 30.[2] Two-thirds of these murders were gang-related. But, as French criminologist Xavier Raufer, states: 'the murders are not Marseille's biggest problem, it's just a symptom. The real problem is monumental corruption.'[3] While Marseille is no longer the prime drug hub for cocaine and heroin, it remains still a crime hub. With a young population, high unemployment, a drug trade now focused on cannabis and generally bleak socio-economic perspectives, the city has upheld its ill reputation for crime and grime. In a recent case of corruption involving the police, it has added a reputation for police corruption to the list when a ring of 30 police officers was busted. The officers extorted 'cash that fund[ed] luxury life-styles of swimming pools and fast cars for officers [who] brazenly waltz[ed] into restaurants […], [ate] and told the boss they weren't paying'.[4] The officers accused made up half of the elite anti-crime squad 'Brigade Anti-Criminalité Nord'. They were arrested on charges of corruption in 2012 for regularly extorting money from drug dealers, knowing full well that these would not be in a position to report them.[5] The officers also took their share of drugs, cigarettes and money from the dealers that they were supposed to keep in check.[6]

Corruption in the Marseille police force had been taken to such extremes that it is not surprising that such activities were possible, but that they were stopped at all. Three different whistle-blowers had reported police corruption cases in Marseille to their superiors prior to the allegations coming to light in 2012, but no action was taken. Instead, the local police chief was promoted to a national security position. Of the 30 police officers suspected to be involved in the case and suspended pending investigation, 16 were later indicted on charges of theft and extortion, and seven were placed under judicial review. In 2013, every one of them was rein-stated, although some with suspensions for up to 15 months, or suf-fered only a modest demotion. The only person not to be reinstated as a police officer was officer Sebastien Bennardo, the whistle-blower. He was made to leave the police force for insubordination.[7]

While systemic police corruption and involvement in crimes should not be regarded as a regular phenomenon in Europe and North America, it would be wrong to regard the Marseille case as an isolated incident. Bribe-taking, turning a blind eye to criminal activity, selective enforcement and the influence of political interests happen at an individual as well as at a departmental level.[8] In the US, media stories since the 1970s have covered corruption in the police when police crime and corruption was rampant. New York holds the record with respect to the number of major police corruption scandals, which appear to come at almost regular 20-year intervals: 1895, 1913, 1932, 1954, 1973 and 1994. The *Knapp Commission Report on Police Corruption*, published in 1972, exposed major corruption in New York City's police force, and set the tone in defining police corruption. During their investigation, the Commission differentiated between 'grass eaters' – officers involved in petty corruption under peer pressure – and 'meat eaters' – officers who aggressively look for opportunities to solicit bribes, like searching drug dealers and pimps (so-called 'shakedowns') with the aim of soliciting bribes to let them go.

From the interviews and findings, the Commission derived a set of reform ideas, some but too few of which were put into place to deter corrupt practices in the long run. Unsurprisingly, corruption in New York's Police Department resurfaced in full force 20 years later. To look into the allegations, New York's mayor appointed Judge Milton Mollen to head a new commission. The Mollen Commission conducted hearings in 1993 and 1994 and in its report concluded that 'When connected to acts of corruption, brutality is at times a means to accomplish corrupt ends and at other times it is just a gratuitous appendage to a corrupt act… [C]ops have used or threatened to use brutality to intimidate their victims and protect themselves against the risk of complaints. We found that officers who are corrupt are more likely to be brutal.'[9] But it was not only the officers on the street who were to blame: parts of the department's internal affairs division, which would in theory have to follow up on all allegations of misconduct in their force, were on the take as well, thus turning a blind eye to brutality and corruption. In effect, corruption turned several police precincts into outlaw outfits.

The Pennsylvania Crime Commission drew similar conclusions in its 1974 report: the 'few bad apples' approach led to supervisors refusing to acknowledge that corruption was a serious problem in their departments, turning a blind eye and – wilfully or not – giving the impression that corruption was tolerated, therefore spreading the practice. While the extent of police corruption was becoming more apparent at that time, the causes for prevalent police corruption were less researched.[10] What did become clear was that corruption not only went hand-in-hand with violence, but also drugs – from robbing drug dealers to soliciting bribes from them in return for protection – and that the police culture of loyalty and secrecy led to a degree of impunity.[11] At the same time, the 'good apples' were vulnerable for corruption not only by criminals seeking to avoid prosecution but also by their corrupt colleagues who were forcing them to stay loyal to the force at all costs.[12] This 'blue wall' or 'blue code of silence' is the downside of the exceptionally strong bond between police forces and their sense of loyalty.

As seen, cases of police corruption can be found on both sides of the Atlantic. Scandals around police corruption have surfaced not only in the US and France, but also in Spain, Britain, Belgium, Germany, Australia and the Netherlands.[13] The cases of police corruption in Europe – like their North American counterparts – do not solely evolve around police bribery, but also around political meddling in police operations and the subsequent inaction of police departments. A mixture of police inaction, (alleged) bribery and political interference were present in two illustrative cases in Belgium and Austria respectively.

In one of Belgium's most notorious criminal cases, the so-called Marc Dutroux affair, alleged corruption and inadequate police action led to the early release of a convicted rapist who then – protected by police incompetence and political influence over the police force – remained free. As a result, four young girls were murdered.[14] A subsequent parliamentary enquiry found political interference indirectly to be a major reason why the girls were not helped by the police. Politicians influenced police promotions, which led to poorly motivated leaders, and interfered with investigations. This, in turn, left the police force unable to prevent the murder of the girls. While there were allegations of Dutroux having bribed police officers, the commission tasked with getting to the bottom of the failure of the justice system in this case noted political meddling, incompetence and an absence of police and prosecutorial coordination as root causes for the multiple failures.[15]

In Vienna, the interaction between police officers and people seeking to gain influence took the form of an obscure private membership club called Friends of the Viennese Police. Founded in 1973, the club states on its website that its aim is to inform the public about the challenging and important work of the police. The website does not give much information about recent activities aside from special cameras worth €110,000 that were donated to the police force by the club in 2014. In 2007, the club came under scrutiny by Austria's investigators as a go-between for 'gifts' and donations to the police. In return for their membership and generous donations, members received benefits such as a sticker with the club emblem. Placed on the owner's car, it was said to bring 'good luck' when being stopped by a police officer. If the sticker did not suffice, a phone call to other club members usually stopped any investigation or tickets for speeding, illegal parking or other offences in its tracks. Its members were illustrious, from well-known industrialists to the former chair of the Austrian central bank (who is the president of the club). Allegedly, even the owner of a well-known brothel applied for membership but was turned down, according to the 'Friends'. It was alleged that the club had also provided travel cheques to Police Chief Roland Horngacher but the club was not found guilty of any wrongdoing or bribery offence.[16]

The extent of police corruption and impunity, naturally, does not go unnoticed by the public. Some 42 per cent of Americans believe that the police are corrupt or extremely corrupt.[17] Even in

Germany, where trust in the police is relatively high, one in five citizens believe their police force is corrupt. In Croatia, it is one in two.[18] But how corrupt are police forces in reality? Unfortunately, as is the case in other sectors, corruption in the police force is by nature difficult to measure. Although surveys such as Transparency International's *Global Corruption Barometer* (cited here) give a good indication of where bribery occurs when the police interact with citizens, it does not measure the influence of corrupt networks within the police, how many officers are part of corrupt rings, let alone how politicians or even organised crime groups infiltrate the force through corruption. Surveys of police officers are inherently difficult due to an often-found wall of silence within the force: it may be against police ethics to engage in corrupt activities, but it is certainly against 'the code' to blow the whistle on other officers, resulting in the aforementioned 'blue wall of silence' that then makes measuring police conduct with respect to integrity very difficult. When officers at the FBI National Academy in the US were asked to contribute to an anonymous survey on corruption, none of the 49 officers chose to respond, showing that reporting and detecting corruption within the police is even more difficult than it is for other civil service entities.[19] This not only makes it difficult to determine the number of corruption cases in the force, it also prevents a classification of corrupt activities.

One might be tempted to look at the number of officers sentenced for corruption. This approach relies on two factors: that corruption is actually being reported (either by the police officers themselves, a colleague or the citizen involved, all of which are rather unlikely scenarios), and in a second step, that there is a functioning and effective justice system that holds corrupt police personnel – and others – to account. Both of these together will only work in the best of circumstances but not in countries with weak governance of the judicial sector and the police. State and local prosecutors rely on police investigations and build up relationships with police officers whom they may later be reluctant to prosecute.

The higher up the chain the corruption cases go, the more likely they are going to touch upon vested interests, therefore making it less likely that they will be investigated and/or prosecuted – thus making it very unlikely that they will be recorded. A higher than global average number of police officers sentenced might therefore not necessarily be viewed as negative: it could also be indicative of a police force that is investigating its own transgressions and a justice system that deserves its name.

Structural causes for police corruption and the police's reluctance to investigate corruption (both internally and externally) are a lack of coordination between departments, absence of transparent decision making and an emphasis on reactive rather than proactive investigations. Political influence – for example, influence in promoting (or demoting) police staff, reorganising departments or meddling in the chain of investigation – are causes we have already described. Another example of outside influence is infiltration by organised crime groups, as we will see in Chapter 8. These external influences have a profound impact on police services in many countries but go beyond bribery. Influence-peddling occurs particularly where no strong oversight systems exist, making it possible for individuals to exert influence over police work.

On the bribery side, opportunity is a well-documented cause of corruption not only in law enforcement. Looking at the case of drug-related police corruption, a 1998 report by the US General Accounting Office found opportunity to be a motive, as well as greed and a streak of vigilante justice. In contrast to non-drug-related corruption, officers were more often found to act in small groups that were not necessarily indicative of a systemic departmental failure, but were at the same time well beyond the 'bad apple' explanation of just a few officers acting outside the law. This suggests that while corruption differs somewhat both in extent and in the type of related police work, a systemic approach to uprooting corruption within the force is more likely to succeed than insisting on the 'few bad apples' approach.[20]

For example, the reality of corruption across and within states and cities in the US differs widely. Cities such as Milwaukee and Kansas City have long had a reputation for low corruption and police misconduct, carrying forward a proud tradition of integrity. This tone from the top, where it is made abundantly clear that corruption or other integrity failures will not be tolerated by superiors and other colleagues, keeps new recruits on the right path, whereas corrupted departments and a culture of turning a blind eye will eventually tempt even the most honest and principled recruit to try their luck or risk missing out, or feel left out by colleagues. Other departments have also gone virtually corruption-free for decades.[21] Police departments that do not have the luxury of a longstanding code of ethics that is lived and breathed by every police officer need a variety of tools to identify the ethics and corruption problems they have and to address them. In the follow-up of severe corruption cases it is often a commission – as in the case of New York and Philadelphia – that looks into the police structure and work in detail, assesses corruption risks and recommends reforms and professional standards. These can lead to reforms on the local or national level, and there have even been reform attempts from the EU level. For Romania, the EU set up a multinational advisory group to work on police reforms, led by the UK and Spain, which concentrated on developing a disciplinary system (including a police code), powers to investigate corruption, the collaboration with civil society organisation to regain trust, and implementing an overall anti-corruption strategy. Surveys conducted within the EU study and reform packet showed that there was little understanding within the Romanian police forces of what was the expected professional standard.[22]

Belgium and the UK were two of the first countries in Europe to introduce professional standards as part of major police reforms (in 2001 and 1999 respectively) following corruption scandals. While the UK is one example of repeated police reforms and enquiries to tackle corruption in the force, the figures collected by the police complaints body reveal that the problem has not gone away: between 2008 and 2011, around 1,200 complaints with regard to corruption were made in the UK, according to the UK's Independent Police Complaints Commission.[23] This represents less than one percent of all recorded complaints made to the Commission, but the figures showed an increase over time.[24] As with other reporting and transparency measures, this may be a good thing: more complaints may mean that people are reporting things that they previously did not report, which in itself would be a good sign. However there is opacity surrounding follow up and very little sign of offending officers being taken to court. The lack of information is a serious barrier to meeting public concern.

Another finding was from both the Knapp Commission and Pennsylvania Crime Commission in the 1970s is, to a lesser extent, still true today: police officers charged with corruption are less likely to end up in court and on trial for corruption than other criminals. In the 1970s, of the police departments that were found to be highly corrupt, barely 1 percent of officers were brought to justice, indicating that fighting police corruption was not only the job of police forces but that it was also reliant on independent prosecutors and an independent and well-functioning judicial system.[25] And on the other side of the judicial divide, the situation appears even less transparent:

Judges on the line: How corruption creeps into the justice system

A particularly vivid case of corruption within the justice system – from police investigation all the way to the court room and on to the prison system – is the Pennsylvania 'kids for cash' case. Luzerne County, PA, is home to some 320,000 people. Situated some 130 miles north of Philadelphia, it has a history of coal-mining, textile industry and corruption. It was home to the Bufalino crime family, who had been active in Luzerne County since Prohibition times and had links to the American Cosa Nostra. The organisation had a good grip on coal-mining and trucking, and ran all organised crime activities in north-eastern Pennsylvania.[26] Since 1994, the organisation had been led by William 'Big Billy' D'Elia. Active in solid waste business and racketeering, he had links to two county judges: his long-time friend Judge Michael T. Conahan, and Judge Mark Ciavarella.[27] The financial entanglement of the three men and around 30 other officials and businessmen brought to light what became known as the 'kids for cash' scandal: kickbacks paid to Judges Conahan and Ciavarella that led to the unusually harsh sentencing of more than 3,000 teenagers.[28]

In essence, the scandal unravelled a network that had formed to build private prison facilities, which were then filled by juveniles who were all sentenced by county Judge Mark Ciavarella. It started as a noble enough idea: Judge Ciavarella was unsatisfied with the public correctional facilities and wanted new ones built. Known for his no-nonsense stance on crime, he was for a long time celebrated by the local community. To push the prison development along, Ciavarella met with an attorney and investor in 2000 and connected him with a local developer. Judge Michael T. Conahan – the mobster's friend – signed an agreement to house juvenile offenders in a new facility. The following years saw a tug-of war of the judges, investors and officials over the existing state facility, eventually closing the existing facility and favouring the – more expensive – newly built private one against the advice of even the auditor general. It took eight years after the initial meeting for the network and meddling to unravel, when investigations by a local newspaper uncovered the financial ties between Judges Conahan, Ciavarella and the investor. In the course of the investigations, it became apparent that Conahan and Ciavarella had been paid $2.8 million as 'finder's fees'.[29] Their ill-fated organised crime money-laundering efforts were the network's undoing.[30] After the scandal broke, Conahan was sentenced to 17 years in prison, and Ciavarella for 28 years – due to their age this amounted practically to a lifetime imprisonment.

There are two tragedies about this case: the first one is that it took years for the truth to come to light, thanks to a network of complicit or at least silent officials who did not blow the whistle on what was happening. The second tragedy is a longer-lasting one: a generation of teenagers in Luzerne county who have lost faith in the integrity of the judicial system due to their experience.

The underlying conflict of interest that drove Judge Ciavarella to convict youths to far harsher sentences for financial profit is not singular in the criminal justice system.

While straightforward bribe-paying might be extremely rare in North America and unusual in most but not all parts of Europe, two types of influence peddling do occur: judges or police officers using their influence for financial – or other – gain; and other organisations or parties, including politicians, trying to influence (and minimise) police investigations and judges' rulings. There are a number of ways in which courts are vulnerable to corruption: through outsiders influencing who gets to sit on the bench in the first instance; through anybody corrupting the laws and procedures of the court; and occasionally through straight bribery. All three can be seen in North America and Europe.

In the US, the process of determining who gets to sit on the bench has been heavily influenced by the 2010 Citizens United ruling (see Chapter 2) and the subsequent unregulated flow of cash into elections. This has also affected the state-level judiciary, increasing the pressure on judges prone to deliver verdicts favourable directly or indirectly to their backers.[31] Other countries, such as Bulgaria, face a network of organised criminals and vested interests in the country who have succeeded in penetrating the judiciary to sway judicial decisions their way and influencing laws in the early stages.

Lastly, judicial systems are vulnerable to not only getting corrupted themselves, but many countries' judicial processes are making it all too easy for corrupt companies and individuals to escape very lightly. One symptom of a system not catering to its original intent – such as deterring corrupt behaviour through sentencing – is the idea of plea bargains. When plea bargains are struck, prosecutions are not brought to trial if the defendant pleads guilty to the crime or a lesser crime. There are no total figures for the US for both the state and the federal level, but overall an estimated 95–7 per cent of all cases that do not get dismissed early on end in plea bargains and never go to trial. On the US federal level, 97 per cent end in plea bargains.[32] This frees the courts as it shortens procedures and puts fewer trials in front of juries.

However, it also comes at a price. First, it means that defendants get a reduced sentence if they admit to a lesser crime – even if they were not guilty, they might be tempted to admit a crime to avoid the maximum sentence. Plea bargains also point to another potential dilemma: defence attorneys find themselves in a conflict of interest. To be successful, they not only need to be excellent at their jurisprudence, to some extent they also rely on having good relations – or at the very least not bad ones – with the sitting judges, and good relations with the prosecutors are helpful. This good relationship with the prosecution is particularly important if deals like plea bargains are hammered out between the defence attorney and the prosecutor. The system of plea bargaining thus may make it more attractive for the defence attorney to advise pleading guilty than to jeopardise a good working relationship. Moreover, other systemic traits such as mandatory sentences for some offences have led to prosecutors having relatively more power than defence attorneys. Lastly, in terms of transparency, plea bargains are abysmal: they are deals struck behind closed doors with very limited options for review and checks. Sentences are not decided by judges but by prosecutors. Taken together, plea bargains make the US criminal justice system arguably a less fair place than was intended by the framers of the Constitution. Like the election of judges, which will be examined below, the system of plea bargains has never really caught on in other countries, except – perhaps ironically – in contexts such as international bribery.[33]

Electing judges

Another issue of judicial independence and proneness to influence is the question of whether judges who are elected and need to fund their election campaigns can be truly independent. Or, perhaps more importantly, whether citizens trust them to be truly independent.

American judicial elections have their roots in the panic of 1837, a financial crisis caused, among other things, by massive overspending by corrupt governors and legislatures. The crisis gave way to a long overhaul of state constitutions between 1846 and 1954, resulting in then twenty states adopting judicial elections to shield judges from party cronyism and patronage of the interests of a few by having them democratically elected and thus guaranteeing that they serve citizens' interests.[34] Then, cronyism-based elections gave way to non-partisan selection and merit-based appointments, and for much of the twentieth century, US state judicial elections and appointments were little-discussed on either the federal or the state level.[35] This is until the Citizens United ruling, when money started pouring into judicial campaigns.

On the federal level, the selection of federal judges is simple: they are nominated by the US president and must be confirmed by the Senate. But the majority of judicial decisions in the US are made not at federal but at state level, with more than 100 million cases filed in state courts annually compared to 1 million filed federal cases.[36] Consequently, the majority of judges in the US are state judges, in total around 30,000, of which 85 per cent will stand in at least one election. The type of elections differ as each state has its own regulations for judicial appointments and elections. They range from retention elections where voters are asked periodically whether appointed judges should remain in office, to fully-fledged competitive elections.[37] The idea of retention elections was to strike a balance between judicial independence and accountability. Competitive elections, in contrast, were initiated to put emphasis on judges' accountability and work very much like their political counterparts, with the distinction that some states chose to have partisan elections whereas others run non-partisan elections. Thirty-nine states currently elect at least some of their judges.[38] Judicial elections, while unusual for Europeans, were able to insulate judges from rigged appointments, and enabled accountability towards the citizens they served.[39] With regard to preventing corruption of judges, the issue currently at stake in the US is not whether judges should be elected but rather whether allowing financial contributions for judicial elections really serves the aim of judicial independence. This has been a hotly debated subject for the past three decades with ever-increasing intensity. Essentially, it is a debate about whether players should be able to pay for the election of their referee.

The discussion intensified particularly after Citizens United in 2010 (see Chapter 2) because the ruling not only had an effect on the election of politicians, but also on the election of judges. The argument was that if a state chose to put judges up for election, it would be contrary to the First Amendment to limit the amount of money anyone could contribute to judicial campaigns. Since the Citizens United decision, it has not been unusual for state judges to raise six- or seven-figure numbers for their election campaigns. Campaign spending on judicial elections skyrocketed, more than doubling the amount of money spent in races from $83 million in the nine years from 1990 to 1999 to $206 million from 2000 to 2009. Of the last six state Supreme Court election cycles, three surpassed $45 million.[40] Bitter, negative ad cycles and spending by outside groups are also features the judicial elections have in common with political elections. Unsurprisingly, the bulk of the donations do not come from individual voters but from business interest groups, lawyers and lobbyists.[41] And if judges raise hundreds of thousands of dollars or more from particular interest groups, is it reasonable to expect that their rulings will be impartial?

Public opinion suggests otherwise. In 2002, 70 per cent of Americans said they thought that 'campaign contributions influence judicial decisions'.[42]

> 70 per cent of surveyed judges expressed concern that in some states nearly half of all Supreme Court Cases involve someone who has given money to one or more of the judges hearing the case.[43]

A survey by *New York Times* reporters Adam Liptak and Janet Roberts of state judges found that in Ohio over a 12-year period, justices voted in favour of their contributors more than 70 per cent of the time.[44]

Sandra Day O'Connor is a former member of the US Supreme Court who has taken a very critical public position on the US judicial system at state level. She has commented that with 'so much money going into influencing the outcome of a judicial election… it is hard to have faith that we are selecting judges who are fair and impartial'.[45]

There are also specific cases that suggest otherwise. One is that of Massey Energy and the company's then-chairman Don Blankenship. Over the course of ten years, coal company Massey was in a legal battle over a contract with Harman Mining Company, who were driven into bankruptcy as a result of the cancellation of a contract by Massey. Harman's owner, Hugh Caperton, took the case to court, where Harman Mining was eventually awarded $50 million in damages for fraudulent misrepresentation, concealment and interference with contractual relations by a jury in West Virginia. Blankenship, who wanted to appeal the verdict, saw his chance in 2004 when West Virginia's Supreme Court Justice Warren McGraw was up for re-election. Blankenship donated

$3 million to the challenger, Republican candidate Brent Benjamin, while at the same time substantially funding a not-for-profit that ran advertisements accusing the incumbent of getting a child rapist out of prison. The Massey-funded challenger Benjamin won and overturned the lower court's verdict, making Blankenship's investment worthwhile. It was later found by the US Supreme Court that State Supreme Court Justice McGraw should have excused himself and overturned the decision, sending it back to West Virginia where Massey Energy ultimately prevailed.[46] Theodore B. Olson, former US solicitor general and attorney on behalf of Caperton, later remarked: 'The improper appearance created by money in judicial elections is one of the most important issues facing our judicial system today.'

Evidence also supports the assumption that money influences the judiciary. Looking at judicial campaign contributions and case decisions across the US, 'the more campaign contributions from business interests justices receive, the more likely they are to vote for business litigants appearing before them in court'.[47] This holds true for the relationship between business contributions and the voting patterns of justices in partisan and non-partisan systems, but – interestingly – not in retention election systems.[48]

However, one story the data does not reveal is whether this risk is the same for all judges, or whether it depends on the level of the court. The decision taken in Citizens United to treat campaigning as free speech, thereby making limits on campaign spending by companies and interest groups illegal, is supported by many who argue that to make judicial elections fairer, Citizens United should be overturned, but the judicial election system kept in place. One proponent of this is Supreme Court Justice Anthony M. Kennedy, who argued in the Citizens United ruling that politicians were more trustworthy than judges,[49] and warned of the dangers of judicial campaign spending giving rise to 'a debt of gratitude'.[50] This may well be the case, but in the meantime unlimited outside spending will continue to increase the problem and lead to distrust. And while it is unlikely that judicial election procedures will be abolished in the foreseeable future, the opposite is being discussed. In the 2015/16 presidential campaign, Republican presidential candidate Ted Cruz suggested that a Constitutional Amendment should be discussed subjecting the justices of the US Supreme Court to periodic judicial-retention elections. Cruz was aiming at reining in judges who judge cases according to their personal ideological preferences.[51] This would subject Supreme Court appointments to the abuses identified at the state level and that currently characterise campaign finance.

Influencing judicial decisions through targeted election funding is not a universal problem, however, as the system is an almost uniquely American one. Except for the election of a very small number of judges in France, Japan and Switzerland, no other country has introduced judicial elections.[52] Nevertheless, a number of European countries face judicial corruption that makes the US debate of how to select judges seem almost like a minor problem.

Eight years after joining the European Union, Bulgaria still has serious battles to fight for transparency and accountability. A defunct judiciary has led to criminals in organised crime groups going unpunished, and has failed to check impunity of public officials and businesses alike. Prosecutors getting bribed to drop charges is as regular a phenomenon as using lawyers to funnel money into the court system to obtain a ruling in a company's or individual's case.[53]

Judicial systems often reflect a nation's history. Bulgaria has experienced both the Ottoman millet system and the communist system. Millets were judicial courts that allowed for self-rule for their religious communities. A system meant to serve diverse groups ultimately led to serving the biggest religious group. Under the rule of the Bulgarian Communist Party (1946–89), the concept of an independent and accountable judiciary was rejected, and the regime had full control over the judiciary, tweaking the law and the justice system according to their needs.

The post-Soviet 1991 Constitution, for the first time, set out to achieve a true separation of powers. This long history of distorted justice, unsurprisingly, left a distrust of the judiciary among ordinary Bulgarians.[54] In national polls, Bulgarians rank their justice system among the least trustworthy and most corrupt areas of public life. The Agency for Social Analysis in Bulgaria found in 2011 that 85 per cent of Bulgarians believe that the courts protect the rich and the powerful as opposed to protecting the everyday citizen. Within the EU, the country's judiciary gets the worst rating in terms of perceived judicial independence among EU member states, according to the European Commission's 2015 Justice Scoreboard.[55] The distrust cuts through the entire justice chain: 75 per cent of Bulgarians think police are working under political pressure and every fourth Bulgarian thinks the police take bribes; 74 per cent of Bulgarians are convinced the courts are subject to political pressure, and 36 per cent that the magistrates themselves are corrupt.[56]

The feeling was shared by the controversial Vanyo Tanov, head of Bulgaria's customs agency. During an inquiry he reported to a parliamentary commission in April 2008 that whenever his agency was looking into black market cases, the name of a state office from customs to tax authorities to ministries always came up with it. After his testimony, members of the Bulgarian Parliament decided that the information they had heard should be sent to the Prosecutor's Office. There were clear indications in the testimony that organised crime groups had influence in law enforcement agencies far beyond leaking information. There were attempts to interfere directly with the investigation of criminal activities as well as efforts from some politicians to prevent investigations.[57] The warning signs were made even clearer by the European Union in 2012 when the European Commission warned that several judicial appointments had been made that raised questions with regards to the judges' independence and judges who were found to accept bribes but escaped justice.[58]

Gaining political influence over the judiciary in Bulgaria has become a priority for political parties coming to power. Laws have even been introduced to change the magistrates of the Bulgarian Supreme Judicial Council after elections. This naturally puts political pressure on the judiciary to survive. In addition, the relatively small size of the judiciary – with 1,700 prosecutors and 2,300 judges – fosters a strong sense of solidarity and mutual protection among its members, especially at the local level.[59] This is one reason why the corrupt do not face justice: judges can be bought. But even if a judge wanted to behave impeccably, there are institutional obstacles that generally shield the powerful from the law.[60] Between 2000 and 2011, one prime minister, three deputy prime ministers, four ministers of agriculture, two ministers of defence, one minister of health, three heads of the National Reserve, two heads of the Communications Regulations Commission, as well as directors of the Agriculture Fund, the National Health Insurance Fund, the National Revenue Agency, the Road Infrastructure Fund and the National Security Service have been indicted. Of those, only one-third were convicted – a figure that is much lower than the national average across all cases (50–80 per cent). Of the 30 per cent convicted in the first instance, no one was convicted in the final court decisions, making the conviction rate for cabinet ministers and executive agency heads 'nil'.

However, corruption of the court system is not the only factor that undermines justice. Corruption can also flourish in spite of the fact that justice systems are trying to fight it. In Romania, Lucian Papici was known as a successful prosecutor. As the director of the National Anti-Corruption Agency, Papici had worked on a number of high-profile investigations, including heavyweights such as media owner Dan Voiculescu and former senator Catalin Voicu, who headed a large influence network undermining the Romanian justice system.[61] Voiculescu was a member of Parliament for the Social Democrats – the party of Prime Minister Victor Ponta – from 2004 to 2012. As a former presidential adviser and general in the security service he was well connected and said to be at the centre of a web that infiltrated the justice system, for which he was issued a seven-year prison sentence. According to prosecutors, Voiculescu had corrupt judges including a High Court justice in his pocket, and obtained favourable verdicts in several criminal cases involving influence peddling, document forgery and complicity in trafficking, at his call. The High Court judge who was sentenced for corruption is still eligible for a state pension that is ten times the average salary in Romania.[62]

In 2013, Lucian Papici investigated Romania's deputy prime minister, Liviu Dragnea, on charges of electoral fraud. Dragnea had allegedly ordered the transportation of people to polling stations to ensure impeachment of President Traian Basescu. Dragnea was sentenced to one year probation but became the party leader of the Social Democrats in 2015 after the prime minister was indicted for alleged forgery, complicity in tax evasion and money-laundering while he worked as a lawyer from 2007 to 2011. This was a step too far: Papici was fired by the prime minister just days after he had been reappointed to a second three-year term. Along with him, the prosecutor general was removed from his position.[63] This case demonstrates how easy it can be for politics to play into the justice system: prosecutors or judges can get appointed or fired depending on how well they serve the interests of an elite or network rather than the general public. As a consequence, where this happens, criminals and organised crime networks as well as corrupt officials escape investigation, prosecution and jail. Corrupting the justice system is a crucial factor for criminals and networks to achieve impunity. Likewise, seeing that justice is generally not achieved angers citizens and makes them cynical not only about the justice system but about the state more widely. This is not an easy cycle to disrupt.

For police forces and the judiciary to work in a just, accountable and transparent manner, influence-peddling has to be stopped at all levels – from a local police chief or court all the way up into national institutions. Even the hint of more than sporadic individual corruption has a lasting negative impact on people's trust and the prosecution of crimes. As in other sectors, strong ethical leadership is crucial. However, a number of countries in Europe still find their political elites entangled in corrupt networks and influence-buying, making 'strong leadership' an even harder task.

On both sides of the Atlantic there are existing problems surrounding corruption in both the police and the judiciary. In the US, the widespread election of judges, and the increasing costs of election and re-election expose the judicial system in many states to distortions created by partisan interests. In Western Europe, doubts about the quality of investigations and consequently of evidence in the courts, and in Eastern Europe, issues surrounding the politicisation of the courts combine to create serious public doubt about the quality of justice and the extent to which it is undermined by corruption.

A fair judicial system, and a police force capable of enforcing it, are generally considered to be critical to the established systems of Western democracy. If the law itself is faulty, it can be revised, but enforcement by the courts and the police will always be crucial. The fact that more than 2 million prisoners (or 0.7 per cent of the population) are held in jail in the US – many of them serving controversial sentences – is itself an indication of a failed justice system. Failings within both the police and the judiciary in Europe – and especially in the 'accession' countries of Eastern Europe – generate a widespread perception that the legal system is still susceptible to corruption. In both cases, the concept of fair justice as integral to society is wide of the reality.

8

Organised Crime: A Perennial Spectre

In a map of organised crime in the 'West', the traditional hotspots would be Italy or the Balkan region in Europe, Mexico and cities such as New York, Baltimore and Marseille. This distorts the true picture of today's organised crime networks, which are dealing in many more places. Such criminal activities range from illegal fishing off the coast of Italy to border smuggling of illegal goods and human trafficking in South-East Europe, to gangland murders in Dublin and organised crime rings in Manchester, as well as a cheese heist's connection with organised crime in Wisconsin and drug-related organised crime in the Bay area of California.[1] While the underlying crimes are vastly different, they share the defining factor of being committed by structured groups for profit,[2] and by using violence or extreme violence and corruption as their modus operandi. To conceal their crimes, organised crime networks' profits are often laundered from criminal activities into the legal economy. Although there still are national organised crime networks, there is an increasing globalisation of networks. For example, in Germany in 2014 there were 571 investigations into 8,700 suspects with 104 nationalities linked to organised crime.[3] The costs of organised crime and corruption are high: the European Parliament estimates that organised crime as facilitated and enabled by corruption costs the EU up to €71 billion annually.[4]

But not only does corruption facilitate organised crime, it also makes it possible for organised crime networks to conceal their dealings. In a recent case, IKEA and Harvard University have been involved in such a deal in Romania. Romania's vast and beautiful forests were nationalised in Soviet times and have undergone a restitution programme since the 1990s that has been riddled with corruption and organised crime, when whole networks forged papers alleging that their families had once owned these forests. Harvard University's Management Company saw these forests as an investment opportunity and started purchasing land in 2004. By 2010, the university was the biggest private owner of forests in Romania. It bought parts of the forests through an elaborate network of offshore companies, and eventually sold 98 per cent of the land to IKEA at a loss. As Romanian prosecutors looked into land fraud and organised crime in the country's forests deals, they also uncovered that there were big questions around the legal ownership of the Management Company's (and, through the sale, IKEA's) forest land, and in March 2016 investigating one particular purchase by the Managenent Company of 3,000 hectares which have a historic association with money-laundering and organised crime charges.[5]

Corruption is necessary to sustain organised crime, as exemplified by a local drug kingpin who pays off police officers, international human traffickers who pay off officials, and international organised crime groups who capture administrations in South-East Europe. Organised crime now embraces not only 'traditional' activities such as gambling, prostitution, smuggling and trafficking, but has also infiltrated the renewable energy sector, the food sector and cyberspace. Although this book separates the issues of police corruption, the interface between organised crime, corruption and police work is complex. In many countries, organised crime and corruption are fought by the same police units. The tentacles of organised crime sometimes reach into the judiciary as well. Likewise, organised crime is closely linked to betting and corruption in sports (discussed in Chapter 9), and environmental crime (Chapter 10). There is even a link between organised crime and the food industry, which both points back to the roots of organised crime in Sicily and is still topical today. Other 'traditional' business areas that are often affected or even taken over by organised crime are the construction sector (see Chapter 4) and the distribution of counterfeit products.

The 1980s and 1990s saw large-scale trials of traditional mafia groups in both Italy and the US that fought organised crime networks but also meant that these groups went on to stake out new horizons. As long as money can be laundered quite easily, corruption and crime are profitable partners. Many organised crime networks have jumped on the opportunities offered by new technology: cybercrime and the exploitation of financial transfer systems for money-laundering particularly into the secrecy jurisdictions discussed in Chapter 6. These and other tools have been so successful that the UN's main agency for fighting corruption and organised crime, the United Nations Office on Drugs and Crime (UNODC), estimates that the latter generate up to 1.5 per cent of global GDP.[6] This chapter will examine some of the operations of organised crime as facilitated by corruption.

Dubrovnik in Croatia is known for its pristine beaches, picturesque alleys and houses, and the castle on the hilltop. Historically, the countries of South-Eastern Europe, or more accurately the Balkan peninsula, have also been known for their share of political turmoil or, as Winston Churchill put it more eloquently: 'The Balkans produce more history than they can consume.' The region is made up of 13 countries,[7] as many languages and more ethnicities, many of which have fought each other at some point in their history even before the idea of the modern nation state existed.

This region had a label attached to it after the Balkan Wars of the 1990s: 'gangster-states'.[8]

With settlements in the Balkans dating back to prehistoric times, the region is also home to Europe's first advanced civilisation and has been a trade route for many centuries. Transport and distribution are two features for which the region is still famous – or rather infamous – today. Since the 1990s, the Balkan countries have been a major stopover point for organised crime ranging from the drug trade (heroin in particular) to trafficking and migrant smuggling, as it was relatively easy to circumvent inspections and detection through payments to the authorities in charge.[9] Where politics may have failed to unite groups across borders, the aim of maximising profits through organised crime has achieved just that. Even more, organised crime has truly become a globalised trade: drugs from Central Asia are smuggled to Western Europe via the Balkans and Central Europe, and organised crime groups from Europe source material in Latin America to sell it to North American buyers. Besides the Balkans, key trade and organised crime hubs in Europe range from ports such as Amsterdam and Rotterdam to entire regions like north-western Italy and south-western France, as well as large cities and tourist areas for investments of organised crime proceeds, such as the Costa del Sol.[10]

Smuggling and banditry is not a modern phenomenon – smuggling of opium goes back at least a century. What has changed are the power structures: after the fall of the Soviet Union in 1989, a power vacuum was exploited by fast-organising crime groups, which have grown solid roots among the political elite, the judiciary and law enforcement agencies throughout the region, constantly pushing and changing spheres of influence and centres of power.[11] Or, as described by a leading Bulgarian political scientist in Misha Glenny's book *McMafia*:

> Our territory has always nestled between huge ideologies, between Orthodoxy and Roman Catholicism, between Islam and Christianity, between capitalism and communism. Empires riddled with hostility and suspicion for one another, but home, nonetheless, to many people who want to trade across the prohibited boundaries. In the Balkans, we know how to make those boundaries disappear. We can cross the roughest sea and traverse the most forbidding mountain. We know every secret pass, and, failing that, the price of every border guard.[12]

The 1990s were a decade of major changes throughout Europe, and as new regimes were established – often in a power vacuum – organised crime groups quickly bought themselves into power structures and took over in many countries throughout Central and South-East Europe. With these networks, crime and corruption expanded in the countries in the region, and both have proved equally difficult to uproot. Bulgaria is one such example where an entire state structure was interwoven with organised crime, which in turn was facilitated by corruption. The way in which organised crime and corruption reinforce each other and take hold of state structures has not only enabled the drug trade and human trafficking to flourish, but has also undermined the state system. Former Bulgarian Interior Minister Bogomil Bonev remarked: 'One of the reasons our criminal groups became so powerful is that they were organised by the state itself.'[13] They achieved the ultimate form of corruption: they captured regions and an entire state.

When Bulgaria entered the European Union in 2007, it did so as the most corrupt European member state – together with Romania – and as the European state with the most pervasive organised crime problem.[14] While there have been high-profile arrests of criminals especially since the late 2000s, these have not been matched by prosecutions. Virtually none of the powerful organised crime networks have been prosecuted, due to systematic failures in investigations, prosecution and the judicial system.[15] Meanwhile, drug trafficking through Bulgaria continues and the country remains an important hub for cocaine, heroin and synthetic drugs from South-West Asia to Europe.

The drug trade makes up for the highest value criminal activity in South-East Europe. Around 80 tons of heroin pass through the region to reach consumers in West Europe every year. At wholesale level on arrival, these drugs are worth more than the national economic output of several countries in the region.[16] But trade routes and channels for smuggled drugs, once established, are usually used for more than one type of product, and many organised crime networks are involved in trading more than one illegal type of good. Usually bribes are used to facilitate the activities, often targeting mid-level officials to look the other way. As in other countries, corruption in Bulgaria is used to obtain information, avoid prosecution and to protect crime networks. In the case of cross-border smuggling, corruption directly correlates with smuggling: bribes are necessary to provide ease in crossing borders; for example, by avoiding customs searches.[17] By using corruption to facilitate the drug trade, organised crime networks manage to both avoid and weaken the structure and efficacy of customs and police agencies alike.[18] The high value of the drugs traffic across borders is a continuous threat to the integrity of poorly paid border guards.

In one recent Romanian example, police raided crossings at the border with Serbia, arresting around 100 border patrol agents, police officers and smugglers. The arrested were thought to be part of a well-connected smuggling operation, with links to political parties in Romania, including those politicians appointing border and customs chiefs. Essentially, the trafficking operations and organised crime uncovered by the investigation were used to funnel back campaign finance into political parties to ensure political power. While indicative of networks' bribery and use of customs and law enforcement, it is also indicative of the other triangular link between organised crime, corruption and law enforcement: where systems are made corruption-proof and investigations cannot be bought, organised crime can be uncovered and punished.[19]

Many of the issues surrounding the drug trade in Europe are, of course, shared by the US, especially on its Mexican border. High-Intensity Drug Trafficking Areas, or smuggling hot spots exist on the US–Mexico border, and they are the hubs for multi-agency prevention and intervention programmes.[20] Along this border near the southern tip of Texas in Hidalgo County in the Rio Grande Valley, a young narcotics cop, Jonathan Treviño, was described by his father as the 'hardest-working narcotics investigator in Hidalgo County'. Hard-working he certainly was. His father Lupe Treviño, who happened to be Hidalgo County's sheriff, had set up a special task force to combat drug trafficking in 2010, which Jonathan was appointed to lead. He had credentials as a decent cop but the appointment reeked of nepotism. The task force was nicknamed Panama Unit and initially Jonathan and the friends and colleagues he recruited for his team demonstrated impressive results and broke up an above-average number of drug operations. However, within a short time the unit started getting busy for its own profit, stealing shipments from drug dealers and selling them to rival gangs. They also became local guns for hire for a drug lord, and they started stealing drugs from competitor gangs for him. The unit made lots of money, which they concealed from their friends and families and would spend at gambling and party trips to Louisiana, Las Vegas, and at race tracks and sports events. 'I just felt like we were untouchable', Jonathan later told Josh Eells from *Rolling Stone*, who wrote a profile of the case and the Treviños.[21] They were not. When the Panama Unit started stealing from the gangs who were paying them and a special investigations unit was set up to look into the Panama Unit's activities, matters deteriorated and the unit was busted in a sting operation.[22]

The case resulted in Jonathan Treviño and nine county sheriff deputies and police detectives pleading guilty or being convicted. Jonathan was sentenced to 17 years in prison. His father, Sheriff Lupe Treviño, was later sentenced to five years in federal prison – not for any involvement with the Panama Unit deals, but for money-laundering. He had taken around $20,000 of illegal drug money from a Texas drug trafficker, Tomas 'El Gallo' Gonzalez, as contributions for his 2012 re-election campaign. 'El Gallo' food produce company served as a front business for a major marijuana and cocaine smuggling racket: up to 700 pounds of marijuana and up to 100 pounds of cocaine were packed in each of the company's vegetable trucks. El Gallo was rumoured to have links to the Mexican Zetas drug cartel. Sheriff Treviño's conviction put an end to an apparently highly successful and acknowledged career in law enforcement, which followed a series of similar convictions of law enforcement agents.[23]

The US Customs and Border Protection Agency, like other border and customs agencies, has been struggling with corruption in its ranks. As the biggest US law enforcement agency, it is tasked with protecting the nation's borders and preventing terrorist or organised crime networks from entering the country. There are 60,000 staff patrolling borders. Between 2004 and 2011, 132 of them were arrested or indicted for corruption-related charges. According to an internal report by the Office for Homeland Security, they 'misused their positions for personal gain by misusing government computer systems, passing sensitive information, stealing money and property, or deliberately circumventing operational procedures'.[24] The statistics indicate that while corruption in customs and border controls is an issue to be taken seriously not only in Central and Eastern Europe but also in in the United States as it can undermine large-scale operations, it is also possible to contain corruption risks in the ranks; for example, by providing job security and attractive pay.

For organised crime networks, the American market for cocaine continues to be important: with $34 billion annually, it accounts for around 40 per cent of all global cocaine revenue and is thus a market of which all organised crime groups want to get a slice. The EU, in comparison, accounts for approximately €8 billion in cocaine revenue each year.[25]

In terms of making drug trafficking big business, the Cosa Nostra had a head start with drug trafficking to the US. The mafia had long been dealing in foodstuff between Europe and North America and had established channels, so it was no coincidence that the major heroin distribution network the mafia established in the 1970s and 1980s used pizzerias as its heroin distribution points.[26] By the early 1980s, the Cosa Nostra was in charge of 80 per cent of the (heavily increased) refining, shipping and distribution of heroin in the north-east of the US. In Italy, organised crime was able to draw on its strong networks and state capture in some cities. A popular saying goes: '*Tutti colpevoli, nessuno colpevole*' – if everyone is guilty, no one is guilty – indicating that the mafia families were so woven into the social and economic fabric of the country that they were virtually impossible to prosecute – that is, until the 1980s.[27] Like all successful organised crime groups, the mafia works through a mixture of legal and illegal businesses, and resorts to corruption to influence public tenders either through paying bribes to win contracts or by getting their own people into state procurement positions.[28]

France is also no stranger to organised crime. The island of Corsica has long been an infamous organised crime hub, as has the port city of Marseille in Southern France (see Chapter 7). Corsica became particularly notorious in the 1960s and 1970s during the height of organised crime wars when the Corsican mafia ran a scheme called the French Connection – supplying the United States with heroin from Turkey that was refined in Marseille. The French Connection was uncovered and disrupted in the 1970s and organised crime activities on Corsica and Marseille have decreased since but never disappeared, and have lately resurfaced.

Due, in part, to its excellent location and climate, but also to the increasing attractiveness of real estate for money-laundering purposes creating a housing bubble, land prices on Corsica have risen fivefold from 2010–15. This makes land a sought-after investment and has also attracted organised crime bosses, making it a key base for their activities. Between 2005 and 2013, there were 85 gangland killings in Corsica. Either out of fear or bound by a code of silence that the mafia in Italy calls '*Ómerta*', the locals remain quiet about what is happening on their island – and because there is no solid witness protection programme in France, it is unlikely that the people in the know will ever speak.[29]

The French government at first was slow to acknowledge the problem but had to act in 2012, when the killings were no longer mafia-internal but affected Corsica's political class. Within a short time, two prominent Corsicans were shot: a well-known defence lawyer who had worked for the Corsican nationalists and was therefore thought to be untouchable (he was killed on his way to work), and the head of the Corsican Chamber of Commerce, Jacques Nacer. The latter was assassinated on the street by two shots to the head and one to the chest while he was locking up his shoe business in the city. As the president of the Chamber of Commerce, Nacer was in charge of Corsica's air- and seaports. He was the 17th homicide victim in Corsica that year, making the island's per capita homicide rate the highest in Europe.[30] The most lucrative activities for Corsican organised crime gangs are smuggling, diversion of public funds, racketeering and gambling. Illegal construction, especially along the coastline, is rampant.

Shortly after the murder of the defence lawyer, the French prime minister announced a strategy to fight Corsica's rampant crime levels and pointed out the links with corrupt activities: 'Economic and financial dealings are behind most of the murders... particular attention will be paid to the fight against money laundering, especially in the fields of property and including sport as well as the procedures for public contracts and urban authorisations.'[31] The French government announced a ten-step plan to fight organised crime in Corsica by bolstering special investigative resources on the island, but it is likely that organised crime groups will keep finding ways to make money with and launder money through real estate as long as possible. By 2016, there has been no indication of decreased activity.

Organised crime in cyberspace

One activity that certainly has increased in recent years is cybercrime. The internet has changed how we act and interact, making the web both a profitable and easy place for business, both legal and illegal. Organised crime groups have discovered the opportunities provided by the web for their activities. The internet now serves both as a conduit to perform 'traditional' organised crime activities, and new forms of crimes such as fraud (including spam mails), child pornography, malware attacks and hacking – the term 'cybercrime' has been coined for the latter activities. In cybercrime there is often an overlap between these new groups and established organised crime networks.[32]

Both Europol and Interpol have stressed how the internet facilitates the activities of traditional organised crime groups.[33] They have also acknowledged that the extent of these activities is largely unknown because traditional organised crime investigations and law enforcement are in many cases separate from cybercrime investigations units. This results in the internet dimension of organised crime activities running the risk of being overlooked where these investigations capabilities are not closely linked. This is especially true where the internet is used by 'traditional', i.e., non-cybercrime groups, such as smugglers to communicate between buyers and sellers. The web thereby enables various separate crime groups to coordinate, and to market their services. Disturbingly, the internet has also enabled sex traffickers to select their victims, and to control and deceive them.

But the internet has also affected the organisational structures of organised crime groups: before the internet, the process of establishing contacts, making payments and delivering products had to be carried out by trusted minions or middlemen. Online communication, online payment systems (both in the legal and illegal sphere) and to some degree more available shipping options have depleted hierarchy levels in many organisations.[34] Many such activities are not carried out in the internet access points the normal web user knows (also known as the 'surface web'), but rely on the use of the so-called 'deep web' and 'dark web'. The deep web is for the most part not a playground for criminals: 'deep web' only describes the part of the web not found by search engines, which includes most databases that are available online, as well as search options on websites such as travel websites, and companies' intranets. The deep web is accessible without special software, e.g. by typing in a web address. The 'dark web' is a small part of the deep web. In contrast to the deep web, within the dark web, networks can be created that can only be accessed by trusted peers and are used for illegal activities. This is where users are anonymous and, through the use of special (encryption) software, cannot be traced. It is the underworld of the World Wide Web.[35] The dark web is thus used whenever detection through the regular web is too risky, which, in some cases, is surprisingly rare. Quite often criminals do not even bother using the dark or even the deep web as they do not feel that there is a risk of them being detected.[36]

Mafia-style organisations nowadays use the web to avoid wire-tapping but are more hesitant to replace traditional illicit organised crime methods with cyber-based activities, although this varies by organisation: the Camorra is more open towards using the web and involving people from outside the 'family' structure than other mafia networks. Lower down the hierarchy, the Camorra's members are increasingly using the web (and deep web) as a crime tool, which might be explained with an age gap: mafia bosses tend to be older and less web-literate. The younger lower-level members have been brought up with the internet, and use Facebook not only to communicate with their friends, but also to detect patterns and trace their victims.[37]

The human toll of trafficking and smuggling

A key target of organised crime, whether facilitated through the deep web or otherwise, is human trafficking. Here again corruption is one of the main facilitators of human trafficking and human smuggling, because high corruption levels in a country or region mean that it is easier to bribe police officers, immigration officials or the judiciary. Within Europe, the demand for cheap labour and sexual services has made human smuggling and trafficking a rapidly growing illicit trade[38] with an estimated market of €35 billion.[39] There are an estimated one million forced labourers in the European Union alone, most of whom are from the EU itself, and many of whom are forced into slavery-like conditions.[40] The figures for the United States do not look brighter: it is estimated that 100,000 girls are victimised (i.e., forced into sex labour) by sex traffickers each year, often by people they know.[41]

Most human trafficking within Europe is conducted with the aim of sexual exploitation. Fuelled by corruption, Bulgaria is one of the main source countries for victims of human trafficking within Europe, together with Romania, Ukraine and Russia.[42] The criminal structures for sex trafficking range from independent pimps trafficking a handful of girls to large trafficking organisations with multi-layer structures, which make up a majority of the 'market'. Whereas some of the money earned may stay with the prostitute – anything from nil to 50 per cent – the lion's share of the proceeds goes to the criminal network, and can reach up to €1.3 billion per year.[43] The links between corruption of public officials, trafficking and prostitution, and organised crime are found throughout Europe: in France, two separate cases involved police officers running and obtaining free services from prostitutes; near Madrid, Spain, 26 local police officers were involved in extortion from prostitutes, bars and businesses; in Greece, police officers were believed to be participating in a sex-trafficking ring that smuggled hundreds of women from Eastern Europe and the Balkans to Greece; in Germany, police officers who frequented brothels were vulnerable to blackmail by organised crime groups.[44] These examples demonstrate, again, the delicate balance between law enforcement, organised crime and corruption.

The 'agromafia', or how organised crime enters supermarkets

Where corruption is high, markets tend to fail and vice versa. When this happens, labour migration rates rise as the state of the economy and/or political situation in countries decline, leaving few perspectives or economic security for citizens. Organised criminal groups are able to take advantage of this by offering transit to countries where work can be found. Migrant smugglers are often part of a wider network that functions like an organised crime network. They rely on word-of-mouth recommendations but as people are often indebted to them, an overly rosy picture of the situation in the destination country is often painted, with dire consequences as one UK migrant from an Eastern European country reports:[45]

> I was out of job for 3 to 4 months. I did not have any money. Then I saw an advertisement in the newspaper that there is a need for workers in the UK. So I decided to go. I have called that agency. They confirmed that there are work opportunities. I came to the agency, they told me how good it is in the UK… sweet life. Wages are very high. I had to pay £350 or £400. They suggested to take with me £100 or £200 until I receive my first wage. I paid this money. I had to borrow £400. I have borrowed it from all of my relatives [laughs] and friends. I got into such a debt, that I had to repay it for a very long time. I came to England. They told me that someone will meet me in the airport. Someone will have a card with my name written on it. When I arrived in the airport no one was waiting for me.

> I called the agency and told them that there was no one waiting for me. They asked me to wait and promised to get in touch with the guy. They said not to worry, that everything will be fine. I waited... then I understood that they have fooled me.[46]

Migrant smuggling is not only an issue from the Middle East and North Africa to Europe – although in numbers this has been by far the bigger since mid-2015 than smuggling within Europe. However, it also exists within the EU. The town of Wisbech in Cambridgeshire, one hour north of Cambridge, is an old market town with a population of 30,000 and is notable for its Georgian architecture. It was also the home of the British abolitionist and leading anti-slavery campaigner, Thomas Clarkson (1760–1846), who helped end the British slave trade in 1807. Clarkson would be appalled had he lived to see history repeat itself, in a way, in his hometown. In recent years, the town has become infamous for a large influx of immigrants who work under slave-like conditions, which certainly constitutes human trafficking. Of the 30,000 inhabitants of Wisbech, one-third are illegal immigrants who have arrived in recent years, leading to a major housing crisis and criminal exploitation of the migrants. When a multi-agency raid in 2013, code name Operation Pheasant, raided properties they discovered 220 cases of migrant exploitation by gangmasters, poor housing conditions for migrants, and benefit offences. Workers were not given their passports or payslips by gangmasters but forced to work mostly in agriculture (picking fruit or vegetables) without even knowing their hourly wage.[47] In this way, migrant exploitation constitutes a link to the food market

The experience of the trafficked people in Wisbech is not a unique experience but it points to problems of criminality and corruption in the food industry. This should not be entirely surprising: the origins of the Cosa Nostra were in Sicilian agriculture during the time of rapidly expanding demand for lemons in the US. Likewise, the origins of the fictional Corleone family in *The Godfather* were based on the import of Italian olive oil to the US through a company founded by Vito Corleone to front the family's illegal activities.[48] While the lemon business is arguably less crime-prone these days, the same cannot be said for the olive oil industry. During the days of the Roman Empire, annual olive oil consumption was around 50 litres per person in the moneyed classes. As a percentage of income, people spent as much on olive oil as they do on petrol today. Romans also made sure that what they were receiving was actual olive oil: every container included information on the weight of the oil, the farm where the olives were pressed, the merchant who shipped the oil and the official who verified this information. In theory, it would have been easy to bribe the official to mislabel the oil. But it is much easier nowadays to make huge profits by replacing virgin oil with other oil.[49]

This is by no means a new business. For decades, the Cosa Nostra, 'Ndrangheta and other organised crime groups have been tampering with olive oil, passing off vegetable oil as much more expensive extra virgin olive oil, making olive oil the most fraud-prone food product. It is a valuable business, as olive oil is five times as expensive as other vegetable oil. To detect fraud, most European countries have their own testing facilities where food is tested for fraudulent ingredients – an organised crime investigation squad in food science labs. Detection rates are low, however, as there are not enough specially trained investigators to counter the well-organised criminals.[50]

In Italy, the turnover from the so-called 'agromafia' rose by 12 per cent between 2012 and 2013 and amounted to €14 billion annually as organised crime took over more businesses, partly fuelled by huge European and American demand for 'authentic' Italian products such as virgin olive oil, mozzarella and Parma ham, which is expensive in production but reaps high profits when tampered.[51] The National Federation of Italian Farmers sees agriculture and food as a priority investment field by organised crime groups that control the distribution and sometimes even the production of foodstuffs, and bribe overseeing bodies and personnel. Through extortion and intimidation, they can infiltrate existing brands and products. Italian authorities believe as much as 15 per cent of the turnover from agriculture to be illicit, stemming from the distribution and production of milk and butter, mozzarella, meat, coffee, sugar, mineral water, flour, bread, butter and, above all, fruit and vegetables.[52] In July 2012, Giuseppe Mandara, the self-proclaimed 'Armani of mozzarella', was arrested on charges of adulterating his prized cheese. His company, the Mandara Group, mixed cow milk with the creamier and more expensive buffalo milk, from which mozzarella is made. In addition, he mislabelled his product. His strategy of defence was easy but unfortunately for him was recorded on a wiretap: 'We'll pretend we're stupid, then we'll be OK.' His company was based near Naples in the Caserta region, a Camorra stronghold that prompted Pope Francis to renounce the mafia and corruption on his visit there in 2014. It therefore came as no surprise to many that Mandara was alleged to have ties to the Camorra, which was said to have helped him with a credit to bridge financial difficulties in the 1980s (one of the ways in which the mafia gets a foot into legitimate businesses).[53] The prosecution's case, however, collapsed and Mandara was free to return home, only to be rearrested in 2014 on similar charges. Again, they did not stick.

The Cosa Nostra, Camorra and 'Ndrangheta influence over the food, fruit and vegetable market, which is particularly profitable in Southern Italy, is getting stronger. One estimate suggests that up to one-third of all farmers in the regions of Basilicata, Calabria, Campania, Puglia and in Sicily have some relation (voluntarily or not) with organised crime, or are affected by theft of machinery, livestock or tools, and take part in fraudulent claims of EU funds or illegal extract from local water supplies.[54]

Organised crime in the form of theft and resale of equipment or food stock also affects French farmers. For example, a highly specialised organised crime gang targeted dealerships and stole John Deere tractors to resell them in Germany, Hungary and

Romania. By the time the crime ring was dismantled in 2012, they had made more than €3 million profit. In addition to that, farmers have seen their potato fields, peach orchards and vineyards harvested illegally, prompting the president of France's leading farmers' union to write to the minister of the interior: 'Our rural areas find themselves facing a new form of organised looting. It is time to take action… What was yesterday pilfering has become a very organized system. Despite all precautions being taken, the situation is getting worse.'[55]

In the US and neighbouring Mexico, drug cartels have also started to see the profitability of food businesses. A drug cartel known as the Knights Templar has taken over lime farms and controls a large portion of lime exports to the US. Prices have tripled, as have the cartel's profits. As in the case of the Cosa Nostra, citrus fruit can be a powerful driver of corruption.[56]

* * *

Organised crime is the orphan child in the combat against corruption: accepted as an issue but never prominent. This is regardless of the facts that both human trafficking and the widespread distribution of harmful drugs are two of the most glaring evils of our time, that the profits of organised crime escape taxation and often buttress secrecy jurisdictions, and that the corruption of government institutions is often a part of the system. This low profile is partly because organised crime is sometimes regarded as just part of the informal economy – accounting for more than 10 per cent of GDP across the rich OECD countries – and partly because consumers often gain access to lower-priced goods (such as counterfeit watches, medicinal products or DVDs) that would otherwise not be available and that they can pick up easily on the street. In other contexts, where markets have been captured (such as the wind farms in Sicily discussed in Chapter 10, or construction rackets in big cities, discussed in Chapter 4) prices to the consumer or the state can actually increase, while the revenue is still defrauded. This situation persists in spite of outstanding and courageous investigations and prosecutions over the past 30 years – particularly in the US, Canada and Italy – and regardless of the network of international agencies (notably Europol, Interpol and UNODC) partly designed to fight it. The cases discussed here confirm the necessity for ever-stronger international collaboration on the issue and for its integration with the fight against corruption.

9

Foul Play: Corruption in Sport

Fixing and corruption in sport has a long history. If you were to go to the site of the ancient Olympics in Greece you would find, outside the ruins of the stadium, remains of statues to their Gods. The statues were paid for by athletes and coaches who were caught cheating.

Declan Hill, investigative sports journalist[1]

The 98th Olympics in 388 BCE was an exceptional sporting event and a grand spectacle. But unlike earlier Olympics, it also saw the first major bribery scandal: the boxer Eupolus of Thessaly bribed three opponents into losing against him. The aftermath of this fraud laid the foundation for the first Olympic rules: the Games were to be won by swiftness of foot and strength, not by money. However, even this commitment proved to have a limited life. The idea of fair and impartial sports was completely reversed when Nero bribed all judges in the 67 CE Olympics and walked away with more than 1,800 first-place prizes.

The modern era of sports has been hit by three main issues: match-fixing, doping and a lack of governance of international sports. The idea that sport should not be controlled by finance has been ignored in many sports on many occasions in recent decades. The rules of fairness should still apply today but have continuously been broken in recent years. Sports sponsorship on a giant scale is a new paradigm in which corruption can flourish in areas that include the rigging of deals to allocate international events to the highest bidder. These were brought to the fore in 2015 by the arrests of Fédération Internationale de Football Association (FIFA) officials, the report of the International Athletics Foundation (IAAF) on doping, and the exposure of the International Olympic Committee's (IOC's) cases of kickbacks to select committees for the Winter Olympics in Salt Lake City. These high-profile incidents are indicative of the substantial problem the sports sector has with governance of its organisations as well as governance of events that affect and influence sports at a global scale. At the same time, there are issue-specific governance problems, such as doping, which affect individual sports (cycling and athletics[2] would be the most prominent examples) at a global scale, or national sports teams. Lastly, these problems mask a deeper malaise at levels with a lower profile, whether they are governance of grassroots sports or corruption of individual matches and games, particularly through match-fixing.[3]

Clearly these recent developments do not serve spectator sports well: viewers and fans are increasingly speaking out against such corruption. Where money influences the games, the unpredictability of outcomes – one of sport's greatest charms – and the belief in fairness is destroyed.[4] This enriches a few but is not in the best interests of the majority of athletes, clubs and fans.[5]

Match-fixing: Betting on the right team

Around €1.4 billion in sports betting takes place around the world every day, or up to €500 billion per year. Global sports betting as an economic activity is therefore larger than the sports economy made up of sports events, infrastructure construction, licensing and sporting goods itself (estimated at €350–450 billion per year[6]). An estimated 80 per cent of betting takes place illegally on the black market, i.e. it is not regulated.[7] Organised crime dominates the black market gambling syndicates, which are primarily operating out of Asia. As a result, money bet with a local, illegal bookie in Europe or the US can find its way to funding far more dangerous activities: as much as $140 billion annually is laundered through illegal sports betting.[8]

Recent years have seen widespread instances of match-fixing in different sports across the world, and the increase of money flowing through online gambling has contributed to the ease and increased stakes in match-fixing. Thanks to the internet, gamblers can bet on matches anytime, anywhere, of any size. Gamblers and fixers are infiltrating Europe, with fixing cases in Bulgaria, Greece, Hungary, Italy, Poland, Russia and Turkey placing in serious doubt the credibility of many matches in their leagues. Match-fixing does not just occur in countries deemed to be particularly corruption-prone but scandals have also occurred in Austria, Belgium, Finland, Germany, Norway and Switzerland. The majority of reported match-fixing cases occur in football, but there are also cases in motor racing, basketball, cricket, horseracing, snooker and tennis.

The structure is simple enough: money is put on a particular outcome, and match-fixers pay players to influence the outcome of the game. The middlemen of match-fixing tend to be locals or insiders of the football world such as players or agents who know the players or referees. They get paid by organisers of the 'fix' – often in Asia, where the gambling market is significantly bigger than in Europe and the US – who in turn arrange the games for anonymous betting entities. Higher up the chain, complex and opaque betting conglomerates place live-bets on these games, making money on the fixed matches.[9] Although it is difficult to accurately assess the extent to which match-fixing is increasing (more revelations may only mean better monitoring), the weight of the evidence is that the issue is becoming more acute. For example, a new phenomenon is that there are detailed accounts of how match-fixing occurs, thanks to tapped phone calls in Italy and Russia and confessions of arrested match-fixers.

One match-fixing scandal in football in Croatia is representative of an increasing numbers of match-fixing stories. Mario Cizmek is an energetic Croatian in his early forties and for 20 years of his life he was a midfielder, starting out as an under-16 national player and going on to play for both Croatian and international clubs. Yet in the space of a few months, a match-fixing scandal destroyed both his football career and ultimately his personal life. Cizmek was struggling financially when he was approached by a match-fixing organiser in spring 2010. His football club had not paid his – or other players' – salaries in over a year. The man who approached him, Vinko Saka, seemed like a patron for him and his fellow players. The trusted local man in his fifties with a shiny BMW offered short-term loans for the cash-strapped players.[10] When he offered money to Cizmek for fixing one match by losing the game, Cizmek says he 'could not believe that [he] could ever run onto the pitch with the intention to lose the match.' He added: 'I felt awful. It was the worst experience for me as an athlete, but there was no way back.'[11] What started as a one-match fix became a series that led to his, his team-mates' and the fixer's arrest. Saka, the match-fixer, pleaded guilty in a plea bargain and is still enjoying his BMW. But Cizmek went to prison and lost his career and his marriage. With the €26,000 that he received, he bought a bunkbed for his children and wanted to spend the rest on paying his taxes. The bunkbed is now all he has to show for a deal that cost him so much, and where the players and spectators lose, while the match-fixers win everything.

Another large European football betting scandal in 2009 involved 320 matches in 12 European countries, the largest number in Germany, Switzerland and Turkey. Of these, 33 matches were international fixtures, including three games in the Champions

League, although fixes in lower divisions were more prevalent.[12] The Union of European Football Associations (UEFA) cooperated with German investigators as 40 UEFA games were under investigation, including 12 UEFA Europa League and three UEFA Champions League fixtures.[13] German investigators from the organised crime task force in Bochum came across the match-fixing network by chance while investigating a Croatian gang on other charges. The leader of the gang, Ante Sapina, was jailed in May 2011 convicted of fixing 20 games.[14] Sapina was tied to Singapore-based syndicates, led by the figures of Dan Tan and Raj Perumal, fixers specialising in international matches, cooperating with Sapina and his brother, and funded by Chinese organised crime groups. The 200-strong criminal gang bribed players, coaches, referees and officials to fix games and then made money by betting on the results.[15] When Perumal was jailed in Finland for rigging the domestic league, he revealed details about the global network of match-fixers based in Singapore.[16] Perumal and Tan went their separate ways and became rivals. Tan was arrested in Singapore in 2013 under suspicion of masterminding a global football match-fixing syndicate.[17]

In another match-fixing sting, Operation Veto, a 2011–13 Europol investigation uncovered 680 fixed matches across the world, 380 of which were suspicious matches in Europe, including a Champions League tie, World Cup and European Championship qualifiers, with fixes in Austria, Finland, Hungary and Slovenia. The majority of allegations, however, concerned lower division matches in Germany, Switzerland and Turkey.[18] German police found bribes averaging up to £86,000 per match to pay off players and referees, and criminals wagered £13.8 million on rigged matches and made £6.9 million in profits on German matches alone.[19] The investigation again revealed the influence that Asian (namely Singapore-based) crime syndicates wield. The Singaporean cartel purportedly made more than €8 million in profits after 'investing' almost €2 million in bribes to fix matches – a handsome profit margin.[20]

These investigations demonstrated the influence of Singaporean organised crime on football. There are thought to be around two-dozen fixers operating out of Singapore, working with local agents around the world.[21] But match-fixing, while most prevalent in European football, has also occurred in other sports: in American football, when a University of Toledo player intentionally fumbled the ball in a bowl game for cash in 2005;[22] in a NASCAR Sprint Cup Series race in Virginia in 2013 in what was called the 'sprintgate' scandal;[23] in the National Basketball Association (NBA) when a referee bet on games and provided insider information in 2007; and a whole series of corruption and match-fixing in cricket, with two players who played in English clubs banned for life in 2014 and a string of other scandals outside Europe.[24]

Tennis has not been exempt from these scandals. In the third quarter of 2015, the European Sports Security Authority flagged tennis as the sport with the most match-fixing suspicious alerts.[25] Long before that there had been serious rumours of match-fixing. Back in 2008, the concern around sports betting and match-fixing was already serious enough to warrant the four leading tennis associations and committees to commission an independent analysis. This brought to light 'patterns of suspected betting activity' in 27 of the 73 matches analysed, and led the commission to strongly suggest a 'uniform anti-corruption programme, with a regulatory structure and an integrity unit'.[26] For example, in 2007, Russian tennis player Nikolay Davydenko was suspected of throwing a match against Argentine Martín Vassallo Argüello. Despite Davydenko winning the first set 6–2, ten times the usual betting amount for such a level of match was then placed on him losing, which he did after losing the second set and then withdrawing due to injury in the third. The Association of Tennis Professionals (ATP), concerned about the impact match-fixing can have on the sport, conducted a lengthy investigation, and cleared both players of wrongdoing in 2008.[27] Similar allegations had occurred in both 2003 and 2006 at Wimbledon.[28] Other players reported that they had been approached with offers of up to $140,000 for winning or losing a match.[29] In January 2016, British media reported the existence of secret files alleging that 16 players ranked in the top 50 had in the past decade been repeatedly flagged to the Tennis Integrity Unit over suspicions that they had thrown matches.[30] Italian prosecutors confirmed in spring 2016 the recent allegations of top players involved in tennis and suggested that more than two dozen top-level players should be investigated by prosecutors and the tennis investigation unit.[31]

The value of bets placed among all sports is third-highest in tennis (after football and about level with cricket), but detecting match-fixing is made difficult because of bets being placed on individual points or sets, not just on entire matches. According to the betting industry, it is also the most vulnerable sport for match-fixing: as bets can be placed on individual points, it is relatively easy to manipulate results without being detected. This is why the Tennis Integrity Unit depends on the data provided by betting companies that can show irregular betting activities. Short of match-fixers or players admitting to fixing matches, this is the only way to detect possible corruption of the sport. Another reason that makes tennis particularly prone to corruption is that, unlike football, it is an expensive game to play. Top players need to make about $150,000 per year to pay for the travel costs of the big ATP tournaments and a full-time trainer. However, outside the top ten ranked players, tennis players do not earn seven-figure salaries.[32]

Corruption in sports related to betting has similarities with some of the causes of petty corruption among government officials and civil servants. Individuals who are poorly paid tend to be easy targets for those looking to gain influence. Perumal's match-fixing syndicate, for instance, would target players and referees in low-wage countries to gain influence.[33] Match-fixing expert and writer Declan Hill proposes that 'a disproportionate number of those who reported approaches from fixers also reported missed wages. Players who are not paid are susceptible to corruption by external criminals and by club managements.'[34]

Worldwide legalisation and regulation of sports betting is the first step in limiting its influence in determining sporting event outcomes. Governments then need to cooperate to 'ensure that betting operators are in full compliance of all reporting regulations so potentially corrupting wagers can be tracked and monitored'.[35] Considering how quickly the European and Asian betting markets have grown and become one globalised market, international cooperation is crucial to regulating it. The illegality and volume of betting in Asia is central to the problem and unlikely to change in the near future.[36] However, legal betting companies are also part of the solution. They gather large amounts of data on individual matches that can be – and are – used afterwards to detect potentially rigged matches.

Faking the game: Doping in Olympic sports

Like many international sports organisations, the International Olympic Committee (IOC) is headquartered in Switzerland. And like other sports bodies, the organisation has seen itself confronted both with allegations of corruption and with cases of doping of Olympic athletes.

In 1998, Olympics corruption made the headlines everywhere.[37] The Sydney bid for the 2000 Summer Olympics saw irregularities and allegations of bribery.[38] Still under IOC President Juan Antonio Samaranch,[39] history was repeated for the Salt Lake City Winter Olympics in 2002: allegations of influence-peddling and corruption among IOC members and agents who allegedly helped cities bidding for the Olympics were investigated by the US Department of Justice, as well as the US Congress and prosecutors in Salt Lake City, Utah.[40] The enquiries found that members of the IOC were paid more than $1 million in cash, real estate, vacations, tickets for the Super Bowl and free college tuition for their children.[41] The US investigation resulted in 15 counts of fraud, conspiracy and racketeering against bid leaders Tom Welch and Dave Johnson.[42]

But while the investigations and trials were still ongoing, the IOC also took action. Besides managing the reputational disaster by apologising to the public and punishing officials, the organisation also soon carried out internal investigations that resulted in IOC members resigning or being expelled. At the same time, the IOC started governance reforms and included external stakeholders in its reforms. The resulting code of ethics saw, for example, a ban of IOC members visiting candidate cities, unless the members also served on the Evaluation Commission (in which case visits were planned through the Commission).[43]

But there was little time for the organisation to feel content. In 2015, one of the most popular sports in the Summer Olympics, athletics, slid into the biggest crisis in its history over a mixture of corruption and doping. This brought weeks and weeks of negative headlines for the sport's governing body, the IAAF, and for national athletics federations such as Russia and Kenya. While doping in sports was not an unknown allegation for athletics, the fact that corruption enabled a system of doping became all too apparent in 2015. Like corruption, doping distorts the level playing field of sports, giving an unfair advantage to those willing to risk their health to gain an unfair edge.

In the same year, one of the most prominent reports on doping in sports was the World Anti-Doping Agency's (WADA) report, which brought to light the problem of doping in athletics and the involvement of IAAF officials in covering up and supporting athletes' doping.[44] The report uncovered the links between Russian athletes and state-sponsored and systematic doping in a very detailed fashion.[45] Implicated in the scandal were Russia's athletic governing body, the Russian Athletics

Federation (also a member of athletics' world governing body), the IAAF, the Russian Anti-Doping Agency, WADA's accredited Moscow laboratory and individual athletes and coaches.[46] The independent commission looked into corruption around positive test results that were not acted upon, payments to medical officials and coaches, corruption that enabled prior notice of doping controls, corruption of competition organising officials, and corruption and extortion around the cover-up of positive doping test results.[47] The commission estimated that a large portion of the then-members of the Russian athletics teams were dopers, including some who competed and won medals in the 2012 London Summer Olympics.[48]

From the evidence of corruption and doping in Russian athletics, certain patterns can be detected that hold true for corruption and doping more generally. First, there is participation of athletes and coaches alike in the system. While some or even many of the athletes willingly take banned substances to enhance their performance and career prospects, deep-rooted doping and corruption also create a climate of fear. Athletes that may not be willing to participate in the systemic doping are cut off from training opportunities or funding by their sports organisations. Second, bribery is used to cover up positive drug tests. Testing for banned substances is a part of every athlete's life, both during competitions but also with unannounced testing outside competition times. When this drug-testing system is undermined by prior information on the out-of-competition testing, athletes' doping is nearly undetectable. Third, there is a social network of national and international sports authority officials, whereby – in the Russian case – the IAAF as the international body failed to follow up on allegations of bribery and doping in the Russian team in an appropriate manner, allowing athletes to compete in the Olympic Games who should have been barred. Fourth, doping goes hand-in-hand not only with corruption but also with organised crime. To traffic and distribute banned substances, crime networks are necessary and Europol has already issued a warning that doping substances are getting increasingly attractive for organised crime networks.[49] And lastly, both corruption and doping are determined by simple cost–benefit calculations, incentives, concerns and spillover effects, so that sports governing institutions need to take this seriously to provide a level playing field for sports.

Even before the WADA report was published, then IAAF President Lamine Diack stepped down.[50] Diack at first categorically denied any wrongdoing by the IAAF and defended the Russian athletics association.[51] He was arrested – together with other IAAF officials (among them his son, and the former director of IAAF's medical and anti-doping department, Dr Gabriel Dollé, and the IAAF's legal counsel Habib Cissé[52]) by French prosecutors in November 2015 for accepting €1 million to cover up positive doping tests.[53]

Diack was succeeded by his deputy for eight years and the praised CEO of the London Olympics, the Briton Sebastian Coe. Coe in turn was caught up in alleged conflicts of interest discussions after taking the IAAF presidency because he refused to give up his roles as special adviser at sports apparel company Nike and as chairman of the company CSM Sports & Entertainment Marketing. One of CSM's customers was Azerbaijan's Ministry for Youth and Sport, which sent the city of Baku in the race for the newly established European Games and won the bid. Both the organisers of the European Games and Coe's company CSM were heavily criticised for helping to give legitimacy to an authoritarian government.[54] Sebastian Coe's potential conflict of interest was voting for Baku to become the host of the European Games while at the same time profiting economically from the bid. Furthermore, CSM helped convince UEFA and Michel Platini to give Baku four of the matches during the European Championship in football in 2020. Coe has denied any conflict of interest.[55]

The doping scandal that was investigated by WADA and that led to the resignation of Diack and the appointment of Coe would not have been uncovered had it not been for investigative journalists and the courage of whistle-blowers, in this case a former Russian athlete and a former Russian anti-doping agency staff member.[56] Like many whistle-blowers, they have paid a steep price for this and had to leave their home and Russia in 2015 due to security concerns. For sports governing bodies to reform their governance systems, comprehensive whistle-blower protection is therefore both a necessity and an opportunity to detect potential integrity threats early on.

Up to the point of the WADA report, the biggest doping scandal had arguably been in cycling. In the same year that the WADA report was published, the international cycling body Union Cycliste Internationale (UCI) published their commissioned report on doping in cycling.[57] This came after years of media coverage and allegations of doping and corruption in cycling, as well as Lance Armstrong's very public interview with Oprah Winfrey in 2013 in which he admitted to having used doping. The report is a review of the governance failures within the UCI that have enabled corruption and doping to take place from the early 1990s to the early 2000s. It states that within this timeframe, doping use in the peloton was so widespread that it was, in effect, impossible for riders not to dope.[58] According to the commission, besides governance problems there were conflicts of interests that included: disagreements between stakeholders over (anti-) doping, poor crisis management and a reputation-damaging election campaign in 2013, where the incumbent[59] relied on loopholes in the UCI constitution after he had failed to win the nomination in the first place. Lance Armstrong, who won the Tour de France seven consecutive times from 1999 until 2005, had held a particularly close relationship with the UCI. This, again, points to one of the problems with big inflows of sponsorship, TV licensing and marketing money into a sport: the body that was supposed to oversee ethical conduct and compliance with anti-doping guidelines made a lot of money for the sport itself and the UCI from Armstrong's and the sport's popularity and thus, arguably, had few incentives to make doping offences public.

For a sport that already suffered from increasing reports of doping and the resulting bad reputation, doping cases meant losing big-name sponsors and TV licence fees as viewer numbers decreased.[60] The lack of UCI governance described in the report was a significant failure.[61] This is despite the fact that the majority of drugs that were taken by cyclists were provided by a small circle of doctors, including a Spanish doctor[62] who was investigated by Spanish authorities in 2006. He had provided drugs not only to cyclists, but also to football, athletics and tennis professionals. For a price, he offered to reveal the names of the Spanish Champions League football teams, London marathon winners, cyclists and Olympic medallists whom he supplied.[63]

To fight corruption and doping in sports on a long-term basis, it is crucial for the world anti-doping agency, WADA, to be effective. The governance reforms it has instigated and the fact that the board members commissioned an independent report and published the critical findings offers hope for the fight against doping across sports. However, WADA can only do this successfully if it is joined in this effort by national sports organisations and their national anti-doping agencies.

Corruption in the FIFA 'family'

We don't go to strangers. If we do have problems in our family, we solve the problems in the family. What happens in our family is not a topic for a jurisdiction outside our family. Regular courts are not a part of our family.

Sepp Blatter, then FIFA president[64]

The headquarters of FIFA – football's world governing body – in Zurich, Switzerland, were built as the symbolic home of football, and FIFA's 211 member associations. In line with the self-confidence of the organisation, it is a huge and imposing building. Outside the building are semi-transparent panels that currently appear like a mockery of the scandals that have evolved around the football governing body's corruption and money-laundering arrests and allegations. Like FIFA's executives, the building did not come cheap at CHF 240 million (€220 million).[65]

In October 2015, the FIFA executive board met at these headquarters for an extraordinary meeting that was indeed 'extraordinary'. Following allegations of bribery by US authorities[66] against FIFA's president Sepp Blatter and of deep-rooted corruption in FIFA in relation to the awarding of football World Cups, the meeting agenda (as a rare beacon of transparency published on their website) read as if it was a routine meeting: the acting president's report, reports from the audit and compliance committee, FIFA's operations and the FIFA standing committees, among others.[67] It was not an ordinary meeting, however, as it followed the raid of FIFA's previous meeting in a Swiss hotel in May 2015, when Swiss prosecutors arrested seven FIFA officials.[68] The allegations of the US authorities seemed to confirm what journalists had long suspected: that the allocation of the 2018 and the 2022 World Cups (to Qatar and Russia, respectively) were not decisions based on the best pitches, but were bought by extensive bribery. US authorities had investigated the matter after British journalist Andrew Jennings handed over incriminating material to them. US authorities then started looking into allegations of racketeering, wire fraud and money-laundering conspiracies, as well as criminal mismanagement.[69]

The resulting 47-count indictment by the US District Attorney of Brooklyn in May 2015 read like a who's who of the world's largest football associations: two then current FIFA vice-presidents, the then current and former presidents of the Confederation of

North, Central American and Caribbean Association Football (CONCACAF), and another seven defendants.[70] Initially, and to the disbelief of many, Sepp Blatter was spared and even re-elected as FIFA's president. To others, this was not so surprising: there were not many – journalists or otherwise – who were willing to take on FIFA. Ultimately, however, Blatter was brought down over allegations of bribery around a contract with CONCACAF from 2005, which handed over TV rights for the football games in the Americas below market value. In addition, a 'disloyal payment'[71] of $1.8 million to his successor in the making and then head of UEFA (Europe's football association) Michel Platini was scrutinised. In December 2015, the still incumbent if suspended President Blatter and president-in-waiting Platini were banned from FIFA positions for eight years. A 40-year rule of hand-picking and grooming the next FIFA president, starting with João Havelange, ended with Blatter's fall that year.

The fact that FIFA managed to uphold its system of bribery, nepotism and lavish expense accounts for such a long time is indicative of the influential network that had been built around the world's most popular sport. US investigators have classified the FIFA system as a 'racketeer-influenced and corrupt organization' (RICO)[72] – the legal speak for a criminal network or syndicate that has taken over an otherwise lawful organisation. This is what has been built up since the 1970s under then FIFA President João Havelange[73] and after him under Blatter: a finely calibrated network of vote-buying and influence-peddling that, in line with RICO, has become a criminal enterprise as a result of its use for systematic corruption. In essence, the US government is saying that FIFA became an organised crime network.

This network was built around a range of players: the FIFA president as a nearly authoritarian decision maker; TV licensing, sponsorship and marketing revenue from sponsors and sports marketing agencies; and the regional and national football associations as both voting powers and profiteers from the marketing and licensing revenue. To obtain TV rights, sports marketing firms such as the now-defunct International Sports and Leisure (ISL) and FIFA had built relations over a long time and bribes greased the deals. ISL was founded in Germany in the 1980s as the result of an already-lucrative business idea that was established in Adidas' headquarters under the department name 'sport political department'. Its first contract was with the International Olympic Committee. ISL, who held the TV rights to World Cups including those held in 2002 and 2006, was proven to have paid out bribes to football officials in return for votes between 1992 and 2000. Around $100 million in bribes were paid. They are said to have included targets such as then FIFA President Havelange himself, as well as then Vice-President Issa Hayatou (later acting FIFA president from October 2015 to February 2016, and also on the board of the IOC, which reprimanded him over the ISL kickbacks[74]), and former IAAF President Lamine Diack.[75]

FIFA's Ethics Committee, which was only established in its current form in 2011, had repeatedly failed to perform its investigatory and oversight function. The most striking example of this was the censorship of the Garcia report in 2014.[76] The Garcia report, which was compiled after an investigation into the World Cup 2010 bids for the 2018 and 2022 tournaments amid repeated allegations of bribery, could potentially have provided insight into FIFA's system but was held back by FIFA, and will not be published until the Swiss investigations into these bidding processes are concluded – a process that is likely to take years.

Among the large number of FIFA officials who were allegedly involved or even indicted for bribery and money-laundering, some were more prominent than others. In Europe, Charles 'Chuck' Blazer was, until 2015, only known to those who follow world football very closely. The American was the CONCACAF general secretary from 1990 to 2011 and was a member of the FIFA Executive Committee from 1997 to 2013. Following an FBI investigation into his business dealings that started in 2011, he pleaded guilty to ten

charges of racketeering, tax evasion, money-laundering and violation of financial reporting at a 2013 US hearing.[77] The hearing
documents were sealed because Chuck Blazer had been a confidential informant for the FBI since 2011. The information he provided – together with the detailed work of investigative journalist
Andrew Jennings – ultimately led to the arrest of the seven FIFA
officials at a Swiss hotel in May 2015. Blazer admitted that he and
other FIFA executive committee members accepted bribes to help
South Africa win its bid for hosting the 2010 World Cup. He is now
banned for life from football activities.[78]

Another FIFA executive who got tangled up in the bribery allegations is Germany's Franz Beckenbauer. Revered by the
German public as one of the world's greatest football players and
trainers – he is one of only two persons to have won the World
Cup both as a player (1974) and as a manager of the West German
national team (1990) – Beckenbauer was also instrumental in winning Germany's bid for hosting the 2006 World Cup. Nicknamed
the 'Kaiser', he embodies the image of a successful player-come-
official, and it would be difficult to overstate his celebrity status
in Germany. When allegations of bribery around the 2006 World
Cup bid came up in October 2015, they included Beckenbauer's
name and an almost-struck contract in the run-up to the bid
selection with CONCACAF for preferential treatment. The FIFA
scandal, which had already been followed closely by the German
media, suddenly had a new dimension that cost the head of the
German football association, the Deutscher Fußball-Bund (DFB),
his position. Both the DFB and Beckenbauer have categorically
denied the allegations,[79] but the football association contracted an
international law firm to undertake an independent evaluation of
the allegations. The resulting report raised as many questions as it
answered: it found that €6.7 million was transferred to Qatar by
Beckenbauer. Whether or not the money was used to pay bribes
for winning the 2006 World Cup remains an open question.[80]
However, in the wake of the FIFA corruption scandal, FIFA finally

commissioned an investigation into the 2006 World Cup allegations in March 2016. After much outside pressure and many questions unanswered, the investigation into 'possible undue payments and contracts' relating to the 2006 World Cup awarding process was long overdue.[81]

The system that Havelange and Blatter built and presided over transformed football into a global industry with significant revenue and popularity. This came at a high cost: football TV rights were not only sold to the highest bidder, but to the ones paying the highest bribes to FIFA officials. In addition, serious allegations linger around (potential) football World Cup hosts buying votes for their countries. For football fans, it seemed unthinkable that Qatar, a place with summer temperatures much too high for a football tournament, would be able to win the bid for hosting a World Cup. Nevertheless, the country will be hosting the 2022 World Cup, although with the event moved to November–December. The sum of the proven and alleged corruption cases leaves outsiders wondering: will there be a way to clean the system of its corruption and focus on the sport again? The answer is: not unless FIFA starts taking its deep-rooted lack of governance and its corruption problems a lot more seriously than it has so far, be it from within – at headquarters or through national football associations – or led through outside pressure such as sponsors, fans and the regulatory regime within Switzerland, now under revision.

Tackling integrity challenges in US college American football and basketball

Strong oversight by an independent organisation to tackle one particular corruption and integrity challenge is not taking place on the level of US college sports either. Where sports at college in Europe is primarily a degree-focused activity,[82] the sports environment in North America and particularly the US is a lot more competitive and professionalised. University sports, or college sports to use the vernacular, have been a proud tradition in the US since the 1890s. Athletics departments[83] at colleges are much more than traditional (European) sports clubs: they bring a sense of identity to students and alumni, and the games and results of the most successful college sports teams are followed at a national level. A good example of this is 'March Madness', college basketball's most-watched tournament, which is broadcast by CBS Sports. The tournament is organised by the National Collegiate Athletic Association (NCAA), an umbrella organisation and governing body for college sports that represents 1,200 colleges and various sports, the most televised of which are college basketball and American football. It generates nearly $1 billion in revenue annually.[84]

Athletes in college sports are, in theory and on paper, students and not professional athletes, but in reality US colleges go to extreme lengths to secure the most promising talents for their sports teams, and offering full scholarships to universities is only part of this deal. In return, the college team's coaches – in the case of state universities usually the best-paid civil servants in the state often with million-dollar contracts – expect full commitment to the team, leaving little if any time for student athletes in top division basketball or American football teams to pursue an academic path at the same time.

In essence, college sports teams are being run like professional teams: they profit from nationwide TV licensing fees and merchandise, and athletics departments enjoy relative freedom within their college structures. This structure is meant to be governed through the NCAA to ensure students' (athletes') safety and interests, but in reality several recent scandals have undermined their credibility. Student athletes at the University of North Carolina at Chapel Hill were over years given passes for exams and classes that they were not really taking. Practices like these still did not help to get a sufficient number of athletes, particularly black athletes, to pass enough courses to graduate:

the system of nearly professional student athletes works for the benefit of the system and potentially for the benefit of the few athletes who make the cut from college sports to a professional career. However, it fails many others in that it does not pay them for their athletic performance and at the same time makes it more difficult for them to pursue an academic degree. Success is measured on the field, not in the classroom: a system that works for professional sports but cannot be the credo of an academic institution.[85] And while the NCAA has rules on students' academic performance and on what can be paid to them by teams, the problems are manifold, with a number of cases indicating that the governance of college sports needs an overhaul:

> At Syracuse [University], officials pressured a professor to change a grade for the star center. At Florida State, players were handed answers to quizzes. At Michigan, administrators appeared to cover for an independent studies scam led by a faculty member with courtside seats. At UCLA, an advisor for the basketball team resigned in disgust when he claimed he saw a pattern of illicit grade changing. At Louisville, prostitutes and strippers were reportedly used to lure in talented high school players.[86]

Similar to the cases of FIFA and the IOC described above, the problems in college athletics can be boiled down to governance issues. The management system is made up by those with vested interests in the athletic side of universities, independent boards without accountability to trustees, and faculty representation that tilts towards athletics-friendly faculty, and not enough representation of (former) athletes. In contrast to FIFA, however, the NCAA has a lot more stakeholders and members, making reform processes slow. However, as college sports are making headlines not only for events such as March Madness but also for letting student athletes down academically while making millions of dollars in profit from them, it is perhaps time the NCAA stepped up their game.

Nobody is governing the sports governing bodies

At the core of sports' current reputation and corruption crisis is the governance of professional and amateur sports: the lack of governance in tennis that has kept a lid on alleged match-fixing in international tournaments; the lack of governance structures in athletics that has failed to prevent systemic doping; the lack of governance structures of the world football body FIFA and its constituent national bodies that has led to World Cups being awarded to the highest bidder; and the lack of governance of college sports in the US, particularly American football and basketball, that fails student athletes academically and benefits the income of universities.

What is sports governance and why are sports bodies so prone to corruption? The European Commission in 2013 has provided one of several existing definitions that, for the purpose of this chapter, captures the essence of sports governance as 'the framework and culture within which a sports body sets policy, delivers its strategic objectives, engages with stakeholders, monitors performance, evaluates and manages risk and reports to its constituents on its activities and progress including the delivery of effective, sustainable and proportionate sports policy and regulation'.[87]

Put simply, governance of sports describes how and whether an organisation is being run properly, including rules, compliance and performance, and whether these components serve the organisation's members.[88] It is useful to think about it on three levels: the first level looks at how a sport and a sports organisation (such as a sport governing body) is organised. This includes internal governance structures, such as rights and responsibilities, inclusion and participation of stakeholders, independence of board members and potential conflicts of interest. The second level describes the governance of athletes and events; for example, how an organisation deals with doping and the selection processes of hosts for sports events, as well as transparency in construction of sports facilities. The third level describes systems of discipline: how are the rules and bylaws structured in terms of transparency and oversight, and how are preventative measures such as investigative powers, whistle-blowing and sanctions against transgressions against the codes handled?[89]

But what aspects of the governance structures and the structure of sports make sports so prone to corruption? The first factor is that generally the overall governance structures of sports federations and associations are very weak. They provide little transparency and thus minimise the chances of detection of forms of corruption. The second factor is a common imbalance between the interest of the sport and the sport as big business. Third, sports organisations, as we will see, exist in a strange legal limbo in that they are neither corporates nor classic not-for-profits. Legally, sports bodies are a special type of not-for profit organisation, and therefore are not held to the same legal standards as are businesses, governments or even regular not-for profits and international organisations (such as the UN). This is, among other things, to ensure that sports organisations are free of political interference and pressure both in their countries and at the international level. However, many sports organisations have in the absence of outside interference let themselves be influenced excessively by a few insiders. In addition to more external independence, sports bodies generally have fewer internal and external stakeholders than listed companies. For example, with few exceptions, executive committees of sports governing bodies are usually only made up of member associations. With respect to legal obligations, 65 international sports governing bodies are based in Switzerland, where they are taking advantage not only of tax and property privileges, but also of a relatively lax legal framework regarding organisational governance and corruption. In Switzerland, corruption is a crime for public officials – including referees – but individual citizens cannot be prosecuted for corruption.[90] This has an effect on sports governance because employees and officials of sports governance organisation are not public officials, meaning they cannot be held accountable for corruption in Switzerland. Neither can individuals be prosecuted for match-fixing if the fixing was conducted via an online platform (as it usually would be). As a result, sports organisations with a lack of governance, transparency and accountability have been able to flourish in Switzerland.

The questions of transparency and accountability are central to understanding not only the issues sports governing bodies face, but also to the reactions to these developments. Consumers of sports – spectators buying tickets for matches or paying for TV subscriptions to watch international football matches – have no way to check basic information about a sport governing body's financial data, including the remuneration of the president or the per diems paid to board members (up to $500 per day on top of the $200,000 per annum[91]). In a majority of cases, there are no term limits for executive board members, no non-executive directors on the executive committees, and only recently have conflict of interest guidelines been introduced by some organisations. Only 23 of 35 organisations evaluated in a 2015 sports governance report have an ethics committee that monitors compliance.[92] Only five of these have an ethics committee that operates independently from the executive committee.[93] Only four out of 35 organisations had a selection process for their executive board that includes a selection committee and integrity checks. Where there are in-house governance and anti-corruption investigations, there is hardly any transparency around these investigations. And it is no understatement to say that what has been found with regards to FIFA's lack of governance is only the tip of the iceberg: the same 2015 study found that FIFA's was the second best of the sports bodies examined. Taken together, these governance structures make international sports federations the lawyer, judge and jury with respect to their own affairs, without external oversight or proper reporting or governance mechanisms to challenge their decisions.

When comparing corruption in national and international sports to corruption in the corporate sector, there is a consistent difference: most of the big corruption cases in the private sector, although not all of them, are the result of corruption on the national or local level, conducted usually not by headquarter employees but by national or regional managers. The reverse is usually the case in sports: it is the members of the sports governing bodies themselves who have made the most headlines for alleged corruption or unaccounted money flows in recent years. This is true for football's world governing body, FIFA (and its regional and national members, who are in turn governing bodies); the IOC (around the awarding of the 2002 Winter Olympics to Salt Lake City); weight-lifting (the International Weightlifting Federation, IWF)[94], volley-ball (the International Volleyball Federation, FIVB)[95] and cycling (the international cycling union, UCI).

As the external rules on transparency and reporting that apply to companies and governments do not currently apply to sports governing bodies – based in Switzerland or elsewhere – only their members, sponsors and external scrutiny and pressure have the potential to influence reforms. However, national member associations rarely have an incentive to push for reform if they are involved in the same deals and profit from the same financial arrangements as the international body. Sponsors such as Adidas and Coca-Cola are more likely to put the pressure on behind closed doors as corporate communications departments are not keen to see the sports body their companies have sponsored investigated for various forms of corruption. But the intense scrutiny by expert groups and the media, particularly in 2015, means that even legal changes are on the horizon: Switzerland has introduced changes to its legal system to allow for better oversight of international sports bodies, with an anti-corruption law known as 'lex FIFA'. According to the new legislation, still pending in early 2016, prosecution of individuals will be possible within some boundaries. The new legislation will also tighten money-laundering rules to apply to officials of sports governing bodies. In an even stronger move, cash payments exceeding CHF 100,000 (roughly €90,000) will require the buyer to be registered by the seller. All of these legal changes will, if implemented, make it more difficult to bribe or launder money through sports governance bodies.[96] Two Swiss lawyers writing about the legal changes sum up their necessity and the balance of sports autonomy and political non-interference with oversight:

> In the past sport organisations in Switzerland always asserted their autonomy, and until now the state has granted this autonomy. With autonomy comes responsibility, however, and whether this responsibility has been lived up to or not in the past remains an open question. Given that an organisation of the stature of FIFA was apparently unable to do so, it seems the only logical consequence that the state should now try to intervene in a regulatory way.[97]

The corruption challenges for sport mentioned in this chapter, particularly governance issues and the pervasiveness of match-fixing, can be seen at the grassroots level of sports as well – that is non-professional sports including local sports clubs. However, grassroots sport is important in terms of participating numbers and the sheer number of widely dispersed governing bodies as well as the overall economic importance of grassroots sports. Furthermore, it is at the grassroots level that corruption, resistance to corruption and good governance and the leading principles of fair game become tangible for most people. Reforms are urgently needed to address the current credibility crisis of national and international sports.

Governance reforms made by organisations such as the IOC including a new code of ethics, new rules of conduct for Olympic bids and enhanced financial transparency and reporting, as well as the recognition that doping and match-fixing are sports' biggest threats, are encouraging.[98] The same can be said for the legislative changes introduced in Switzerland, which are a sign of national and international responsibility for sports governance. As always with sports, legislation influencing sports needs to be measured carefully as to not obstruct the independence of sports, but new legal frameworks are certainly necessary specifying both transparency and independent oversight.

On the detection side, a much tougher line on sports betting, especially in the largely unregulated betting places such as Singapore, is needed. On the prevention side, the influx of money into sports has made many fans suspicious of the intentions of clubs, club owners and sports governing bodies. To address the potential conflict of interest between sports and marketing decisions, sponsorship decisions need to be more clearly separated from sports management, and financial disclosure (including salaries of executives and presidents of governing bodies) is required to address the often conflicting ideas of commerce and marketing against the not-for-profit statutes of sports governance bodies.

But not only does there need to be institutional reform. It is up to the grassroots level, fans and athletes to continue to take on leadership in good sports governance and to exert pressure on their national (and through them international) sports federation to clean up sports from corruption. Ways forward have been shown by such not-for-profit organisations as Transparency International Germany[99] and Play the Game[100] who have worked for more than ten years on pressurising sports governing bodies to take the issues of match-fixing, doping and bribery more seriously. Corruption in sport has become a reality, especially in Europe, which is deeply distressing to the global public and can only add to the disillusion with institutions designed to work for the common benefit but that abjectly fail to do so.

10

Murky Waters: Environmental Corruption

In December 2015, the United Nations Climate Change Conference in Paris convened the world's leaders, thinkers and practitioners on climate issues. 25,000 delegates from 195 countries – from governments to academics, and companies to the not-for-profits – met in France to discuss achieving a legally binding and universal agreement on climate, with the aim of keeping global warming below 2°C. The Paris Agreement was signed by 195 nations declaring their goal to cut greenhouse gas emissions to net zero by 2100. This is to be achieved, mainly, by shifting from fossil fuels to renewable energy such as wind or solar power. The agreement was lauded as a breakthrough.

The Paris conference was also a promising event for 30 international companies: car-maker BMW was the 'headline partner', or main sponsor, with other sponsors being the Carbon Trade Exchange, energy companies Vattenfall and Cogar International, and financial services companies such as Moody's and the Spanish bank Santander, as well as renewable energy companies. The list of companies is a pretty accurate reflection of corporate interests in the debate around reducing carbon emissions but excluded – with the exception of Vattenfall – traditional energy producers.[1]

Paris was the 21st meeting of its kind, the so-called Conference of Parties (COP21) and after many failings since the achievement of the Kyoto Protocol,[2] it was lauded as a breakthrough agreement. One thing the delegates in Paris gave little attention to and that may just undermine the outcome of the conference was corruption and the environment, or corruption in and around climate change.

The corrupting effect works in two ways: it can directly threaten the environment, as is the case of lax environmental controls or it can impede mitigation. In the first case corruption leads, as we will see, to environmental degradation. Examples of this are through the too cosy linkage between regulators and companies in the US, and through illegal waste dumping on both sides of the Atlantic. Environmental crime, facilitated by corruption in the areas of licensing, customs, fraudulent certificates and others, has detrimental consequences for the environment and citizens alike.[3] But environmental corruption can also undermine actions that were devised to protect the environment, such as corruption in the renewable energy sector, carbon trading (also a regulation of sorts) or climate finance.[4]

Links between the environment and corruption are elusive but real on two levels: first, in terms of consequences, and second, in terms of mitigation – previous agreements and legislation on the environment in both Europe and the US have been undermined by various forms of corruption. Corporate lobbying in both cases has undermined well-conceived instruments such as the emissions trading regime in the EU, as will be discussed in the case of the Czech Republic.

It is important to note that the degree of public debate around climate change in general differs in Europe and North America. In Europe it is generally accepted that climate change is man-made and the discussion has long turned to mitigation and adaption, whereas in the US the question whether climate change is real is still much more controversial – so much so that during the 2016 presidential campaign, Republican candidates Ted Cruz and Donald Trump both questioned the science of climate change.[5] What unites both sides of the Atlantic, however, is that environmental corruption is currently given too little public attention.

Companies and environmental oversight

Duke Energy is the largest utility or, to be more specific, electric power holding company in the United States. Headquartered in Charlotte, North Carolina, it has been in business for more than 100 years.[6] Its responsibility for the murky waters of the Dan River in North Carolina and Virginia is a case illustrating just how corporate lobbying and regulatory capture can have detrimental effects on the environment. The case is a particularly dramatic demonstration of the dangers of non-transparent political party funding, environmental licensing, political appointments and cronyism, and lobbying – factors that frequently come together in the environmental sector and can lead to disastrous outcomes.

The Dan River in North Carolina and Virginia is a 344 km broad-flowing river passing a few towns and communities. For one of these towns, Danville, it is the source of local drinking water. The river runs from North Carolina past a little town called Eden into Virginia and then back into North Carolina, where it empties into a lake. Mainly used for canoeing, kayaking and hiking along its trails, it was included into the Virginia Scenic River System by the Virginia Department for Conservation and Recreation in 2012. Not even two years later, it became famous for being the scene for a major environmental disaster: a coal ash spill caused by Duke Energy in February 2014. The coal ash spill was the third largest coal ash spill of its type in the history of the United States and occurred in Duke Energy's retired coal steam station in Eden, North Carolina, and fed into the Dean River.

According to the prosecutor who later brought the case against the company, Duke had ignored several warnings about possible problems at its coal ash site, thereby illegally polluting the area and resulting in a burst pipe under the site that led to 70 km of the Dan River being covered by dark sludge. The burst released 39 million tons of coal ash and 20,000 gallons (75,000 litres) of toxic water into the river and threatened drinking water and aquatic life. Coal ash – the residue of energy production from coal – is often mixed with water to form a slurry, which is then stored in impoundments commonly called 'coal ash ponds'.[7] It contains a number of metals such as arsenic and mercury, and must therefore be contained in these ponds. However, the US environmental regulator, the Environmental Protection Agency (EPA), has classified it as generally 'non-toxic'.

Throughout the US, there are currently around 1,000 coal mines and 600 coal energy plants, which provide the most important source of energy in the US (39 per cent of all generated energy), followed by natural gas, nuclear energy, and hydropower.[8] It is up to US states to regulate how coal ash is stored as there is no federal regulation. After the coal ash spill in North Carolina, it was alleged that the state regulator had gone soft on companies like Duke.[9] Environmental activists had handed over evidence to the regulators in North Carolina, the North Carolina Department of Environment and Natural Resources, in 2013, proving that there were groundwater spills originating from Duke's coal ash pond but no action was taken by the regulator.

Duke, like most companies, is active in the political arena to lobby for its causes, which more often than not involves environmental legislation. The company provides funding to political candidates through a Political Action Committee (PAC) called DUKEPAC. Through DUKEPAC, the company and its employees have contributed significant campaign funding for both parties, with roughly two-thirds going to Republican candidates. However, the very nature of PACs, or their bigger and less transparent brothers, Super PACs, makes it impossible to know how much money went to which candidate. While some contributions can be tracked, indirect contributions to other PACs that support causes for candidates do not have to be publicised. But one thing is clear: Duke Energy was the employer of Republican Governor Pat McCrory for 28 years. McCrory had also received more than $1 million in campaign contributions from Duke Energy, plus an unknown amount that went to PACs supporting causes that McCrory stood for.[10] It was during his governorship that the coal ash spill happened. The regulators failed to act. In a strange way, the Dan River spill was helpful for the campaigners: the sweetheart deal that Governor McCrory had offered Duke – fines of merely $99,111 as a settlement for environmental damage, without obligation to clean up the pollution – was not sustainable after the Dan River spill's public outcry. Duke settled the lawsuit with a plea bargain and paid $34 million for environmental projects. In addition, the company was placed under a five-year probation and subject to monitoring of its compliance programme.[11]

It would be easy to dismiss what happened in North Carolina as a one-off case of close ties between a governor, his influence over regulatory bodies, and a particular interest group. The coal ash spill cannot be directly related back to any individual oversight or regulatory laxness. However, it left many people wondering how special interests groups were able to influence supposedly independent supervisory or regulatory agencies – a process often referred to as 'regulatory capture' – where the benefits of a programme or decision go to a (small) group but are borne by a large group of people, notably taxpayers.[12]

From a related perspective, the Koch brothers of Koch Industries (one of the largest privately held companies in the US, involved in a range of products and commodities from refinery to chemicals, electronic components to energy, see also Chapter 2)[13] have either made serious attempts at regulatory capture or succeeded in such capture over several decades. Nevertheless, the company has not managed to avoid major lawsuits. In 1997, the Department of Justice levelled 97 counts of an indictment against Koch Industries for covering up the discharge of 91 tons of butane from a refinery in Christ Church, Texas. In this case the company was fined $296 million and four employees were sent to jail for a total of 35 years. The EPA has been a particular target of the Kochs who, for instance, sought to prevent the EPA classifying formaldehyde as having 'known carcinogen elements', even though the National Toxic Agency had confirmed the accuracy of this description. Koch Industries employees also said in an interview that they had lied to regulators about oil pipeline leaks and spills. One jury found the company guilty of 25,000 false claims to the government. This is a record of a company with a dubious record in relation to the environment and public health, whose high level profitability has enabled its owners to have a critical influence in elections at every level in the US.[14]

Patterns similar to that of the Duke case and of the Kochs' fight with the EPA can be seen on the other side of the Atlantic, too. A case in point is that in the Czech Republic involving the energy giant ČEZ, leading politicians and the subversion of targets designed to restrict emissions.

The ČEZ Group (Skupina České Energetické Závody) is a Czech electricity conglomerate of various firms and companies operating mainly in the Czech Republic and other countries in Central and South Eastern Europe. It is 70 per cent owned by the Czech government with the remaining shares being traded on the Warsaw and Prague exchanges. The company was founded in 1992 and is now one of the ten largest energy companies in Europe. It is also the utility company with the highest total shareholder return in the world.[15] In 2009, ČEZ made a record net profit of CZ 52 billion crowns ($2.1 billion), which is roughly 10 per cent greater than the net profit of the five largest Czech banks combined.[16]

In recent years the company has been the subject of harsh criticism for its growing political influence, power and leverage, often manifest in its meddling with Czech politics (and vice versa),[17] including environmental policies with far-reaching consequences beyond national borders.[18] This point was illustrated in major scandals surrounding the hasty approval of a controversial law on carbon emissions by the Czech Parliament in 2013, dubbed the 'Tuscan Affair' (based on the location of some key meetings) by the Czech press.

A key figure in this case was Martin Roman, ČEZ's CEO from 2004 to 2011, who accumulated considerable influence over Czech politics and state administration; to the extent that he has been described as the most influential man in the Czech Republic and was given the nickname 'half-prime minister'. His influence was said to be greatest over Czech Prime Minister Mirek Topolánek, who was in office from 2006 to 2009. The 'Tuscan Affair', which came to light during a carbon emissions trading scandal, exposed this connection centred around the price of emissions under the European Union's Emissions and Trading Scheme (ETS).

Within the ETS, the European Commission gives out a limited number of CO_2 emission allowances to polluting industries. Companies that use up less of their allocated allowances are free to trade and sell them to other firms, creating a market for the trade in carbon credits. This is intended to set a market price for CO_2 emissions that eventually leads companies to reduce their emissions.

Ahead of the EU climate change summit in December 2008, a Czech delegation of members of the Topolánek government and key people from the Czech industry – at the forefront ČEZ and its CEO Martin Roman – invited more than 200 guests from the EU political scene to celebrate the 'kick-off' of the Czech EU presidency in Brussels. At the climate change summit, all 27 EU countries agreed to cut carbon emissions by 20 per cent by 2020,[19] to source 20 per cent of their energy from renewable resources, and to increase energy efficiency by 20 per cent compared to 1990. However, the Czech Republic[20] managed to get special treatment over the allocation of carbon emission allowances to Czech companies: for the

sake of investing in 'green' technologies and, above all, counter-
acting the effects of the global recession and euro crisis, only 30
per cent of emission allowances were to be auctioned, whereas the
remaining 70 per cent could still be given out for free.[21]

The exemption means that the Czech Republic was able
to give out free emission allowances to its companies as long as
the companies invested the 'saved' amount into environmentally
friendly technology.[22] This gave Czech companies a competitive advantage. The law putting this exemption into place was a
huge lobbying success for ČEZ and a severe failing by the Czech
Environmental Law Service.[23] A few weeks later, the lobbying
efforts came to light: Martin Roman and key ČEZ officials and
lobbyists were photographed at a holiday get-together in Tuscany
– on a yacht and at an extravagant villa – with Czech politicians
and members of Parliament, among them Topolánek, who had
resigned as prime minister just months earlier following a vote of
no-confidence.[24]

The affair was given particular attention because the Czech
bill establishing the European Trading Scheme exemptions was
approved in such a hurry and with such unusual speed compared
to other bills – and even before the EU issued official implementa-
tion guidelines. Moreover, the application deadlines for the quali-
fying technology modernisation projects were set for such a short
timeframe that an application for any 'bigger' modernisation project could hardly be prepared in a timely manner.[25]

Further scrutiny by the EU Commission of the policies
implementing transitional free allowances for energy companies in
the Czech Republic[26] revealed that the Czech government, which
decided to allocate for free more than 108 million allowances
between 2013 and 2019, not only failed to correctly implement its
obligations under the EU regime, but was in breach of the main
aims and objectives.[27]

According to a 2011 study by Sandbag, a UK-based global
climate think tank, ČEZ is the only 'carbon fat cat' in the European

energy and power sector with a surplus of 4.7 million allowances worth approximately €80 million. While some companies carried over surplus allowances from phase II (2008–12) to phase III (as of 2013), others – like ČEZ – are continuously given free allowances according to sector-specific benchmarks. Notwithstanding these forms of subsidies, the Czech Republic has among the highest electricity prices on a purchasing-power basis in Europe.[28] In fact, protests over rising electricity prices involving ČEZ and its Eastern European subsidiaries were also staged in Bulgaria and Albania in 2013.[29]

As a result of interest peddling, legislative loopholes for companies such as ČEZ have effectively undermined the idea of carbon trading and emissions reductions (although it remains a key part of the follow-up agenda to the Paris climate change conference). As the Czech case demonstrates, lax regulation and powerful lobbying can have a substantial effect on strategies designed to control the impact of climate change. This is a classic case of the undermining of public policy – a functioning carbon emissions market – for corporate gain.

Corporate deception made in Germany

In the US, the transportation sector is the second-largest greenhouse gas producing sector, after the energy sector itself.[30] Within transportation, most greenhouse gas emissions are the result of the combustion of petroleum-based products such as gasoline or diesel. Half of the transport emissions are caused by passenger cars and light-duty trucks, as well as sports utility vehicles, pickup trucks and minivans.[31] In Europe, the figures are comparable: road transport causes around 20 per cent of Europe's CO_2 emissions, and is the only sector in the EU where emissions are still rising. To curb this development, the European Union has set binding emissions targets for automobiles. One part of this legislation was the requirement for car-makers to state the car's CO_2 emissions to enable consumers to choose the most environmentally friendly option, should they wish to do so.[32]

Car-makers on both sides of the Atlantic have been trying to find ways to devise more emission-efficient cars without compromising on the 'Fahrvergnügen' – the German word for enjoying the drive – or design, and while trying to meet customers' demands for ever-more powerful engines. At the same time, they have also been trying to lobby policymakers on making the emission standards not too stringent. And in some cases, the rules have been avoided altogether.

Volkswagen (VW) is the second largest car-maker in the world, after Toyota. With its brands (Audi, Seat, Skoda, Bentley, Bugatti, Lamborghini, Ducati and Porsche), plus commercial vehicles, the company produces 10 million cars per year, giving it a 12 per cent global market share in passenger cars. In 2015, the Volkswagen figure that made headlines was another one: 800,000 – the number of cars that were suspected of having tampered with emissions test results.[33] To deceive the authorities and stay within emission limits, VW had manipulated cars with a 'defeat device'. In what was later called the 'diesel dupe',[34] Volkswagen had installed software in its type EA 189 diesel motors that was able to detect when tests were being run and adapt the car's fuel emission accordingly. The result was that the test results were within emission limits, while the cars emitted up to nine times as much when on the road.[35] Eleven million cars with this software were sold, eight million of them in Europe.

Environmental groups have long criticised European testing, claiming that 90 per cent of diesel vehicles in Europe did not meet the emissions requirements: US standards are stricter than their European counterparts. The US Environmental Protection Agency (EPA) and the US Department of Justice fined heavy-duty engine-makers for using 'defeat devices' as far back as 1998, demonstrating that the tactics were not new. Similarly, it was the EPA and not its European counterparts that

Figure 1 Ownership structure of Volkswagen

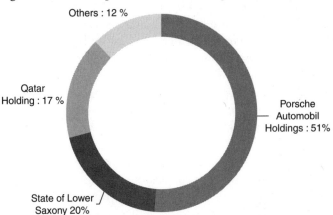

Others : 12 %

Qatar
Holding : 17 %

Porsche
— Automobil
Holdings : 51%

State of Lower
Saxony 20%

issued a 'Notice of Violation' in September 2015, alleging that VWs and Audis equipped with 2.0-litre engines and manufactured between 2009 and 2015 circumvented EPA standards, and a second notice was issued in November 2015 for 3.0-litre engine models since 2014. The company admitted shortly after that it had used the device in all of its US 3.0-litre diesel models since 2009.[36] In the wake of the scandal, the EPA also asked German luxury car manufacturer Mercedes-Benz to explain its cars' emission levels after a class-action lawsuit against the company was filed in the US alleging that Mercedes used a similar defeat device in its exhaust.

In Germany, the 'dieselgate' scandal highlighted both problems within the company – although in early 2016 it was sticking to the 'bad apple' excuse – and problems on the political level. Volkswagen, owned in part by the German state of Lower Saxony (see Figure 1), has traditionally had close links with German politics and politicians, and Germans were left to wonder whether the company had enjoyed special treatment.

Germany's opposition Green Party went so far as to claim that the German government knew of the defeat devices, and that VW – and the German car industry more generally – had huge influence over German policies and even emission targets. The administration denied the allegations and stated that it had ordered an inquiry.[37] However, the commission conducting the inquiry – whose composition is not public – is, according to news reports, anything but a neutral actor. It is made up of four employees of the German Transport Ministry (who are, arguably, unlikely to look into the allegations of political influence peddling), three members of the Federal Office for Motor Vehicles (again, arguably not particularly likely to press for an investigation of its own potential failures), as well as one academic (who has previously worked for the automotive industry).[38]

On the European level, the scandal showed a deficiency in testing methods and oversight and threw doubt on the ability of the Commission and national governments to manage an EU-wide emissions control regime for vehicles, which has itself been the subject of intense lobbying. A much clearer response came from the US where the courts took on the Volkswagen case and set the company a deadline to fix 600,000 cars or face the possibility of a bench trial in the summer of 2016.[39]

It is clearly possible that other comparable cases will come to light in which manufacturers seek to deliberately bypass emission rules by clever technical fixes, a practice that has been detected among other vehicle manufacturers in the past. This is clearly the corruption of established standards for corporate gain at the expense of both shareholders (obliged to assume the cost of huge fines) and reputation, making a mockery of corporate shareholder responsibility.

Crime, corruption and the environment: The ecomafia

The practice of environmental crimes such as illegal waste dumping, waste trafficking, illegal logging, unreported fishing and wildlife trafficking can be found on both sides of the Atlantic. Corruption is integral to these crimes.[40] Like other areas of crime, corruption and trading in influence, all actors are represented when it comes to the environment including public officials, private-sector employees and organised crime. Whether they are in the business of tempering with solar subsidies, waste management or water services, the benefit of the few comes at a high cost for consumers, taxpayers and the environment.

The most famous news story in recent years to combine the words 'waste' and 'chaos' took place in Naples, Italy. The city became not only infamous for the existence of the Camorra but also the ill-smelling consequences of their role in contract-buying and selling in the public waste management system. Naples became the best-publicised example of corrupted waste management services with a proper waste management crisis in 2008 when mountains of litter were not picked up by the mafia-controlled waste management organisation. This in turn threw the entire city into chaos. In 2014 it became even worse: toxic commercial waste was dumped in the periphery of Naples by a waste management organisation and set on fire to eliminate it. The public outcry over the potential environmental and health impact was so strong that even Pope Francis voiced concern, and the US Navy moved personnel from outside Naples to other bases for fear of contaminated water.[41]

The crisis was a result of the effect of corrupt networks of organised crime and local authorities collaborating in waste collection services. The impact was not only an environmental one: a 2012 study showed that if Milan and Rome were able to reduce environmental and other corruption to an 'average value', the two cities could save €10–50 million per year respectively.[42]

This is not an exclusively Italian problem. Environmental crimes such as waste dumping are a problem in other parts of Europe as well, and are also often found as a conjunction of legal businesses and organised crime groups, sometimes in conjunction with bribery-induced city officials.

In Northern Ireland, a 38-people strong Environmental Crime Unit was set up in 2008 to prevent illegal waste dumping and organised crime activities in the waste sector. It was acknowledged that this was becoming a lucrative business and thus an increasing problem in Northern Ireland, ranging from waste collection to the running of skips, illegal landfill and illegal burning of waste, making Northern Ireland 'the dirty corner of the United Kingdom'.[43] It was also recognised that an increasing number of illegal waste cases involved organised crime groups, who set up and use waste management companies as an add-on to their other business. Despite increased efforts, the Environmental Crime Unit was unable to prevent the activities of an organised crime group that resulted in 500,000 tons of illegally dumped waste – stretching 1.4 km – near Northern Ireland's city of Londonderry. The waste facility, in the town of Mobuoy, was the result of ongoing illegal waste management over years. The clean-up of the site could cost taxpayers up to £100 million. The persons responsible for dumping the waste at the site are unknown, but the quantities of waste dumped there suggest that whoever ran this sophisticated operation evaded at least £34 million in taxes and dues to local government.[44]

Similar cases have occurred across the Atlantic, too, with proven organised crime involvement. In 2013, Carmine Franco, also known as 'Papa Smurf', was indicted and sentenced for extortion, loan sharking and stolen property offences, among others. Together with another 11 members of three La Cosa Nostra crime families in New York (the Genovese, Gambino and Lucchese crime families), Franco managed, by extortion, to use a legal waste business to front his illegal waste business and keep his illegal activities undetected. He had previously been barred from running any type of waste company, so Franco's only way to keep a hand in the business was to threaten business owners of legal businesses in New York and New Jersey with violence and extortion, and to use their businesses for his activities. The crime family and Franco thus avoided any kind of official connection to the businesses. In addition, some of the controlled owners committed crimes separately including fraud, making the entire enterprise a mix of legal to illegal business in various forms.[45] The problem of corruption in waste management led New Jersey's authorities to commission an investigation into the subject, the result of which was presented in a 2011 report that made explicit reference to 'vulnerability to corruption in the recycling and disposal of contaminated soil and demolition debris that pose serious potential environmental and public health consequences'.[46]

On a transnational scale, electronic waste from the US and Europe is illegally mislabelled and shipped to developing countries by organised crime groups. Batteries are mislabelled as mixed plastic scrap and end up on waste dumps in Africa, contaminating the environment and bringing their dealers millions in profit from a market that is estimated to be worth $19 billion annually.[47] A new term for this kind of 'business' was coined: the 'ecomafia'.

The ecomafia is, like 'classic' organised crime lines of activities, a business-savvy enterprise that exploits weaknesses of individuals and markets alike. Over the past ten years, the ecomafia has become active in environmental fields such as investing in wind power and renewable energy more widely.[48] A lack of transparent procedures and authority in this area has led to the mafia paying off local officials and supervisory bodies that are supposed to guard the environment. The scale of this led to Europol leading an inquiry in 2009–10 into the activities of organised crime and corruption in this sector, and a new body of academic literature and press attention.[49] A key result was the examination of the wind energy sector. In Italy, as elsewhere, renewable energy and its production is state-subsidised to encourage companies (and citizens) to produce energy from renewable sources and limit the dependency on oil and gas. This has become an unexpectedly lucrative business for some, as energy that is fed into the grid can bring high profits on top of the subsidies. Italy's wind farms are particularly lucrative as the power sold into the grid brings the highest return worldwide with €1.80 per Kwh.[50] These subsidies are financed both by the Italian government and the European Union, which has pledged to achieve 20 per cent of renewable energy production by 2020, thus encouraging member countries to switch to green energy. The Italian government estimated that wind energy would increase from an annual 89 Kw tons (of oil equivalent – a measurement unit for renewable energy) in 2008 to 250 Kw tons of oil equivalent in 2013,[51] therefore tripling the amount of energy produced within five years by increasing the number of wind farms. Coupled with the guaranteed feed-in price of €180 per MWh where the UK, for example, paid around €120,[52] renewable energy was becoming an ever-more attractive business of which one mafia boss in Sicily claimed that nobody would build a single wind turbine unless he agreed to it.[53] The wind farms were then used both to generate profits but also to launder money, which caused the Italian anti-mafia agency to investigate and freeze €1.3 billion of assets of businessman Vito Nicastri in 2013. Nicastri had operated 43 energy companies that had strong-armed land-owners in Sicily into letting the companies use their land to run wind turbines, and bribed public officials to get permits. It was the largest seizure of mafia-related assets in Italy's history, and Nicastri was shown to have ties to both the Cosa Nostra and the 'Ndrangheta.[54] He was convicted on counts of false tax returns and fraud against the state to four years in prison in 2015.[55]

Indeed, Nicastri's case points to a bigger problem: while the aim of increasing the supply of renewable energy on the EU-level is a laudable one, it requires large amounts of money as economic incentives, such as subsidies, to achieve its 2020 aim. As with other systems where large amounts of money change hands in a short time, this brings huge corruption risks. On the EU level, the European Regional Development Fund (ERDF) committed to allocate a massive sum of €295 billion in grants for renewable energy, to be paid to companies and audited by the different national authorities. However, there is often too little oversight of this money, resulting in large amounts being skimmed off, as in Nicastri's case. Similar schemes have been uncovered in Spain, where investigations showed €110 million paid as 'commissions' to public officials of the People's Party (PP) in Castile and León, and other European countries such as Bulgaria and Romania.[56]

Wherever one stands on climate change and environmental issues, one truth should stand undisputed: corruption harms the environment, and current mitigation and adaption mechanisms themselves are at risk of foul play. This chapter has shown how climate change mitigation mechanisms such as the EU's Emissions and Trading Scheme have themselves fallen prey to influence and rent-seeking by politicians and the private sector. In the same vein, the increase of renewable energy sources such as wind farms in Europe, while good for the environment, have been exploited by organised crime groups and other profiteers. In addition, regulatory capture or influencing of regulatory policy has led to environmental disasters such as the coal ash spill at Duke. Except for environmental crimes such as waste disposal, none of these issues have found much traction in the mainstream discussion. However, if policymakers are serious about tackling climate change, tackling the corruption risks in the environmental sector will be crucial.

11

A Challenge to the West

Corruption in the West is the spectre at the feast, largely unrecognised but with an uncanny ability to determine what actually happens. It has permeated society in ways that cannot be ignored. The situation places the great anti-corruption reforms of the late nineteenth and early twentieth century in serious jeopardy. Corruption also has a global impact: the ways in which European, American and Canadian companies trading abroad may engage in bribery to win contracts is widely noticed in emerging markets.

Where very well-known brand companies are publicly exposed as having bribed in emerging markets, local companies in those markets may conclude that there is little need to reform their own practices. The substantial attempts by the World Bank and other development finance agencies to clean up public tender processes in emerging markets can easily be set back when cases exposing corruption in the construction sector (such as Montreal or Rome) reach the international media. Organised crime groups, such as those in Mexico, are enabled and emboldened by the presence of distribution networks in the US and Europe. Political observers, alive to trends in Europe and the US, can see that supposed high standards in campaign and electoral finance are being deeply eroded. The cumulative impact of cases such as these means that the West's own perception of itself – as less corrupt than emerging markets – is scarcely held south of the Rio Grande or the Mediterranean.

And corruption in the West also has an impact at a more personal level. Sports fans may find that the results of matches at the highest level are determined by offshore betting syndicates or the systematic use of performance-enhancing drugs, as the World Anti-Doping Agency's (WADA's) report of 2015 showed so clearly. Small- and large-scale private investors may find that major failures in corporate governance have written off a once-valued share, as in Volkswagen or BP. Depositors may see the collapse of their savings in institutions such as Northern Rock or Countrywide, even if rescued at the last minute by government intervention at the taxpayers' expense. On the political front, voters are increasingly dismayed that big funders can determine the size of campaigns, as in the US, or that parties can enrich their leaders from party funds, as in Spain, or misuse funds awarded by the state for the purpose of campaigning, as in Italy and Hungary.

The corporate world, too, creates dilemmas for individuals. In boardrooms, a non-executive director with a mandate for the company's ethics may wake at nights wondering whether he or she really knows what is happening at the point of sale – whether the product is medicine or helicopters. A CEO in the construction industry with the best of intentions and seeking to expand his company's turnover may despair at the tenacious hold of organised crime in cities as diverse as Montreal, Brussels and Rome.

But organised crime may strike at individuals with equal force. A migrant labourer, escaped from Eritrea or Honduras, may be bound to his or her 'trafficker' for many years. The comfortable retiree, secure in middle-class life, may find a bank balance removed overnight as organised hackers – just as likely to be local as thousands of miles away – raid an account.

Are two of the biggest issues of the day – inequality and climate change – immune to corruption in the West? The facts suggest the opposite. The network of 'secrecy jurisdictions', as the 'Panama Papers' confirmed, ensures that the very wealthiest individuals can hold and multiply their wealth outside the framework of taxes and transparent reporting. Strategies to address climate change focus on the case for reducing CO_2 emissions and for the promotion of renewable energy. But the former has clearly been undermined by fraudulent testing systems among vehicle manufacturers and the latter by discrete manipulation of the wind power market as well as giant loopholes in the oversight of climate change financing.

This is a context in which the credibility of the attempt to curb corruption in the West is being called into doubt by its own citizens. Seen from the rest of the world, the picture is even less credible. What is the underlying dilemma, and what can be done?

The dilemma

In the US, the intentions of the framers of the Constitution to avoid political corruption have been partly undermined in the course of history. The framers regarded the emergence of factions geared to special interests as anathema and could not foresee an era in which formal lobbying would be such a strong determinant of congressional legislation. In fact, special interests have defined themselves very effectively through both campaign finance and the lobbying industry. The 27 member countries of the EU have a different set of problems in addressing political corruption, reflected in Western Europe in the diversity of electoral systems, and the frequent inadequacies of the investigative and justice systems; and in Central and Eastern Europe by the fragile foundations on which the new liberal democracies have been built. Further, the arrival of the 'single market', a success in economic terms, has created opportunities for organised crime that were previously hard to access.

These constitutional and political dilemmas are reinforced by conflicts between the public and private sectors that undermine measures designed to curb corruption. Conflicts of this kind include, for example, the deliberate undermining of emissions control systems in Europe, a necessary part of resistance to climate change, and the inability of the EPA in the US, as the responsible agency, to make public its analysis of fracking. Separately, in no case is the clash between public and private interests in both the US and Europe shown more clearly than in the issue of secrecy jurisdictions. The growth of these financial escape holes over the past 40 years has been to the benefit only of a private and corporate elite and cannot possibly be defined as in the American or European public interest. Yet these jurisdictions have prospered and are a source of reassurance if not a magnet to the corrupt.

A further dilemma characterises the world of sport. Here, the age-old fascination of physical prowess has been mixed with the phenomenon of globalisation, ensuring the freedom of movement of athletes and betting rings and turning the commercial sponsorship of sport into a corporate bonanza. Recognition of the dilemma of the conflict of interest between athletes, the public and commercial interests is the first step to confronting the corruption that now characterises key parts of the sports world.

But the ultimate dilemmas surrounding corruption in the countries of the West are nearly always personal. The argument that 'the system made me do it'[1] is hardly an excuse in the US and most of the EU. Individuals at the top of banks, and on their trading floors, make free choices, as do corporate managers seeking to defy clearly defined public regulations, as do those who choose to deposit funds in secrecy jurisdictions. Individual choice and integrity is governed by ethical tradition and the strength of the law and its applications. In the case of contemporary corruption, both the strength of the ethical tradition and the strength of the law and its application is in doubt.

What can be done?

The overarching principle in seeking to override these dilemmas must be one of systemic change in which the consequences of an individual choice to behave corruptly are much clearer. This is a triple issue of regulation (and legislation), compliance and 'governance' (both of companies and sports organisations). In each of these instances there will be a need for first, improved measures of prevention and prosecution; second, for an end to a cult of secrecy; and third, for action by civil society.

The battle for improved regulation extends to both the regulations themselves and to their enforcement. We have argued that the recent moves to near total deregulation of campaign finance in the US lays society open to the corruption of influence. In Europe the wide range of systems designed to control political finance are scarcely effective in a range of countries. In parallel with this situation the forces of lobbying need to be better regulated in both Europe and the US.

Although regulation of the banking and finance sectors has been improving there is a long way to go. We have shown how progress in both the US and Europe has fallen short of what the public might legitimately expect where huge quantities of taxpayers' money have been deployed to bail out errant banks. But the wide distribution of responsibility in the US between eight different regulatory bodies, and continued resistance to the separation of retail and investment banking display the inertia towards reform. In the Eurozone, the establishment of the 'Single Supervisory Mechanism' is a welcome development, but early indications are that it is as slow as the British regulator (the Financial Conduct Authority) to take on the issues of in-house compliance.

In the broader corporate sector, the questions of regulation raised in Chapter 4 predominate. What more can be done to ensure that the cases involving huge fines and large companies can be brought to an end, other than by the 'gentlemen's understandings' that characterise deferred prosecution agreements. In each of the sectors we have discussed there are important initiatives towards more effective self-regulation – by, for example, disentangling political finance from the construction industry and (in some countries) the mafia, which will require much tougher judicial follow-up.

Ending a cult of secrecy is still critical to the fight against corruption. The tradition of secrecy survives in many political finance systems whether through 'dark money' vehicles as in the US, or the anonymity of donations below defined levels in the EU, both of which undermine the public interest. Executives continue to seek to immerse themselves in secrecy until prosecution services or the media challenge them directly. But the ultimate tradition is that of the secrecy jurisdictions themselves, who have made secrecy a selling point, and who are now rightly under unprecedented threat. In each of these cases, an end to secrecy as it has been practised is necessary to the defeat of corruption.

Civil society has already made its mark on these issues. The moves by Transparency International and Global Witness in the early 1990s have led to a burgeoning coalition of interest groups whose progress is represented by their collective role in creating corruption benchmarks, monitoring conventions, holding the public and private sector accountable and, perhaps most importantly, in shining a light on corruption and empowering citizens to speak out. Others have followed, like Global Integrity and the Sunlight Foundation in the US, and – within the realm of civil society but on the media side – crucial investigative journalist networks such as the International Consortium of Investigative Journalists, the Bureau of Investigative Journalism and the Organized Crime and Corruption Reporting System.[2] At the state level in the US, citizen mobilisation against different forms of corruption is widespread – represented by organisations such as Represent.us in Massachusetts (pioneering an Anti-Corruption Bill) and Common Cause in Illinois.

The challenge

How much does the ongoing threat from corruption matter? The anti-corruption movement has for a long time spoken of a 'world free of corruption'. It is indisputable that such a world would be able to channel many more resources to the provision of health care and education at the 'grassroots' across the developing world; that the arms race for large- and small-scale arms would be dramatically impeded; that the incentives for human trafficking would be severely undermined; that terrorist cells that use corruption to acquire funds could be thwarted; that key mechanisms that drive global inequality could be seriously restricted; and that the likelihood of mechanisms to address climate change being undermined by corruption could be reversed.

The credible mechanisms to create this world have passed from outright rejection (the World Bank in the early 1990s), to deep scepticism (*The Economist* in 1994) to apparently enthusiastic acceptance (the G20 in 2015). Further, support from the public for the anti-corruption movement in a range of countries – where such support is often dangerous – has never been higher. That support is now linked to a steadfast determination to unmask corrupt elites who drive the process. It would be a supreme irony for Europe and America to abandon the progress they have made in addressing corruption just at the time when global acceptance of the need for action has made such strides. There is no one measure to achieve this, but a series of steps to consolidate past gains and map those for the future. Corruption is both insidious and dynamic and, once it has a hold, is always more likely to intensify than diminish. The fight against it requires constant vigilance, political courage and an unerring eye for cracks in the system. There can be no justification for ducking the challenge.

Notes

Chapter 1: Corruption and its Perils

1 Transparency International, *Global Corruption Barometer*, Berlin, 2013, available at www.transparency.org/gcb2013.

2 Ibid. These findings for Europe are in line with the results of a survey commissioned in 2015 for 'Public Integrity and Trust in Europe', Hertie School of Governance, Berlin 2015, Tables 2 and 3.

3 Peter Olsen-Phillips et al., *The Political One Per Cent of the One Per Cent in 2014: Megadonors Fuel Rising Costs of Elections*, Open Secrets, Center for Responsive Politics and Sunlight Foundation, Washington, DC, 30 April 2015.

4 Among the 32,000 mentioned in Chapter 1, about one-third supported Democratic Party candidates and two-thirds Republican candidates; see Olsen-Phillips et al., *The Political One Per Cent of the One Per Cent in 2014*.

5 Tax Justice Network (TJN) is a leading analyst of these and provides the following 'loose definition': a 'secrecy jurisdiction provides facilities that enable people or entities to escape (and frequently undermine) the laws, rules and regulations of other jurisdictions elsewhere, using secrecy as

a prime tool'. In most cases the absence of taxes on capital or income is a further defining characteristic. See Tax Justice Network, *Financial Secrecy Index*, 2013.

6 Gabriel Zucman, *The Hidden Wealth of Nations*, University of Chicago Press, Chicago 2015, p. 35.

7 Tax Justice Network, *Financial Secrecy Index*.

8 Board of Governors of the Federal Reserve Bank System, March 2016.

9 Zucman, *The Hidden Wealth of Nations*.

Chapter 2: The Rising Price of Power

1 Which prevented corporations from making any contributions to federal campaigns.

2 Ronald Collins and David Skover, *When Money Speaks: The McCutcheon Decision, Campaign Finance Laws and the First Amendment*, Scotus Oak Park, Illinois, 2014, Chapter 7.

3 Opinion delivered by Chief Justice Roberts on *McCutcheon vs the FEC*, April 2014.

4 'Reaction to the Supreme Court's Campaign Finance Decision', *New York Times*, 2 April 2014, available at http://thelede.blogs.nytimes.com/2014/04/02/reaction-to-supreme-court-decision/?_r=0 (last accessed on 23 November 2015).

5 Super PACs can support both causes and run advertisements favourable to candidates, but cannot make direct contributions.

6 Matea Gold and Anu Narayanswamy, 'How "ghost corporations" are funding the 2016 election', *Washington Post*, 18 March 2016.

7 Open Secrets, *The Money Behind Elections*, based on Federal Election Commission Reports. Totals include direct expenditure by candidates, party committees, '527 groups', outside spending reported to the FEC and 'overhead' expenditure by PACs and Super PACs.

8 Federal Election Commission, Statistics Division.

9 Russ Choma, 'The One Percent of the One Percent Over Time, Open Secrets', Centre for Responsive Politics, Washington, DC, 13 May 2015.

10 A phrase attributed to James Madison in *The Federalist*, No. 52.

11 Both were representing the American government in Paris and London respectively.

12 Jon Meacham, *Thomas Jefferson: The Art of Power*, Random House, New York, 2012, pp. 257–8.

13 Bill Allison and Sarah Harkins, *Fixed Fortunes: Biggest Corporate Political Interests Spend Billions, Get Trillions*, Sunlight Foundation, Washington, DC, 2014.

14 These values evidently build on those of their father, Fred Koch, who assisted in building 15 oil refineries for Soviet Russia in the 1930s but was finally disillusioned with Stalin and became deeply opposed to the Soviet regime.

15 Jane Mayer, *Dark Money: The Hidden History of the Billionaires behind the Rise of the Radical Right*, Doubleday, New York, 2016.

16 Ibid.

17 By, for instance, making grants to the United Negro College Fund and the National Association of Criminal Defence Lawyers. Mayer, *Dark Money*, p. 361.

18 A target set at the Kochs' 'donor summit' held in January 2015 and explained by James Davis of Freedom Partners as being spread around the multi-pronged network. Mayer, *Dark Money*, p. 377.

19 Elizabeth Warren, *A Fighting Chance*, Scribe, London, 2015, pp. 280, 287.

20 Center for the Advancement of Public Integrity, Columbia Law School, *Oversight and Enforcement of Public Integrity: A State by State Study*, New York, 2015.

21 Laurence Cockcroft, *Global Corruption: Money, Power and Ethics in the Modern World*, I.B.Tauris, London, 2012, pp. 91–3.

22 Named after 1907 legislation that allowed the governor to appoint 'independent' panels.

23 'Tarnished silver', *The Economist*, 31 January 2015.

24 Benny Weiser and Susanne Craig, 'Sheldon Silver, ex-New York Assembly speaker, is found guilty on all counts', *New York Times*, 30 November 2015.

25 William Rashbaum and Susanne Craig, 'Ex-New York Senate leader, and his son are convicted of corruption', *New York Times*, 12 December 2015.

26 Ibid.

27 Otto Kerner Jr, Dan Walker, George Ryan and Rod Blagojevich.

28 Thomas J. Gradel and Dick Simpson, *Corrupt Illinois: Patronage, Cronyism, and Criminality*, University of Illinois Press, Champaign, 2015, p. 90.

29 Ibid., Table 1.2, p. 6.

30 Charles Flaherty (1991–6), Thomas Finneran (1996–2004) and Salvatore DiMasi (2004–9).

31 Columbia Law School – Center for the Advancement of Public Integrity, *Oversight and Enforcement of Public Integrity*, Massachusetts, 2015.

32 Thomas Edsall, 'Can anything be done about all the money in politics?', *International New York Times*, 16 September 2015.

33 Peter Eigen, *The Web of Corruption*, Campus Verlag, Frankfurt, 2003, p. 130.

34 Parliamentary Paper (Bundestag-Drucksache 14/9300), available at http://dip21.bundestag.de/dip21/btd/14/093/1409300.pdf.

35 Eva-Maria Thoms, 'Köln, wie es stinkt und kracht', *Die Zeit*, 13 May 2004, available at www.zeit.de/2004/21/M_9fllskandal.

36 Parliamentary Paper (Bundestags-Drucksache 17/12340).

37 Associated Press, 'Jacques Chirac found guilty of corruption', *Guardian*, 15 December 2011, available at www.theguardian.com/world/2011/dec/15/jacques-chirac-guilty-corruption.

38 Kim Willsher, 'Nicolas Sarkozy loses appeal over wiretaps in corruption case', *Guardian*, 22 March 2016.

39 Through the Campaign and Illegal Practices (Prevention) Act.

40 Sir David Garrard, Sir Gulam Noon, Chai Patel and Barry Townsley.

41 His dual loyalties and tax status attracted a great deal of media attention and in 2010 he made a public statement to the effect that he did not pay tax on his international income in the UK.

42 Rajeev Syal, 'Fugitive Liberal Democrat donor, Michael Brown, begins five year prison sentence', *Guardian*, 1 May 2012.

43 Assumes total expenditure by two parties of £40 million at national level and a further £10 million by smaller parties, and a total of £30 million by all candidates at constituency level (where only a minority will spend the total permitted sum of £40,000).

44 Estimate by *Financial Times*, 11 February 2015, p. 3, based on Electoral Commission data.

45 Estimate by *Financial Times*, 5 February 2015, p. 3, based on Electoral Commission data.

46 Rachel Sanderson, 'Renzi vows tougher stance on corruption', *Financial Times*, 12 December 2014.

47 Nearly 10 per cent of the 630 members of the Chamber of Deputies.

48 'Why Silvio Berlusconi still matters, *The Economist* explains', 26 January 2014.

49 Tobias Buck, 'Politicians pilloried amid Spanish sleaze', *Financial Times*, 8 February 2013.

50 'Mariano Rahoy is under new pressure in political scandal', *The Economist*, 20 July 2013.

51 www.upi.com/Top_News/World-News/2015/01/06/Almost-all-political-parties-in-Spain-guilty-of-tax-fraud-financial-crimes/3991420545370.

52 Francis Fukuyama, 'The end of history', *The National Interest*, Summer 1989.

53 OSCE, quoted in 'Eastern, Central and South Eastern Europe and Central Asia', in *Funding of Political Parties and Election Campaigns: A Handbook on Political Finance*, IDEA, Stockholm 2014.

54 Council of Europe, *Recommendations of the Committee of Ministers on Common Rules against Corruption in the Funding of Political Parties and Electoral Campaigns*, 2003.

55 Transparency International Hungary, *Transparency in Campaign Funding*, Budapest, 2015.

56 Viktor Orbán, 'Prime Minister Viktor Orbán's speech at the 25th Balvanyos Summer Free University and Student Camp', website of the Hungarian government, 30 July 2014 (accessed on 22 March 2016).

57 Kester Eddy and Neil Buckley, 'Hungary moves to charge former PMs', *Financial Times*, 3 August 2011.

58 Anton Shekhovtsov, *Is Transition Reversible?*, Legatum Institute, London 2015, p. 14.

Chapter 3: The Power of the Lobby

1 Although the *Oxford English Dictionary* credits the lobbies of the Houses of Parliament as the origin of the term, and it appears in print as early as 1820, the term 'lobbying' certainly gained much wider usage during the Grant administration'.

2 Lee Drutman, *The Business of America is Lobbying*, Oxford University Press, Oxford, 2015.

3 Quoted in James A. Thurber, www.american.edu/spa/ccps/upload/Thurber-Paper-for-AUS-Conference.pdf.

4 Plus others such as the European Council, the Council of the European Union, the European Central Bank, see http://europa.eu/about-eu/institutions-bodies.

5 European Union *Transparency Register*, last accessed on 30 March 2016.

6 Transparency International EU, *Integrity Watch Database*, Brussels, available at www.integritywatch.eu (last accessed on 21 March 2016).

7 Led by Prof Andreas Kortenkamp of Brunel University in the UK.

8 http://ec.europa.eu/smart-regulation/refit/index_en.htm.

9 The EU institution defining the EU's general political direction, consisting of member states' heads of state as well as the European Commission's president, and the Council's own president.

10 In February 2016 the case of Severin was on appeal.

11 Transparency International EU, *Inside Job: When MEPs are Lobbyists*, Brussels, 2016.

12 'Bowles blasted over move to city', *EurActiv*, 8 January 2015.

13 Ibid.

Chapter 4: The Big Business of Corruption

1 Robert Khuzami commented 'the message in this and the SEC's other FCPA cases is plain – any competitive advantage gained through corruption is a mirage' on 7 April 2011 in response to the Securities and Exchange Commission charging Johnson & Johnson (J&J) with violating the Foreign Corrupt Practices Act (FCPA) by bribing public doctors in several European countries and paying kickbacks to Iraq to illegally obtain business. See www.sec.gov/news/press/2011/2011–87.htm, quoted in: Ernst & Young, *Managing Bribery and Corruption Risks in the Construction and Infrastructure Industry*, 2012, available at www.ey.com/Publication/vwLUAssets/Managing_bribery_and_corruption_risks_in_the_construction_and_infrastructure_industry/$FILE/Assurance_%20FIDS_sector_paper_Construction.pdf (last accessed on 6 May 2015).

2 See, for example, OECD, *Foreign Bribery Report: An Analysis of the Crime of Bribery of Foreign Public Officials*, OECD Publishing, Paris, 2014, available at www.oecd.org/corruption/oecd-foreign-bribery-report-9789264226616-en.htm (last accessed on 2 April 2016).

3 Securities and Exchange Commission, *SEC Charges Siemens AG for Engaging in Worldwide Bribery*, Press Release, Washington, DC, 15 December 2008, available at www.sec.gov/news/press/2008/2008–294.htm (last accessed on 3 April 2016); Hans Leyendecker, 'Das ist wie bei der Mafia', *Sueddeutsche Zeitung*, 14 January 2011, available at www.sueddeutsche.de/wirtschaft/siemens-korruptionsaffaere-das-ist-wie-bei-der-mafia-1.1046507.

4 Securities and Exchange Commission, *SEC Charges Siemens AG for Engaging in Worldwide Bribery*.

5 'OECD Convention on Combating Bribery of Foreign Public Officials in International Business Transactions.'

6 OECD, *Foreign Bribery Report*, p. 8.

7 Chartered Institute of Building, *A Report Exploring Corruption in the UK Construction Industry*, London, September 2013, p. 14, available at www.ciob.org/sites/default/files/CIOB%20research%20-%20Corruption%20in%20the%20UK%20Construction%20Industry%20September%202013.pdf (last accessed on 20 November 2015).

8 Ibid.

9 Balfour Beatty agreed a civil settlement of £2.25 million in 2008 with the UK's Serious Fraud Office after allegations of corruption during the building of the Bibliotheca Alexandria in Egypt. See, for example, www.theguardian.com/business/2008/oct/07/balfourbeatty.egypt. AMEC settled with the UK Serious Fraud Office for £4.9 million in 2009; see, for example, www.building.co.uk/i%E2%80%99ll-be-watching-you-serious-fraud-office/3153428.article. Reuters News, 'Bilfinger to pay $32 million over US corruption charges', 9 December 2013, available at www.reuters.com/article/2013/12/09/bilfinger-bribery-idUSL1N0JO1XN20131209 (last accessed on 16 April 2015). KBR, Inc. and Halliburton Co. paid $402 million to settle in the US 2009, to resolve SEC charges that KBR subsidiary Kellogg Brown & Root LLC bribed Nigerian government officials over a 10-year period, in violation of the Foreign Corrupt Practices Act (FCPA), in order to obtain construction contracts. See www.sec.gov/news/press/2009/2009–23.htm. K&L Gates, *Biggest Risk of Corruption in the Construction Industry: The Global Picture*, London 2014, available at www.klgates.com/files/Publication/e3e0dfee-dc39-4ab8-8c4e-14fbab-d10c4e/Presentation/PublicationAttachment/36557fb6-891f-4020-aadd-209aa092c330/Biggest_Risk_of_Corruption_in_the_Construction_Industry_Whitepaper.pdf (last accessed on 20 November 2015).

10 Andy Blatchford, 'Quebec corruption inquiry: Suspects donated $2 million to federal parties', *The Star*, 5 September 2013, available at www.thestar.com/news/canada/2013/09/05/quebec_corruption_inquiry_suspects_donated_2_million_to_federal_parties.html (last accessed on 10 February 2015).

11 Martin Patriquin, 'Quebec's dirty business: kickbacks, "fake" work orders, city employees on the take and other allegations', *Maclean's*, 4 October 2012, available at www.macleans.ca/news/canada/dirty-business (last accessed on 10 February 2015).

12 Kevin Dougherty, 'Engineering firm Dessau blacklisted', *Montreal Gazette*, 20 June 2013, available at www.montrealgazette.com/Engineering+firm+Dessau+blacklisted/8561671/story.html (last accessed on 10 February 2015). See also Daniel Leblanc, 'Fifth firm testifies on illegal donations at Charbonneau Commission', *The Globe and Mail*, 19 March 2013, available at www.theglobeandmail.com/news/politics/fifth-firm-testifies-on-illegal-donations-at-charbonneau-commission/article9972499/ (last accessed on 10 February 2015).

13 'Charbonneau Commission March 11–21: key testimony', *Montreal Gazette*, available at www.montrealgazette.com/corruption/keytestimony Mar11-21.html (last accessed on 10 February 2015).

14 Ibid.

15 Dessau reported itself for fraud in 2011. For the involvement in the corruption scheme, Dessau was blacklisted in 2013 and is thus the only company that was barred from competing for public contracts for five years, despite the proven bribery and corruption dealings of other construction companies.

16 www.thestar.com/news/canada/2013/02/18/quebec_corruption_inquiry_alleged_mafia_gobetween_known_as_mr_sidewalk_testifies.html.

17 See Lee Lamothe and Adrian Humphreys, *The Sixth Family: The Collapse of the New York Mafia and the Rise of Vito Rizzuto*, Wiley, Hoboken, 2008.

18 T. Gabor, J. Kiedrowski, D. Hicks, M. Levi, R. Goldstock, R. Melchers and E. Stregger, *Commercial Construction and OC*, Organized Crime Research Brief No. 27, Public Safety Canada, Ottawa, 2011, available at www.publicsafety.gc.ca/cnt/rsrcs/pblctns/rgnzd-crm-brf-27/rgnzd-crm-brf-27-eng.pdf (last accessed on 2 April 2016).

19 Ibid.

20 Martin Patriquin, 'Quebec's foundation of corruption', *Maclean's*, 19 December 2012, available at www.macleans.ca/news/canada/the-foundation-of-corruption (last accessed on 10 February 2015).

21 Martin Patriquin, 'Montreal is a disaster', *Maclean's*, 29 October 2009, available at www.macleans.ca/news/canada/montreal-is-a-disaster (last accessed on 4 February 2015).

22 Andy Blatchford, 'Quebec corruption inquiry: suspects donated $2 million to federal parties', *The Star*, 5 September 2013, available at www.thestar.com/news/canada/2013/09/05/quebec_corruption_inquiry_suspects_donated_2_million_to_federal_parties.html (last accessed on 10 February 2015).

23 'Romania's motorway blues', *The Economist*, 16 August 2011, available at www.economist.com/blogs/easternapproaches/2011/08/romanian-roads (last accessed on 15 April 2015).

24 Chartered Institute of Building, *A Report Exploring Corruption in the UK Construction Sector*.

25 www.giaccentre.org.

26 www.constructiontransparency.org/home.

27 World Health Organization, *Factsheet*, available at www.who.int/mediacentre/factsheets/fs319/en (last accessed on 18 June 2014).

28 PricewaterhouseCoopers and Martin-Luther-Universitate Halle-Wittenberg, *Wirtschaftskriminalitaet Pharmaindustrie*, 2013, available at www.pwc.de/de_DE/de/publikationen/paid_pubs/pwc_studie_wirtschaftskriminalitaet_pharma_2013.pdf (last accessed on 13 April 2015).

29 Ibid.

30 See, for example, www.globalresearch.ca/evidence-emerges-that-measles-outbreaks-are-deliberately-encouraged-by-big-pharma-to-ignite-vaccine-hysteria/5429853 (last accessed on 8 April 2015).

31 There are nine steps in the life of a drug or medical device: research and development and clinical trials, patents, manufacturing, registration, inspection, promotion, selection, procurement and dispensing.

32 www.phrma.org/sites/default/files/pdf/ChartPack_4%200_FINAL_2014MAR25.pdf, p. 45. Those R&D cost figures are for the US: www.phrma.org/sites/default/files/pdf/ChartPack_4%200_FINAL_2014MAR25.pdf, p. 2.

33 Pharmaceutical Research Industry, '2014 Profile', table 6, 'Domestic sales and sales abroad, PhRMA member companies: 1980–2013', Appendix p. 73, see www.phrma.org/sites/default/files/pdf/2014_PhRMA_PROFILE.pdf.

34 Based on the average USD/EUR exchange rate for 2012 = 1.2848; see http://sdw.ecb.europa.eu/quickview.do?SERIES_KEY=120.EXR.A.USD. EUR.SP00.A.

35 European Federation of Pharmaceutical Industries and Associations, *The Pharmaceutical Industry in Figures*, 2013, available at www.efpia. eu/uploads/Figures_Key_Data_2013.pdf.

36 'AstraZeneca LP agreed to pay $7.9 million to settle allegations that it violated the False Claims Act by paying kickbacks to sell its drugs, the DOJ said', see www.fcpablog.com/blog/2015/2/20/two-astrazeneca-whistleblowers-share-14-million-in-fca-settl.html.

37 In 2015, the SEC charged the New York-based pharmaceutical company Bristol-Myers Squibb with violating the FCPA when employees of its China-based joint venture made improper payments to obtain sales. Bristol-Myers Squibb agreed to pay more than $14 million to settle charges. See US Securities and Exchange Commission, www.sec. gov/spotlight/fcpa/fcpa-cases.shtml.

38 In 2012, Pfizer paid $60.2 million and Eli Lilly & Co. paid $29.4 million to the US to settle allegations they had bribed government officials, including hospital administrators and government doctors, in China and other countries to approve and prescribe their products. See US Securities and Exchange Commission, www.sec.gov/spotlight/fcpa/ fcpa-cases.shtml.

39 In 2016, the Swiss-based pharmaceutical company agreed to pay $25 million to settle charges that it violated the FCPA when its China-based subsidiaries engaged in pay-to-prescribe schemes to increase sales; see US Securities and Exchange Commission, www.sec.gov/spot-light/fcpa/fcpa-cases.shtml.

40 UK pharmaceutical company GlaxoSmithKline was fined $490 million by Chinese authorities for bribery in 2014; see www.fcpa-blog.com/blog/2014/9/19/china-fines-gsk-490-million-for-bribery. html.

41 Richard L. Cassin, 'Quick look at big pharma's U.S. rap sheet', *FCPA Blog*, 7 August 2013, available at www.fcpablog.com/blog/2013/8/7/ quick-look-at-big-pharmas-us-rap-sheet.html (last accessed on 13 April 2015).

42 France, Portugal, Luxembourg, Greece, Italy and Spain.

43 European Parliament, 'Press release: dangerous drugs: better EU safety monitoring in response to Mediator scandal', 11 September

2012, available at www.europarl.europa.eu/news/sv/news-room/content/20120907IPR50815/html/Dangerous-drugs-better-EU-safety-monitoring-in-response-to-Mediator-scandal (last accessed on 20 November 2015). The European Parliament press release states the figures as 500–2,000, and the French Ministry of Health put it at 500.

44 Chris Harris, 'Lobbying a "key corruption risk facing Europe", claims report', *Euronews*, 15 April 2015, available at www.euronews.com/2015/04/15/lobbying-a-key-corruption-risk-facing-europe-claims-report (last accessed on 20 November 2015).

45 Jean-Claude Jaillette, 'Scandale: la corruption ordinaire des laboratoires Servier', *Marianne*, 23 July 2013, available at www.marianne.net/Scandale-la-corruption-ordinaire-des-laboratoires-Servier_a230668.html (last accessed on 20 November 2015).

46 Jaillette, 'Scandale'.

47 Angelique Chrisafis, 'France shaken by fresh scandal over weight-loss drug linked to deaths', *Guardian*, 6 January 2013, available at www.theguardian.com/world/2013/jan/06/france-scandal-weight-loss-drug (last accessed on 20 November 2015).

48 'French court finds pharma firm Servier negligent in deadly drug scandal', *MedicalXpress*, 22 October 2015, available at http://medicalxpress.com/news/2015-10-french-court-pharma-firm-servier.html (last accessed on 20 November 2015).

49 Anne Jouan, 'Mediator: pas de procès avant 2018', *Le Figaro*, 5 May 2015, available at www.lefigaro.fr/actualite-france/2015/05/05/01016-20150505ARTFIG00180-mediator-pas-de-proces-avant-2018.php (last accessed on 20 November 2015).

50 Note: Three companies (GSK, Johnson & Johnson and Abbott) were responsible for approximately two-thirds (66 per cent) of financial penalties during the current study period. GSK, once again, topped the list with $3.1 billion alone in settlement monies paid in the United States between 2 November 2010 and 18 July 2012; see www.citizen.org/documents/2073.pdf (table 4).

51 US Department of Justice, *GlaxoSmithKline to Plead Guilty and Pay $3 Billion to Resolve Fraud Allegations and Failure to Report Safety Data: Largest Health Care Fraud Settlement in US History*, press release, 2 July 2012, available at www.justice.gov/opa/pr/glaxosmithkline-plead-guilty-and-pay-3-billion-resolve-fraud-allegations-and-failure-report (last accessed on 3 April 2016).

52 'GlaxoSmithKline fined $3bn after bribing doctors to increase drugs sales', *Guardian* www.theguardian.com/business/2012/jul/03/glaxosmithkline-fined-bribing-doctors-pharmaceuticals (last accessed on 30 July 2016).

53 See 'GlaxoSmithKline to pay $3bn in US drug fraud scandal', *BBC News*, 2 July 2012, available at www.bbc.co.uk/news/world-us-canada-18673220 (last accessed on 12 April 2015).

54 Ibid.

55 US Department of Justice, *GlaxoSmithKline to Plead Guilty*.

56 Adam Jourdan and Ben Hirschler, 'China hands drugmaker GSK record $489 million fine for paying bribes', *Reuters*, 19 September 2014, available at www.reuters.com/article/2014/09/19/us-gsk-china-idUSKBN0HE0TC20140919 (last accessed on 15 April 2015); Ben Hirschler, 'Exclusive: GSK faces new corruption allegations, this time in Romania', *Reuters*, 29 July 2015, www.reuters.com/article/us-gsk-romania-corruption-exclusive-idUSKCN0Q32A920150729.

57 Sergio Sismondo, 'Key opinion leaders and the corruption of medical knowledge: what the Sunshine Act will and won't cast light on', *Journal of Law, Medicine and Ethics*, 14(3), 2013.

58 www.opensecrets.org/lobby/search.php.

59 This order is reversed if the pharmaceutical and health care sectors (at $503 million) are taken together.

60 GlobalData, *US Pharmaceutical Market Value Will Approach $550 Billion by 2020, says GlobalData*, 17 March 2015, available at http://healthcare.globaldata.com/media-center/press-releases/pharmaceuticals/us-pharmaceutical-market-value-will-approach-550-billion-by-2020-says-globaldata (last accessed on 3 April 2016); Research and Markets, 'United States Healthcare, Regulatory and Reimbursement Landscape Report 2015', 1 April 2015, available at www.businesswire.com/news/home/20150401005435/en/Research-Markets-United-States-Healthcare-Regulatory-Reimbursement (last accessed on 27 June 2016).

61 The Loi Bertrand (no. 2011–2012) was adopted on 29 December 2011 and has been complemented by Decree no. 2013–414 of 21 May 2013.

62 Such as Transparency International UK's Pharmaceutical & Healthcare Programme, or the work done by the Sunlight Foundation.

63 www.opensecrets.org/lobby/clientsum.php?id=D000000104.

64 http://special.defensenews.com/top-100.

65 http://companies.defenceindex.org/docs/2015%20Defence%20 Companies%20Anti-Corruption%20Index.pdf.

66 www.dw.de/probe-into-german-greek-arms-deals-reveals-murky-side-of-defense-sales/a-5890375.

67 Compared with the Ministry of Finance's 2014 report, www.iu.qs.com/2014/02/impact-of-the-financial-crisis-on-greek-higher-education.

68 www.dw.de/probe-into-german-greek-arms-deals-reveals-murky-side-of-defense-sales/a-5890375.

69 www.zdf.de/ZDF/zdfportal/blob/30625198/1/data.pdf.

70 www.demotix.com/news/1152445/former-greek-minister-defense-akis-tsochadzopoulos-arrested-home#media-1152415.

71 www.spiegel.de/international/europe/greece-arrests-two-suspects-in-submarine-bribery-case-a-944446.html (last accessed on 2 February 2015).

72 www.spiegel.de/international/europe/greece-arrests-two-suspects-in-submarine-bribery-case-a-944446.html.

73 www.defenseindustrydaily.com/greece-in-default-on-u-214-submarine-order-05801.

74 www.macropolis.gr/?i=portal.en.the-agora.412&cid=24 (last accessed on 2 February 2015).

75 www.hellasforce.com/en/former-defence-minister-tsochatzopoulos-linked-huge-extortion-ring.

76 www.telegraph.co.uk/news/worldnews/europe/greece/9129234/EU-accused-of-hypocrisy-for-1-billion-in-arms-sales-to-Greece.html; https://euobserver.com/defence/115513 (last accessed on 21 January 2015).

77 www.deutschlandradiokultur.de/korruption-dolce-vita-und-deutsche-waffen.976.de.html?dram:article_id=296651.

78 As measured by military spending as percentage of GDP; www.theguardian.com/news/datablog/2015/jan/20/greece-election-2015-the-politics-and-economics-in-numbers (last accessed on 21 January 2015).

79 Jan Grebe and Jerry Sommer, 'Greece: high military expenditures despite the financial crisis', *BICC Focus*, 2010, available at www.bicc.de/publications/publicationpage/publication/greece-high-military-expenditures-despite-the-financial-crisis-158 (last accessed on 21 January 2015).

80 As a percentage of GDP.

81 Transparency International, *Defence Companies Anti-Corruption Index*, London, 2015, available at http://companies.defenceindex.org (last accessed on 8 April 2016).

82 Originally developed by Transparency International, Integrity Pacts have lately also been recognised by the European Union as useful tools; see http://ec.europa.eu/regional_policy/en/policy/how/improving-investment/integrity-pacts.

Chapter 5: The Bankers' Story: An End to Trust

1 Specific charges against banks and individuals for interest rate 'rigging' have focused on this as the product of a form of cartel, as manifested in fines levied by the EU anti-trust authorities totalling €669 million on six banks and one interdealer broker imposed by December 2015.

2 From 5.5 per cent in 1970. Source: IMF.

3 William K. Black, *The Best Way to Rob a Bank is to Own One*, University of Texas Press, Austin, 2005.

4 Gretchen Morgen, 'Inside the countrywide lending spree', *New York Times*, 26 August 2007.

5 Charles W. Calomiris and Stephen H. Haber, *Fragile by Design: The Political Origins of Banking Crises and Scarce Credit*, Princeton University Press, Princeton, 2014, p. 23.

6 Wholesale Access, *Mortgage Brokers*, 2006, pp. 35, 37.

7 Center for Public Integrity, www.publicintegrity.org/2009/05/06/5449/roots-financial-crisis-who-blame.

8 Simon Head, *Mindless: Why Smarter Machines Are Making Dumber Humans*, Basic Books, New York, 2014, p. 84.

9 Permanent Subcommittee of Investigations of the US Senate (chaired by Sen Levin), *Wall St and the Financial Crisis: Anatomy of a Financial Collapse*, April 2011.

10 Ibid.

11 *Credit Ratings and Structured Finance, Wall Street and the Financial Crisis: Anatomy of a Financial Collapse*, Permanent Subcommittee on Investigations, US Senate, 2011, p. 32.

12 Ibid., p. 17.

13 Ibid.

14 SEC Chairman Christopher Cox before Senate Committee on Banking, Housing and Urban Affairs, (S.Hrg 110-1012), 23 September 2008.

15 In interviews in 2010, Bill Clinton said he had been wrong to follow the advice against regulating derivatives (Harris Evans, ABC News, 17 April 2010).

16 S. Johnson and J. Kwak, *Thirteen Bankers: The Wall Street Takeover and the Next Financial Meltdown*, Vintage Books, New York, 2011, p. 135.

17 Eventually inserted into the Consolidated Appropriations Act of 2001.

18 'Barclays LIBOR deal raises settlement pressure on banks', *Financial Times*, 13 October 2014.

19 Quoted in Lindsay Fortado, 'Trader tells court of his "rage" over transatlantic LIBOR probe', *Financial Times*, 13 July 2015.

20 Lindsay Fortrado, 'UBS trader nicknamed Rain Man tells court bosses knew of rigging', *Financial Times*, 7 July 2015.

21 David Enrich and Jenny Strasburg, 'Rabobank is fined, CEO is out in Libor settlement', *Wall Street Journal*, 29 October 2013, available at www.wsj.com/articles/SB10001424052702303471004579165293824297108 (last accessed 15 June 2016).

22 Nick Hayes was found guilty of rigging the LIBOR rate in November 2015 and given a prison sentence of 14 years, commuted in January 2016 to 11 years. Six brokers associated in court proceedings with the network allegedly run by Hayes were acquitted in February 2016. See 'Jury acquits five of six brokers in LIBOR trials', *Financial Times*, 8 February 2016.

23 Financial Conduct Authority, 'Final Notice', 11 November 2014, available at www.fca.org.uk/static/documents/final-notices/final-notice-citibank.pdf.

24 The others were Bank of America, UBS, RBS and Barclays.

25 The six banks were later fined an additional total $5.6 billion in May 2015 by the Department of Justice and the US Federal Reserve.

26 Quoted in Jill Treanor, 'Barclays may face massive new penalty over currency rigging', *Guardian*, 13 November 2014, available at www.theguardian.com/business/2014/nov/13/barclays-penalty-currency-rigging-banks (last accessed 7 April 2016).

27 See Bibliography.

28 Senate Permanent Committee on Investigations, *Failing to Manage Conflicts of Interest: A Case Study of Goldman Sachs, a Section of Wall Street and the Financial Crisis: Anatomy of a Financial Collapse*, 2011.

Chapter 6: On- and Offshore Secrets

1 Marc Pitzke, 'Offshore leaks: vast web of tax evasion exposed', *Der Spiegel*, online, 4 April 2013.

2 Ibid.

3 Ibid. The participating newspapers were the *Guardian*, *Washington Post*, *Le Monde*, *Sonntagszeitung* and *Süddeutsche Zeitung*.

4 International Consortium of Investigative Journalists (ICIJ), *The Panama Papers, Secrecy for Sale: Inside the Global Offshore Money Maze*, 3 April 2016, available at www.icij.org/offshore.

5 For a full set of defining criteria of secrecy jurisdiction, see the annual *Financial Secrecy Index* of the Tax Justice Network.

6 Which escape either banking or legislative regulation in their country of origin.

7 Global Financial Integrity, Washington, DC.

8 Tax Justice Network, *Where on Earth Are You? Major Corporations and Tax Havens*, March 2009, available at www.taxjustice.net/cms/upload/pdf/0903_Whereonearth.pdf.

9 David Leigh, 'Fugitives, aides, bagmen: meet the "politically exposed" clients', *Guardian*, 13 February 2015.

10 Transparency International UK, *Corruption on Your Doorstep: How Corrupt Capital is Used to Buy Property in the UK*, February 2015.

11 Cynthia O'Murchu, 'Puzzle of who owns property held in offshore vehicles hard to crack', *Financial Times*, 1 August 2014.

12 UNODC estimated total flows from drug trafficking and 'other transnational crimes' at $1.6 trillion in October 2011 (Research Report, October 2011).

13 US Department of the Treasury, *National Money Laundering Risk Assessment*, Washington, DC, 2015.

14 Louise Story and Stephanie Saul, 'Hidden wealth flows to elite New York condos', *New York Times*, 8 February 2015.

15 Zucman, *The Hidden Wealth of Nations*.

16 *Failure to Identify Co-owners Impeding Law Enforcement*, Permanent Subcommittee on Investigations, US Senate, 14 November 2006 (S. Hrg 109-845). Opening statements by Co-Chairs Senators Levin and Coleman.

17 Tax Justice Network, *Financial Secrecy Index*, Report on USA, 2015, p. 8.

18 Ibid.

19 www.parliament.uk/business/committees/committees-a-z/commons-select/public-accounts-committee/news/tax-avoidance-google.

Chapter 7: Justice for Sale?

1 Anti-Corruption Task Force, 1999, Association of Chief Police Officers, UK.

2 John Lichfield, 'Marseille: Europe's most dangerous place to be young', *Independent*, 23 September 2012, available at www.independent.co.uk/news/world/europe/marseille-europes-most-dangerous-place-to-be-young-8166738.html (last accessed on 6 March 2016).

3 Eugenie Bastié, 'Non, ces homicides ne sont pas LE problème de Marseille – c'en est juste un symptôme spectaculaire. Le vrai problème de Marseille, c'est une monumentale corruption', *Causeur.fr* (online), 17 September 2013, available at www.causeur.fr/le-vrai-probleme-de-marseille-cest-une-monumentale-corruption-24187.html (last accessed on 28 October 2015); P. Gounev and V. Ruggiero, *Corruption and Organized Crime in Europe: Illegal Partnerships*, Routledge, London, 2012, p. 108.

4 Henry Samuel, 'Marseille police: crime, corruption and cover-up at the highest level', *Telegraph*, 12 October 2012, available at www.telegraph.co.uk/news/worldnews/europe/france/9605614/Marseille-police-crime-corruption-and-cover-up-at-the-highest-level.html (last accessed on 28 October 2015).

5 AFP, 'Corruption à Marseille: sept policiers ont été écroués', *Le Figaro*, 6 October 2012, available at www.lefigaro.fr/actualite-france/2012/10/06/01016-20121006ARTFIG00274-corruption-a-marseille-sept-policiers-ont-ete-ecroues.php (last accessed on 28 October 2015).

6 'Twelve French police arrested in Marseille corruption probe', *RFI* (online), 3 October 2012, available at www.english.rfi.fr/france/20121003-twelve-french-police-arrested-in-marseille-corruption-probe (last accessed on 28 October 2015).

7 'BAC Nord de Marseille: les ripoux réintégrés... mais pas celui qui a brisé l'omerta', *Le Journal du Siecle* (online), 31 January 2013, available at http://lejournaldusiecle.com/2013/01/31/bac-nord-de-marseille-les-ripoux-reintegres-mais-pas-celui-qui-a-brise-lomerta (last accessed on 28 October 2015).

8 Roebuck and Parker offer the most widely known typology of police corruption, which makes a distinction between corruption of authority, kickbacks, opportunistic theft, shakedowns, protection of illegal activity, the fix (undermining criminal investigations), direct criminal activities, internal payoffs and 'padding' (planting or adding evidence). J.B. Roebuck and T. Parker, 'Typology of police corruption', *Social Problems Journal*, 21(3), 1974, pp. 423–37.

9 Milton Mollen, *Report: Commission to Investigate Allegations of Police Corruption and the Anti-Corruption Procedures of the Police Department*, City of New York, New York, 7 July 1994, available at https://web. archive.org/web/20110721230958/http://www.parc.info/client_ files/Special%20Reports/4%20-%20Mollen%20Commission%20- %20NYPD.pdf (last accessed on 28 October 2015), p. 45.

10 Wesley Skogan and Kathleen Frydl, *Fairness and Effectiveness in Policing: The Evidence*, National Academic Press, Washington, DC, 2004. See also Sanja Kutnjak Ivković and M.R. Haberfeld, *Measuring Police Integrity Across the World: Studies from Established Democracies and Countries in Transition*, Springer, New York, 2015, pp. 6f.

11 P.M. Stinson Snr, 'Police crime: the criminal behaviour of sworn law enforcement officers', *Sociology Compass*, 9(1), 2015, pp. 1–13.

12 Maurice Punch, 'Police corruption and its prevention', *European Journal on Criminal Policy and Research* 8, 2000, pp. 301–24, p. 302.

13 Rositsa Dzehlkova, Philip Gounev and Tihomir Bezlov, *Countering Police Corruption: European Perspectives*, Center for the Study of Democracy, Sofia Bulgaria, 2013, pp. 20f.

14 Olienka Frenkiel, 'Belgium's silent heart of darkness', *Guardian*, 5 May 2002, available at www.theguardian.com/world/2002/may/05/dutroux. featuresreview (last accessed on 28 October 2015).

15 Council of Europe, 'Police powers and accountability in a democratic society', *Criminal Research*, 33, 2000, pp. 75f.

16 Marion Kraske, 'Wiener Sumpf. Die feinen Freunde der Polizei', *Spiegel Online*, 2 July 2007, available at www.spiegel.de/panorama/ justiz/wiener-sumpf-die-feinen-freunde-der-polizei-a-513593.html (last accessed on 13 October 2015).

17 Deborah Hardoon and Finn Heinrich, *Transparency International Global Corruption Barometer 2013*, Berlin, 2013, available at www. transparency.org/gcb2013/report (last accessed on 28 October 2015).

Note that this survey focuses on corruption exclusively, not on suspected racism in a number of police forces.

18 Ibid.

19 Sanja Kutnjak Ivković, 'To serve and collect: measuring police corruption', *Journal of Criminal Law and Criminology*, 93(2), 2003, pp. 593–650, p. 599.

20 US General Accounting Office, *Law Enforcement: Information on Drug-Related Police Corruption*, Report to the House of Representatives, Washington, DC, 1998, available at www.gao.gov/assets/230/225957.pdf (last accessed on 31 July 2016).

21 Ivković and Haberfeld, *Measuring Police Integrity Across the World*, pp. 10f.

22 Stephen Foster, 'Counter corruption: an international perspective', in Allyson MacVean, Peter Spindler and Charlotte Solf (eds), *Handbook of Policing, Ethics and Professional Standards*, Routledge, London and New York, 2013, pp. 144–155, pp. 147f.

23 Independent Police Complaints Commission, *Corruption in the Police Service in England and Wales: Second Report – a Report Based on the IPCC's Experience from 2008 to 2011*, London, May 2012, available at www.ipcc.gov.uk/sites/default/files/Documents/research_stats/Corruption_in_the_Police_Service_in_England_Wales_Report_2_May_2012.pdf (last accessed on 7 March 2016).

24 Dzehlkova, Gounev and Bezlov, *Countering Police Corruption*, p. 47.

25 Ivković and Haberfeld, *Measuring Police Integrity Across the World*, pp. 6f.

26 Dave Jansoski, 'The rise and fall of a mob power', *The Citizens' Voice*, 17 July 2011, available at http://citizensvoice.com/news/the-rise-and-fall-of-a-mob-power-1.1175897 (last accessed on 29 October 2015).

27 Dave Janoski, 'Prosecutor: D'Elia's downfall kickstarted kids-for-cash probe', *The Times Tribune*, 19 February 2011, available at http://thetimes-tribune.com/news/prosecutor-d-elia-s-downfall-kickstarted-kids-for-cash-probe-1.1107444 (last accessed on 29 October 2015).

28 Juvenile Law Center, 'Hillary', available at www.jlc.org/about-us/what-we-do/stories/hillary (last accessed on 29 October 2015).

29 'Timeline of corruption', *The Citizens' Voice*, 6 February 2011, available at http://citizensvoice.com/timeline-of-corruption-1.1100929 (last accessed on 29 October 2015).

30 Janoski, 'Prosecutor'.

31 Maggie Clark, 'Do campaign donations in judicial races influence court decisions?', *Pew Charitable Trusts*, 11 June 2013, available at www.pewtrusts.org/en/research-and-analysis/blogs/stateline/2013/06/11/do-campaign-donations-in-judicial-races-influence-court-decisions (last accessed on 31 October 2015).

32 Jed S. Rakoff, 'Why innocent people plead guilty', *New York Review of Books*, 20 November 2014, available at www.nybooks.com/articles/archives/2014/nov/20/why-innocent-people-plead-guilty (last accessed on 28 October 2015).

33 Other common law and civil law countries have plea bargains, such as Canada, and the UK (to a much lesser degree, and many judges are not fond of plea bargains), Germany and France. However, they are either in a minority of cases and/or leave final sentence-setting up to the court.

34 Jed Handelsman Shugerman, 'Economic crisis and the rise of the judicial elections and judicial review', *Harvard Law Review*, 123(5), 2010, pp. 1063–151: 38 states hold competitive elections or ballot confirmation of an appointment of high court justices; see John Eidelson, 'Big political money now floods judges' races, too', *Bloomberg Business*, 31 July 2014, available at www.bloomberg.com/bw/articles/2014-07-31/big-political-money-now-floods-judges-races-too (last accessed on 9 September 2015).

35 Andy Kroll, 'Is your judge for sale?', *Mother Jones*, November/December 2014, available at www.motherjones.com/politics/2014/10/judicial-elections-citizens-united-karl-rove (last accessed on 10 September 2015).

36 See Bureau of Justice Statistics, www.bjs.gov/index.cfm?ty=tp&tid=30 (last accessed on 9 March 2016).

37 States with retention elections for all level of courts are Alaska, Colorado, Iowa, Nebraska, Utah and Wyoming. States with appellate court retention elections are Arizona, California, Florida, Indiana, Kansas, Maryland, Missouri, Oklahoma, South Dakota and Tennessee. States with retention elections following popular elections are Illinois, North Carolina and Pennsylvania. See also Kroll, 'Is your judge for sale?'.

38 Shugerman, 'Economic crisis and the rise of the judicial elections and judicial review', p. 1063; Liptak, 'Rendering justice, with one eye on reelection'; Streb, *Running for Judge*, pp. 6ff.

39 See, for example, Chris W. Bonneau and Melinda Gann Hall, *In Defense of Judicial Elections*, Routledge, New York, 2009.

40 Joanna Shepherd, *Justice at Risk: An Empirical Analysis of Campaign Contributions to Judicial Decisions*, American Constitutions Society for Law and Policy, Alabama, 2013, p. 1.

41 60 per cent of the 2000–9 spending came from these groups; see Shepherd, *Justice at Risk*, p. 1.

42 James J. Sample, 'Justice for sale', *Wall Street Journal*, 22 March 2008.

43 Quoted in Laurence Lessig, *Republic Lost*, Twelve Hachette Book Group, New York, 2012, p. 229.

44 Adam Liptak and Janet Roberts, 'Campaign cash mirrors a high court's rulings', *New York Times*, 1 October 2006, available at www.nytimes.com/2006/10/01/us/01judges.html?pagewanted=all (last accessed on 23 November 2015).

45 Sandra Day O'Connor, 'How to save our courts', *Parade*, 4 February 2008.

46 Kroll, 'Is your judge for sale?'; *Caperton vs A. T. Massey Coal Co.*, 556 US 868 (2009).

47 Joanna Shepherd, *Justice at Risk*, p. 1.

48 Ibid.

49 See www.nytimes.com/2014/09/28/sunday-review/judges-on-the-campaign-trail.html?_r=0.

50 Adam Liptak, 'Judges on the campaign trail', *New York Times*, 27 September 2014, available at www.nytimes.com/2014/09/28/sunday-review/judges-on-the-campaign-trail.html?_r=0.

51 Jim Geraghty, 'Breaking down Ted Cruz's plan for Supreme Court "retention elections"', *National Review*, 2 July 2015, available at www.nationalreview.com/article/420692/ted-cruz-supreme-court-reelection-amendment (last accessed on 11 September 2015).

52 In Hungary, the chair of the judiciary and the prosecutor general are both nominated by the president but subject to a vote of two-thirds of MPs.

53 Center for the Study of Democracy, *Organized Crime in Bulgaria. Markets and Trends*, Sofia Bulgaria, 2007, p. 36.

54 Wim Van Meurs and Alina Mungiu-Pippidi, *Ottomans into Europeans: State and Institution-Building in South Eastern Europe*, Hurst Publishers, London, 2010, p. 177.

55 European Commission, *2015 EU Justice Scoreboard*, Brussels, 2015, p. 37, available at http://ec.europa.eu/justice/effective-justice/files/justice_scoreboard_2015_en.pdf (last accessed on 9 March 2015).

56 'Bulgarians most dissatisfied in Europe – study', *Sofia News Agency Novinite*, 2 December 2011, available at www.novinite.com/view_news.php?id=134476 (last accessed on 19 November 2015).

57 Nikolai Chavdarov, 'The untouchables: organised crime grows stronger in Bulgaria', *Jane's Intelligence Review*, 23(7), 2011, pp. 38–42, p. 40.

58 European Commission, *Report from the Commission to the European Parliament and the Council. Interim Report On Progress in Bulgaria under the Co-operation and Verification Mechanism*, Brussels 8 February 2012, available at http://eur-lex.europa.eu/legal-content/EN/TXT/PDF/?uri=CELEX:52012DC0057&from=EN.

59 Gounev and Ruggiero, *Corruption and Organized Crime in Europe*, p. 99.

60 Maria Popova, 'Why doesn't the Bulgarian judiciary prosecute corruption?', *Problems of Post-Communism*, 5(5), 2012, pp. 35–49.

61 Daniel Stroe, 'Anti-corruption prosecutor's dismissal troubles political waters in Romania', Independent Balkan News Agency, 3 October 2013, available at www.balkaneu.com/anti-corruption-prosecutors-dismissal-troubles-political-waters-romania (last accessed on 29 October 2015).

62 Transparency International Bosnia & Herzegovina, *Corruption Case Shocks Romanian Justice System*, 11 June 2013, available at http://ti-bih.org/slucaj-korupcije-sokirao-rumunski-pravosudni-sistem/?lang=en (last accessed on 13 October 2015).

63 Freedom House, 'We request the Supreme Council of the Magistracy to take attitude regarding Prime Minister's Ponta meddling with the justice system', 3 October 2013, available at http://freedomhouse.ro/en/index.php/stiri/watchdog/item/151-we-request-the-supreme-council-of-the-magistracy-to-take-attitude-regarding-prime-minister%E2%80%99s-ponta-meddling-with-the-justice-system (last accessed on 29 October 2015); see also www.balkaneu.com/anti-corruption-prosecutors-dismissal-troubles-political-waters-romania/#sthash.O5aQMGKe.dpuf.

Chapter 8: Organised Crime: A Perennial Spectre

1 Matthew Green, 'The black fish: undercover with the vigilantes fighting organised crime at sea', *Guardian*, 24 February 2016, available at www.theguardian.com/environment/2016/feb/24/black-fish-undercover-with-vigilantes-fighting-organised-crime-at-sea; Dan Rossington, 'Gangs made £5bn smuggling migrants into Europe – with the UK a

major target', *Mirror*, 22 February 2016, available at www.mirror.co.uk/
news/uk-news/gangs-made-5bn-smuggling-migrants-7419644;   Beth
Abbit, 'Tameside drug dealers jailed over crack cocaine and heroin
racket', *Manchester Evening News*, 29 January 2016, available at www.
manchestereveningnews.co.uk/news/greater-manchester-news/tame-
side-drug-dealers-jailed-over-10808647; Connor Lally, 'Gang leaders
thrive thanks to global nature of organised crime', *The Irish Times*, 11
February 2016, available at www.irishtimes.com/news/crime-and-law/
gang-leaders-thrive-thanks-to-global-nature-of-organised-crime-
1.2530111; Jeff Turl, 'Drugs charges surge in 2015. Organized crime
a problem says deputy chief', *Bay Today*, 17 February 2016, available
at   www.baytoday.ca/local-news/drugs-charges-surge-in-2015-organ-
ized-crime-a-problem-says-deputy-chief-198642; Ted Miller, 'Police:
massive Wisconsin cheese heist part of organized crime', *WIVB*, 29
January 2016, available at http://wivb.com/2016/01/29/police-massive-
wisconsin-cheese-heist-part-of-organized-crime (all last accessed on 26
February 2016).
2 Definition by the UN Office on Drugs and Organised Crime (UNODC)
and J.S. Albanese, 'North American Organized Crime', *Global Crime*,
6(1), 2004, pp. 8–18, p. 10.
3 Bundeskriminalamt, *Organised Crime: National Situation Report*, 2014, available at www.bka.de/nn_194550/EN/SubjectsAZ/OrganisedCrime/organ-
isedCrime__node.html?__nnn=true (last accessed on 28 February 2016).
4 European Parliament, *Organised Crime and Corruption*, Brussels, March
2016, available at www.europarl.europa.eu/RegData/etudes/IDAN/
2016/558779/EPRS_IDA%282016%29558779_EN.pdf (last accessed on
2 April 2016), p. 9.
5 Daniel Bojin, Paul Radu and Hans Strandberg, 'How Ikea and Harvard got
tangled in a corrupt Romanian land deal', *Huffington Post*, 3 March 2016, available at www.huffingtonpost.com/entry/harvard-ikea-corruption-romania_
us_56d86cbbe4b0000de4039509 (last accessed on 2 April 2016).
6 Or $870 billion (2009 figures); see UNODC, *Transnational Organized
Crime: The Globalized Illegal Economy*, available at www.unodc.org/
toc/en/crimes/organized-crime.html (last accessed on 24 November
2015).
7 Albania, Bosnia and Herzegovina, Bulgaria, Croatia, Cyprus, Greece,
Kosovo, Macedonia (FYROM), Moldova, Montenegro, Romania, Serbia
and Slovenia.

8 Katherine Hirschfeld, *Gangster States: Organized Crime, Kleptocracy and Political Collapse*, Palgrave Macmillan, Basingstoke, 2015, p. 117.

9 European Parliament, *Report on Organised Crime, Corruption and Money Laundering*, A7-0307/2013, Brussels, 26 September 2013, p. 13.

10 Ernesto U. Savona and Michele Riccardi (eds), *From Illegal Markets to Legitimate Businesses: The Portfolio of Organised Crime in Europe. Final Report of Project Organised Crime Portfolio*, Università degli Studi di Trento, 2015, p. 7.

11 European Parliament, *Report on Organised Crime, Corruption and Money Laundering*, p. 13.

12 Ivan Krastev; see Misha Glenny, *McMafia: Crime Without Frontiers*, Vintage/Random House, London, 2008, p. 16.

13 See UNODC, *Crime and its Impact on the Balkans and Affected Countries*, Vienna, May 2008, p. 48. As quoted by Robert Kaplan in 'Hoods against democrats', *Atlantic Monthly*, December 1998.

14 Daniel Smilov, 'Bulgaria: perception and reality', in Kevin Casas-Zamora (ed.), *Dangerous Liaisons: Organized Crime and Political Finance in Latin America and Beyond*, Brookings, 2013, pp. 165–94, p. 170.

15 Nikolai Chavdarov, 'The untouchables: organised crime grows stronger in Bulgaria', in: *Jane's Intelligence Review*, Vol 23 No 07, July 2011, pages 38–42, page 41.

16 UNODC, *Crime and its Impact on the Balkans and Affected Countries*, p. 12f.

17 Samir Rizvo, 'Organized crime and corruption in the Balkans', in S. Butiri and D. Mihailovic (eds), *Evolving Asymmetric Threats in the Balkans*, IOS Press, Amsterdam, 2011, pp. 69–80, p. 72.

18 US Department of State, Bureau of International Narcotics and Law Enforcement Affairs, *2015 International Narcotics Control Strategy Report (INCSR), Bulgaria*, Washington, DC, 2015, available at www.state.gov/j/inl/rls/nrcrpt/2015/vol1/238950.htm (last accessed on 15 June 2015).

19 Stan Cosmin, 'Border police, customs officials detained in smuggling raids', *CNN News* (online), 8 February 2011, available at http://edition.cnn.com/2011/WORLD/europe/02/08/romania.smuggling.raids (last accessed on 16 June 2015).

20 White House, Office of National Drug Control Policy, *High Intensity Drug Trafficking Areas*, available at www.whitehouse.gov/ondcp/high-intensity-drug-trafficking-areas-program (last accessed on 15 June 2015).

21 Josh Eells, 'America's dirtiest cops: cash, cocaine and corruption on the Texas border', *Rolling Stone*, 5 January 2015, available at www.rollingstone.com/culture/features/americas-dirtiest-cops-cash-cocaine-texas-hidalgo-county-20150105 (last accessed on 15 June 2015).

22 Ibid.

23 Jared Taylor, 'Former Hidalgo county sheriff Lupe Treviño: "I did it"', *The Monitor*, 17 July 2014, available at www.themonitor.com/news/local/former-hidalgo-county-sheriff-lupe-trevi-o-i-did-it/article_8f763442-0db8-11e4-ad9e-0017a43b2370.html (last accessed on 15 June 2015).

24 Department of Homeland Security, Office of the Inspector General, *US Customs and Border Protection Has Taken Steps to Address Insider Threat, but Challenges Remain*, redacted version, September 2013, p. 2.

25 Savona and Riccardi (eds), *From Illegal Markets to Legitimate Businesses*, p. 9.

26 John Dickie, *Cosa Nostra: A History of the Sicilian Mafia*, St Martin's Griffin, London, 2004, pp. 358f.

27 Ibid., Prologue.

28 Rizvo, 'Organized crime and corruption in the Balkans', p. 72.

29 Lori Hinnant, 'Corsica organized crime on the rise', *Huffington Post*, 14 January 2013, available at www.huffingtonpost.com/2013/01/14/corsica-organized-crime_n_2472278.html (last accessed on 4 June 2015).

30 Ibid.

31 Kim Willsher, 'France announces plan to tackle Corsican crime wave', *Guardian*, 23 October 2012, available at www.theguardian.com/world/2012/oct/22/france-crackdown-corsica-crime (last accessed on 6 June 2015).

32 Anita Lavorgna, 'Organised crime goes online: realities and challenges', *Journal of Money Laundering*, 18(2), 2015, pp. 153–168, pp. 154f.

33 See the Internet Organised Crime Threat Assessments.

34 Lavorgna, 'Organised crime goes online', p. 158.

35 Jamie J. Bartlett, *The Dark Net*, William Heinemann, London, 2014.

36 Ibid.

37 Lavorgna, 'Organised crime goes online', p. 159.

38 Louise Shelley, 'The globalization of crime', in M. Natarajan (ed.), *International Crime and Justice*, Cambridge University Press, Cambridge, 2011, pp. 3–10.

39 Savona and Riccardi (eds), *From Illegal Markets to Legitimate Businesses*, p. 57. See also www.unodc.org/documents/human-trafficking/UNVTF_fs_HT_EN.pdf (last accessed on 1 August 2016).

40 European Parliament, *Report on Organised Crime, Corruption and Money Laundering*, 2013, p. 14; Christophe Cornevin, 'Jacques Nacer, un notable assassiné', *Le Figaro*, 16 November 2012, available at www.lefigaro.fr/actualite-france/2012/11/16/01016-20121116ARTFIG00441-jacques-nacer-un-notable-assassine.php (last accessed on 6 June 2015).

41 Lauren Gambino, 'The underworld of US sex trafficking', *Guardian*, 26 January 2015, available at www.theguardian.com/world/2015/jan/26/path-appears-sex-trafficking-pbs-documentary (last accessed on 1 June 2015); Louise Shelley, 'Human security and human trafficking', in Anna Jonsson (ed.), *Human Trafficking and Human Security*, Routledge, London and New York, 2011, pp. 10–25.

42 Georgi Petrunov, 'Managing money acquired from human trafficking: case study of sex trafficking from Bulgaria to Western Europe', *Trends in Organised Crime*, 14, 2011, pp. 165–183, p. 168.

43 Ibid., p. 177.

44 Gounev and Ruggiero, *Corruption and Organized Crime in Europe*, Routledge 2012, pp. 79f.

45 J. Townsend and C. Oomen, *Before the Boat: Understanding the Migrant Journey*, Migration Policy Institute, 2015, p. 8.

46 Interview extracted from Sam Scott, Gary Craig and Alistair Geddes, *Experiences of Forced Labour in the UK Food Industry*, Joseph Rowntree Foundation, London, May 2012, p. 41, available at www.jrf.org.uk/sites/files/jrf/forced-labour-food-industry-full.pdf (last accessed on 16 June 2015).

47 Amelia Gentleman, 'Wisbech: the end of the road for migrant workers', *Guardian*, London, 8 October 2014, available at www.theguardian.com/uk-news/2014/oct/08/wisbech-migrant-workers-exploited-gangmasters-eastern-europe (last accessed on 16 June 2015); John Smith, 'Why I found Operation Pheasant an eye opening experience as poor migrant workers are deliberately kept poor', *CambsTimes*, 30 June 2013, available at www.cambstimes.co.uk/cambridgeshire-life/letters/personal_view_why_i_found_operation_pheasant_an_eye_opening_experience_as_poor_migrant_workers_are_deliberately_kept_poor_1_2257527 (last accessed on 16 June 2015); Fenland District Council, 'Big wins for Operation Pheasant' (no date), available at www.fenland.gov.uk/article/9004/Big-wins-for-Operation-Pheasant (last accessed on 15 June 2015).

48 Based on the real-life 'olive oil king' Giuseppe 'Joe' Profaci; see http://godfather.wikia.com/wiki/Genco_Pura_Olive_Oil_Company (last accessed on 10 June 2015).

49 Tom Mueller, 'Slippery business: the trade in adulterated olive oil', *The New Yorker*, 13 August 2007, available at www.newyorker.com/magazine/2007/08/13/slippery-business?currentPage=all (last accessed on 16 June 2015).

50 Ibid.; Jamie Doward and Amy Moore, 'Cartels and organised crime target food in hunt for riches', *Guardian*, 3 May 2014, available at www.theguardian.com/world/2014/may/03/food-fraud-uk-labs-fight-organised-crime-counterfeit (last accessed on 16 June 2015).

51 Barbie Nadeau, 'Has the Italian mafia sold you fake extra-virgin olive oil?', *The Daily Beast*, 14 November 2015, available at www.thedailybeast.com/articles/2015/11/14/has-the-italian-mafia-sold-you-fake-extra-virgin-olive-oil.html (last accessed on 24 November 2015).

52 Maurizio Tropeano, 'Vola il business agromafia: 14 miliardi di euro nel 2013', *La Stampa*, 19 October 2013, available at www.lastampa.it/2013/10/19/economia/vola-il-business-agromafia-miliardi-di-euro-nel-BoW1u9tRmiLf1uSpw111WO/pagina.html (last accessed on 16 June 2015).

53 Michael Day, 'Italy's "Armani of Mozzarella" Guiseppe Mandara arrested over "contaminated cheese" amid accusations of mafia association', *Independent*, 18 July 2012, available at www.independent.co.uk/news/world/europe/italys-armani-of-mozzarella-giuseppe-mandara-arrested-over-contaminated-cheese-amid-accusations-of-mafia-association-7956861.html (last accessed on 16 June 2015).

54 Anita Lavorgna and Anna Sergi, 'Trade secrets: Italian mafia expands its illicit business', *Jane's Intelligence Review*, September 2012, pp. 44–7.

55 Agence France Presse, 'Organised crime targets French countryside', 25 January 2014, available at www.france24.com/en/20140125-organised-crime-targets-french-countryside (last accessed on 16 June 2015).

56 Although the cartel is also looking to gain entry into the avocado trade; see Doward and Moore, 'Cartels and organised crime target food and hunt for riches'; UK Government, *Elliott Review into the Integrity and Assurance of Food Supply Networks – Final Report*, London, July 2014, available at www.gov.uk/government/uploads/system/uploads/attachment_data/file/350726/elliot-review-final-report-july2014.pdf (last accessed on 16 June 2015).

Chapter 9: Foul Play: Corruption in Sport

1 Declan Hill, 'Match-fixing: how gambling is destroying sport', *BBC Sport*, 5 February 2013, available at www.bbc.co.uk/sport/0/football/21333930 (last accessed on 15 March 2016).

2 For the purpose of this chapter, the British term 'athletics' will be the term used for what is known as 'track and field' in the US.

3 Europol, 'Update – results from the largest football match-fixing investigation in Europe', *Europol Media Corner*, 6 February 2013, available at www.europol.europa.eu/content/results-largest-football-match-fixing-investigation-europe (last accessed on 17 November 2015).

4 Richard H. McLaren, 'Corruption: its impact on fair play', *Marquette Sports Law Review*, 19(1), Article 3, 2008, pp. 15–38, p. 16. McLaren also points to biased refereeing as a problem in wrestling, boxing and football and allegations thereof during the Beijing Olympics, see page 16.

5 More information on corruption and sports is also available in Transparency International, *Global Corruption Report: Sport*, Berlin, 2016, which was published while this chapter was being finalised and includes a number of excellent essays on the topics covered in this chapter.

6 See www.atkearney.com/documents/10192/6f46b880-f8d1-4909-9960-cc605bb1ff34.

7 Chris Eaton, 'A sure bet to fix sport', *Huffington Post*, 6 May 2015, available at www.huffingtonpost.com/chris-eaton2/a-sure-bet-to-fix-sport_b_7216418.html (last accessed on 17 November 2015).

8 International Centre for Sports Security, Sorbonne Université Paris 1, Protecting the Integrity of Sport Competition: The Last Bet for Modern Sport, Paris 2014, available at www.theicss.org/wp-content/themes/icss-corp/pdf/SIF14/Sorbonne-ICSS%20Report%20Executive%20Summary_WEB.pdf.

9 One of the best works on the subject is the work of a Canadian investigative journalist: Declan Hill, The Insider's Guide to Match-Fixing in Football, Anne McDermid Associates, Toronto 2013. He is also the author of *The Fix: Soccer and Organized Crime*, which exposed allegedly fixed matches during the 2006 World Cup in Germany between Italy and Ukraine.

10 Associated Press, 'As he waits for jail, Croatian soccer player deeply regrets involvement in match-fixing', *Fox News*, 13 February 2013, available at www.foxnews.com/world/2013/02/13/as-waits-for-jail-croatian-soccer-player-deeply-regrets-involvement-in-match (last accessed on 17 November 2015).

11 FIFPro (World Players' Union), *FIFPro Black Book Eastern Europe: The Problems Professional Footballers Encounter: Research*, Hoofdorp / Netherlands, 2012, p. 135, available at www.fifpro.org/images/documents-pdf/BLACK-BOOK.pdf (last accessed on 17 November 2015).

12 David Forrest, 'Corruption of football by match-fixers', *Football Perspectives*, 13 August 2012, available at http://footballperspectives.org/corruption-football-match-fixers (last accessed on 17 November 2015).

13 UEFA, 'UEFA statement on match-fixing case', 22 November 2009, available at http://web.archive.org/web/20091123061118/http://www.uefa.com/uefa/keytopics/kind=64/newsid=922086.html#newsActions (last accessed on 17 November 2015).

14 Paul Kelso, 'How German police fell on European football's biggest match-fixing scandal by accident', *Telegraph*, 5 February 2013, available at www.telegraph.co.uk/sport/football/news/9851507/How-German-police-fell-on-European-footballs-biggest-match-fixing-scandal-by-accident.html (last accessed on 17 November 2015).

15 BBC News, 'Match-fixing inquiry probes 200 European football games', 20 November 2009, available at http://news.bbc.co.uk/1/hi/world/europe/8370748.stm (last accessed on 17 November 2015).

16 Declan Hill, 'Inside the fixing: how a gang battered soccer's frail integrity', *New York Times*, 1 June 2014, available at www.nytimes.com/2014/06/02/sports/soccer/match-fixing-gang-strikes-at-soccers-fragile-legitimacy.html?_r=3&pagewanted=all (last accessed on 17 November 2015).

17 Jonah Fisher, 'Singapore "match-fixing boss" faces indefinite limbo', *BBC News*, 26 September 2013, available at www.bbc.co.uk/news/world-asia-24238681 (last accessed on 17 November 2015).

18 AFP, 'Investigation into match-fixing uncovers 680 suspicious football matches worldwide', *News.com.au*, 5 February 2013, available at www.news.com.au/national/european-police-agency-say-investigation-into-match-fixing-has-uncovered-680-suspicious-matches-worldwide/story-e6frfkp9-1226570352916 (last accessed on 17 November 2015).

19 BBC Sport, 'Match-fixing: Champions League tie played in England "was fixed"', *BBC Sport*, 4 February 2013, available at www.bbc.co.uk/sport/0/football/21319807 (last accessed on 17 November 2015).

20 Mary Gearin, 'Global soccer match-fixing scandal revealed', *ABC News Australia*, 5 February 2013, available at www.abc.net.au/news/2013-02-04/scale-of-global-soccer-match-fixing-revealed/4500644 (last accessed on 11 November 2015).

21 Paul Kelso, 'How German police fell on European football's biggest match-fixing scandal by accident', *Telegraph*, 5 February 2013, available at www.telegraph.co.uk/sport/football/news/9851507/How-German-police-fell-on-European-footballs-biggest-match-fixing-scandal-by-accident.html (last accessed on 17 November 2015).

22 Associated Press, 'Quinton Broussard pleads guilty', *ESPN*, 26 August 2011, available at http://espn.go.com/college-football/story/_/id/6895890/former-toledo-rockets-player-quinton-broussard-pleads-guilty-sports-bribery-investigati (last accessed on 11 November 2015).

23 Jenna Fryer, 'SpinGate: NASCAR credibility crisis began after Clint Bowyer spun out at Richmond', *Huffington Post*, 16 September 2013, available at www.huffingtonpost.com/2013/09/16/nascar-spingate-clint-bowyer-spun_n_3937392.html (last accessed on 17 November 2015).

24 BBC Sport, 'Naved Arif: ECB bans ex-Sussex & Pakistan A cricketer for life', *BBC Sport*, 18 June 2014, available at www.bbc.co.uk/sport/0/cricket/27904861 (last accessed on 17 November 2015).

25 European Sports Betting Authority (ESSA), *ESSA Q3 2015 Integrity Report*, November 2015, available at www.eu-ssa.org/wp-content/uploads/QR3-BROCHRE-FICHES.pdf?s=123 (last accessed on 11 November 2015).

26 Ben Gunn and Jeff Rees, 'Environmental review of integrity in professional tennis', May 2008, available at www.sportingintelligence.com/wp-content/uploads/2011/01/Integrity-in-tennis.pdf (last accessed on 19 November 2015), p. 45; and McLaren, 'Corruption', p. 19.

27 'Davydenko cleared of match-fixing', *BBC Sport*, 12 September 2008, available at http://news.bbc.co.uk/sport1/hi/tennis/7612536.stm (last accessed on 17 November 2015).

28 In a match between Richard Bloomfield and Carlos Berlocq, and Yevgeny Kafelnikov and Fernando Vicente respectively. See McLaren, 'Corruption', p. 17.

29 McLaren, 'Corruption', p. 17.

30 Simon Cox, 'Tennis match fixing: evidence of suspected match-fixing revealed', *BBC Sports*, 18 January 2016, available at www.bbc.com/sport/tennis/35319202 (last accessed on 18 March 2016).

31 Tara John, 'Prosecutor says 37 top tennis players should be investigated for match-fixing', *Time Magazine*, 15 March 2016, available at http://time.com/4258840/prosecutor-says-37-top-tennis-players-should-be-investigated-for-match-fixing (last accessed on 18 March 2016).

32 Adrian Dennis, 'The secret world of tennis gambling', *The Daily Beast*, 7 May 2015, available at www.thedailybeast.com/articles/2015/07/05/the-secret-world-of-tennis-gambling.html.

33 Hill, 'Inside the fixing'.

34 Ibid.; see also McLaren, 'Corruption', p. 16.

35 Eaton, 'A sure bet to fix sport'.

36 Forrest, 'Corruption of football by match-fixers'.

37 However, a report looking into the allegations stopped short of confirming corruption according to an investigation afterwards. German investigative reporters Thomas Kistner and Jens Weinreich have written a book about corruption and the IOC, *Der Olympische Sumpf – Die Machenschaften des IOC*, Piper, Munich, 2000.

38 BBC, 'Asia-Pacific Sydney Olympics bid "broke rules"', *BBC News*, 15 March 1999, available at http://news.bbc.co.uk/2/hi/asia-pacific/296910.stm (last accessed on 18 November 2015).

39 He was the IOC president from 1990 to 2001. He was succeeded by Jacques Rogge, who was succeeded by Thomas Bach in 2013.

40 Jere Longman, 'Olympics: corruption is extensive, I.O.C. official finds', *New York Times*, 22 January 1999, available at www.nytimes.com/1999/01/22/sports/olympics-corruption-is-extensive-ioc-official-finds.html (last accessed on 19 November 2015). The investigation was headed by Canadian Richard Pound, who also headed WADA's investigative committee into doping and corruption in Russia.

41 Both defendants rejected plea agreements and were acquitted in 2003 when a federal judge threw out the case for lack of evidence in 2003; see Howard Berkes, 'FIFA scandal has echoes of Salt Lake Olympics corruption crisis', *NPR*, 29 May 2015, available at www.npr.org/sections/thetwo-way/2015/05/29/410653814/fifa-scandal-has-echoes-of-salt-lake-olympic-corruption-crisis (last accessed on 19 November 2015). Note that this was much less than the bribery allegations in the FIFA scandal. Lex Hemphill, 'Olympics: acquittals end bid scandal that dogged Winter Games', *New York Times*, 8 December 2003, available at www.nytimes.com/2003/12/06/sports/olympics-acquittals-end-bid-scandal-that-dogged-winter-games.html (last accessed on 17 March 2016).

42 Lisa Riley Roche, 'Salt Lake Olympic scandal "set a precedent" for US prosecution of FIFA', *Deseret News*, 27 May 2015, available at www.deseretnews.com/article/865629546/Salt-Lake-Olympic-scandal-set-a-precedent-for-US-prosecution-of-FIFA.html?pg=all (last accessed on 19 November 2015).

43 Will Jennings, 'Lessons for FIFA from the Salt Lake City Olympic scandal', *The Conversation*, 28 May 2015, available at http://theconversation.com/lessons-for-fifa-from-the-salt-lake-city-olympic-scandal-42493 (last accessed on 17 March 2016).

44 WADA Investigations, *Independent Commission Investigation*, 9 November 2015, available at www.wada-ama.org/en/resources/world-anti-doping-program/independent-commission-report-1. The commission was headed by Richard Pound, with independent commission members Professor Richard H. McLaren and Günter Younger.

45 Conducted by independent experts following a December 2014 documentary by Hajo Seppelt for German public television; see Wada Investigations, *Independent Commission Investigation*.

46 WADA Investigations, *Independent Commission Investigation*.

47 Ibid.

48 Ibid., p. 22.

49 Ibid., pp. 91f.

50 Diack was a member of the IOC from 1999–2013 and then became an honorary member in 2014; he resigned in November 2015 following the launch of a formal investigation into him on allegations of corruption and money-laundering; see, for example, Reuters, 'Former IAAF president Lamine Diack resigns as honorary IOC member', *Guardian*, 11 November 2015, available at www.theguardian.com/sport/2015/nov/11/lamine-diack-ioc-resigns (available at 19 November 2015).

51 Associated Press, 'IAAF president Lamine Diack: Russia will not be banned over doping claims', *Guardian*, 21 April 2015, available at www.theguardian.com/sport/2015/apr/21/iaaf-lamine-diack-russia-doping-allegations-no-ban (last accessed on 17 November 2015).

52 Lamine Diack and his legal adviser Habib Cissé were investigated for corruption charges; Dr Gabriel Dollé was investigated for both corruption charges and charges of aggravated money laundering; see Associated Press, 'Former IAAF anti-doping head Gabriel Dollé under criminal investigation', *Guardian*, 5 November 2015, available at www.theguardian.com/sport/2015/nov/05/gabriel-dolle-iaaf-criminal-investigation (last accessed on 17 November 2015).

53 Owen Gibson, 'Athletics governing body suspends Russia from all competitions', *Guardian*, 13 November 2015, available at www.theguardian.com/sport/2015/nov/13/athletics-governing-bodies-suspend-russia-from-all-competitions (last accessed on 17 November 2015).

54 Andreas Sellíaas, 'Comment: who is the "real" Sebastian Coe?', *Play the Game*, 20 August 2015, available at www.playthegame.org/news/comments/2015/014_who-is-the-real-sebastian-coe (last accessed on 19 November 2015).

55 Owen Gibson, 'Athletics governing body suspends Russia from all competitions', *Guardian*, 13 November 2015, available at www.theguardian.com/sport/2015/nov/13/athletics-governing-bodies-suspend-russia-from-all-competitions (last accessed on 17 November 2015).

56 Julia Stepanow and her husband Vitali.

57 Cycling Independent Reform Commission, *Report to the President of the Union Cycliste Internationale*, Lausanne, February 2015, pp. 161ff, available at www.uci.ch/mm/Document/News/CleanSport/16/87/99/CIRCReport2015_Neutral.pdf (last accessed on 19 November 2015). The commission was headed by Dick Marty, with vice-presidents Peter Nicholson and Ulrich Haas.

58 Cycling Independent Reform Commission, *Report to the President of the Union Cycliste Internationale*.

59 Pat McQuaid who was challenged by Brian Cookson, who won a majority of votes and took over the presidency.

60 In most European countries (except France) and in the US, viewer numbers sharply decreased between 2006 and 2012. Indeed, the two German public television stations did not show the Tour de France from 2012 to 2014 due to doping allegations that had tainted the sport. The impact of the doping scandals on the sport was also tangible in TV licensing fees: while German stations had paid €20 million for the three years 2009–11 they only paid €5 million for 2015 and 2016.

61 Declan Hill, '7 lessons from the IAAF and Russian doping scandals', available at http://declanhill.com/7-lessons-from-the-iaaf-and-russian-doping-scandals.

62 Eufemiano Fuentes.

63 Giles Tremlett, 'Spanish doping doctor ready to reveal role in major sports', *Guardian*, 10 May 2015, available at www.theguardian.com/sport/2013/may/10/spanish-doping-doctor-reveal-sports (last accessed on 19 November 2015).

64 Jens Weinrich, 'The ILS Bribery System', presentation by Jens Weinreich at the Play the Game conference 2009, available at www.playthegame.org/fileadmin/image/PTG2009/Presentations/Jens_Weinreich_-_The_ISL_bribery_system.pdf (last accessed 13 November 2015).

65 FIFA text was last updated in March 2016.

66 Led by US Attorney General Loretta Lynch.

67 Agenda of the extraordinary meeting of the FIFA executive committee, 20 October 2015, available at http://resources. fifa.com/mm/Document/AFFederation/Bodies/02/71/20/13/ ExCo_ExtraordinaryAgendaOctober2015_EN.v.1.0_Neutral. pdf?t=1444909990026 (last accessed on 11 November 2015).

68 The FBI had worked with material and evidence provided by British investigative journalist Andrew Jennings in August 2011. For a thorough overview of FIFA actors and corruption allegations, see Andrew Jenning's book *The Dirty Game: Uncovering the Scandal at FIFA*, Penguin Random House, London, 2015.

69 James Whaling, 'FIFA timeline: How the corruption scandal within football's governing body has transpired', *Daily Mirror*, 9 October 2015, available at www.mirror.co.uk/sport/football/news/fifa-timeline-how-corruption-scandal-6603731 (last accessed 11 November 2015).

70 US Department of Justice, *Nine FIFA Officials and Five Corporate Executives Indicted for Racketeering Conspiracy and Corruption*, press release, 27 May 2015, available at www.justice.gov/opa/pr/nine-fifa-officials-and-five-corporate-executives-indicted-racketeering-conspiracy-and (last accessed on 13 November 2015).

71 David Conn, 'Michel Platini must explain all about Sepp Blatter and FIFA's payment', *Guardian*, 26 September 2015, available at www.the-guardian.com/football/2015/sep/26/michel-platini-sepp-blatter-fifa-payment (last accessed on 19 March 2016).

72 Samuel Rubenfeld, 'Supreme Court RICO Ruling Bolsters Criminal Case Against FIFA', in: *Wall Street Journal*, 23 June 2016, available at: http://blogs.wsj.com/riskandcompliance/2016/06/23/ supreme-court-rico-ruling-bolsters-criminal-case-against-fifa/

73 President Jean-Marie Faustin Godefroid 'João' de Havelange, who ran the football association until 1998.

74 Mark Critchley, 'Sepp Blatter suspended: who is Issa Hayatou, the man set to be Fifa's stand-in president?', *Independent*, 8 October 2015, available at www.independent.co.uk/sport/football/news-and-comment/ who-is-issa-hayatou-the-man-set-to-be-fifas-stand-in-president-a6685756.html (last accessed on 15 March 2016).

75 Owen Gibson, 'João Havelange resigns as FIFA honorary president over "bribes"', *Guardian*, 30 April 2013, available at

www.theguardian.com/football/2013/apr/30/joao-havelange-resigns-fifa (last accessed on 13 November 2015).

76 Jens Seyer Andersen, 'FIFA's new ethics committee fails first test', *Play the Game*, 3 May 2013, available at www.playthegame.org/news/comments/2013/fifa%E2%80%99s-new-ethics-committee-fails-first-test (last accessed on 13 November 2015).

77 His guilty plea read: 'Among other things, I agreed with other persons in or around 1992 to facilitate the acceptance of a bribe in conjunction with the selection of the host nation for the 1998 World Cup. Beginning in or about 1993 and continuing through the early 2000s, I and others agreed to accept bribes and kickbacks in conjunction with the broadcast and other rights to the 1996, 1998, 2000, 2002, and 2003 Gold Cups. Beginning in or around 2004 and continuing through 2011, I and others on the FIFA executive committee agreed to accept bribes in conjunction with the selection of South Africa as the host nation for the 2010 World Cup. Among other things, my actions described above had common participants and results. Between April of 2004 and May 2011, I and others who were fiduciaries to both FIFA and CONCACAF, in contravention of our duties, I and others, while acting in our official capacities, agreed to participate in a scheme to defraud FIFA and CONCACAF of the right to honest services by taking undisclosed bribes. I and others agreed to use e-mail, telephone, and a wire transfer into and out of the United States in furtherance of the scheme.' In case transcript, United States, District Court, Eastern District of New York, *United States of America vs Charles Gordon Blazer*, sealed proceeding, 25 November 2013, 1:13-cr-00602-RJD Document 19, p. 30, available at https://s3.amazonaws.com/s3.documentcloud.org/documents/2093153/blazer.pdf (last accessed on 15 November 2015).

78 FIFA, 'Independent Ethics Committee bans Chuck Blazer from football related activities for life', 9 July 2015, available at www.fifa.com/governance/news/y=2015/m=7/news=independent-ethics-committee-bans-chuck-blazer-from-football-related-a-2662031.html (last accessed on 15 November 2015).

79 'Beckenbauer zu SPIEGEL-Enthüllungen – Ich habe niemandem Geld zukommen lassen', *Der Spiegel*, 19 October 2015, available at www.spiegel.de/sport/fussball/franz-beckenbauer-bestreitet-korruption-bei-wm-vergabe-a-1058377.html. German weekly *Der Spiegel* ran a whole series of investigative reporting around FIFA corruption, in particular

with a view to the 2006 World Cup in Germany and the bidding process for it. Rafael Buschmann, Jürgen Dahlkamp, Gunther Latsch and Jörg Schmitt, 'Freshfields-Ermittlungen gegen DFB: Ein Konto in Sarnen', *Der Spiegel*, 4 March 2016, available at www.spiegel.de/sport/fussball/freshfields-vs-dfb-franz-beckenbauer-schluesselfigur-in-ermittlungen-a-1080783.html (last accessed on 15 March 2016).

80 Associated Press, 'Franz Beckenbauer's ban lifted after agreeing to take part in FIFA inquiry', *Guardian*, 24 June 2014, available at www.theguardian.com/football/2014/jun/27/franz-beckenbauer-fifa-ban-lifted-2018-2022-world-cup-inquiry (last accessed on 15 November 2015).

81 James Riach, 'FIFA opens investigation into Franz Beckenbauer and Germany's 2006 World Cup bid', *Guardian*, 22 March 2016, available at www.theguardian.com/football/2016/mar/22/fifa-franz-beckenbauer-germany-2006-world-cup (last accessed on 24 March 2016).

82 Most European universities do not offer sports programmes unless it is for sports degree programmes such as sports teachers, trainers or sports management – or clubs for pastime activities of students.

83 Athletics departments in the US are a term used for sports departments including a range of sports from track and field (athletics in British English) to (American) football, basketball, tennis, etc.

84 www.usatoday.com/story/sports/college/2015/03/11/ncaa-financial-state-ment-2014-1-billion-revenue/70161386 (last accessed on 2 August 2016).

85 There have been changes by the NCAA to exclude sports teams with very low graduation rates. However, the graduation rate of black student athletes is still well below the graduation rate of white student athletes. See: Shaun R. Harper, Collin D. Williams Jr., Horatio W. Blackmann, Black Male Student Athletes and Racial Inequities in NCAA Division I College Sports, Center for the Study of Race and Equity in Education, University of Pennsylvania 2013, available at: https://www.gse.upenn.edu/equity/sites/gse.upenn.edu.equity/files/publications/Harper_Williams_and_Blackman_%282013%29.pdf

86 Jay M. Smith, 'College basketball: an unhealthy "addiction"', *Huffington Post*, 15 March 2016, available at www.huffingtonpost.com/jay-m-smith/college-basketball-an-unhealthy-addiction_b_9463152.html.

87 European Commission, *Principles of Good Governance in Sport in the EU*, Brussels, 2013, available at http://ec.europa.eu/sport/library/pol-icy_documents/xg-gg-201307-dlvrbl2-sept2013.pdf (last accessed on 18 March 2016).

88 A good overview of sports governance is offered, for example, in Russel Hoye and Graham Cuskelly, *Sports Governance*, Elsevier, Oxford, 2007.

89 The description of the two levels is adapted from Michael Pedersen, 'Sport governance: what are we actually talking about?', *isportsconnect*, April 2013, available at www.isportconnect.com/index.php?option=com_content&view=article&id=18753&catid=191&Itemid=166 (last accessed on 19 March 2016).

90 As of March 2016. There are, as mentioned, legal changes underway in Switzerland. For a good summary of current legislation and planned changes in Swiss laws with respect to corruption, see Lucien W. Valloni and Eric P. Neuenschwander, 'The role of Switzerland as host: moves to hold sports organisations more accountable, and wider implications', in Transparency International, *Global Corruption Report: Sport*, pp. 320–4.

91 Jennings, The Dirty Game, pp. 57ff. See also Stephen Wilson, 'IOC lifts the veil on how much its members receive in allowances and per diems', *Telegraph*, 2 April 2015, available at www.theglobeandmail.com/sports/more-sports/ioc-lifts-the-veil-on-how-much-its-members-receive-in-allowances-and-per-diems/article23761472 (last accessed on 16 November 2015).

92 Play the Game, *Sports Governance Observer 2015: The Legitimacy Crisis in International Sports Governance*, October 2015, available at www.playthegame.org/theme-pages/the-sports-governance-observer (last accessed on 19 November 2015), p. 8.

93 Ibid.

94 Grit Hartmann, 'IWF president under suspicion of financial mismanagement', *Play the Game*, 14 May 2013, available at www.playthegame.org/news/news-articles/2013/iwf-president-under-suspicion-of-financial-mismanagement (last accessed on 18 March 2016).

95 Nick Butler, 'Rio 2016 volleyball test event in doubt after corruption allegations involving FIVB president', *Inside the Games*, 15 December 2014, available at www.insidethegames.biz/articles/1024363/rio-2016-volleyball-test-event-in-doubt-after-corruption-allegations-involving-fivb-president (last accessed on 18 March 2016).

96 Changes regarding money-laundering legislation have long been demanded by the OECD's Financial Action Task Force. The new legislation would include officials of sports governance bodies on the politically exposed persons (PEPs) register that requires enhanced scrutiny for transactions. See Valloni and Neuenschwander, 'The role of Switzerland as host'.

97 Valloni and Neuenschwander, 'The role of Switzerland as host'.

98 See the IOC's Pâquerette Girard Zappelli on this: Pâquerette Girard Zappelli, 'The International Olympic Committee's actions to protect the integrity of sport', in Transparency International, *Global Corruption Report: Sport*.

99 For more on Transparency International Germany's work, see Sylvia Schenk, 'What the anti-corruption movement can bring to sport: the experience of Transparency International Germany', in Transparency International, *Global Corruption Report: Sport*.

100 Publisher of the *Sports Governance Observer* mentioned in the governance section, see www.playthegame.org/theme-pages/the-sports-governance-observer.

Chapter 10: Murky Waters: Environmental Corruption

1 Official website of the Paris Climate Conference, 'Sponsor' section, available at www.cop21paris.org/sponsors-and-partners/sponsors (last accessed on 29 October 2015).

2 The first international agreement to establish legally binding emissions targets for industrialised countries, and to create innovative mechanisms to assist these countries in meeting these targets. Entered into force in 2004.

3 U4 Anti-Corruption Resource Centre, *Environmental Crime and Corruption*, Expert Answer 326, Bergen/Norway, April 2012, available at www.u4.no/publications/environmental-crime-and-corruption (downloaded on 17 June 2015).

4 Climate finance is a rather new instrument on the global level that is conducted, among other funds, through the Green Climate Fund. So far, around $10 billion has been pledged by developed nations to the Green Climate Fund for developing nations. These are to be used for financing mitigation and adaption programmes to combat the effects of climate change. The fund mechanisms and project implementation bear significant corruption risks in themselves that need addressing on an international level.

5 Arthus Neslen, 'Donald Trump warned against scrapping Paris climate deal', *Guardian*, 16 February 2016, available at www.theguardian.com/environment/2016/feb/16/todd-stern-warns-republicans-against-scrapping-paris-climate-deal (last accessed on 25 March 2016).

6 Duke Energy official website, www.duke-energy.com/about-us/history.asp (last accessed on 15 October 2015).

7 Southern Alliance for Clean Energy, Southeast Coal Ash Waste website, available at www.southeastcoalash.org (last accessed on 29 October 2015).

8 Natural gas provides 27 per cent of US energy, nuclear 19 per cent and hydropower 6 per cent. Other renewables make up 7 per cent. All 2014 figures; see the US Government's US Energy Information Administration statistics, available at www.eia.gov/tools/faqs/faq.cfm?id=427&t=3 (last accessed on 14 October 2015).

9 Trip Gabriel, 'Ash spill shows how watchdog was defanged', *New York Times*, 28 February 2014, available at www.nytimes.com/2014/03/01/us/coal-ash-spill-reveals-transformation-of-north-carolina-agency.html?_r=0.

10 Ibid.

11 CBS/AP, 'Duke Energy fined $102 million in coal ash spill', *CBS News*, 14 May 2015, available at www.cbsnews.com/news/duke-energy-fined-102-million-in-coal-ash-spill (last accessed on 14 October 2015).

12 James Q. Wilson, *Bureaucracy*, Basic Books, New York, 1989, p. 76.

13 The website of Koch companies states they are involved in 'refining, chemicals, biofuels and ingredients; forest and consumer products; fertilizers; polymers and fibers; process and pollution control equipment and technologies; electronic components; commodity trading; minerals; energy; ranching; glass; and investments', see www.kochindustriesinc.com/About_Koch/default.aspx (last accessed on 25 November 2015).

14 Asjylyn Loder and David Evans, 'Koch Brothers flout law getting richer with Iran sales', *Bloomberg Business News*, 3 October 2011, available at www.bloomberg.com/news/articles/2011-10-02/koch-brothers-flout-law-getting-richer-with-secret-iran-sales (last accessed on 10 March 2016).

15 Boston Consulting Group, quoted in: Greenpeace Czech Republic, 'legal steps taken by the federated states of micronesia against the prunéřov ii coal-fired power plant – Czech Republic (background information)', Prague 2010, available at: www.greenpeace.org/international/Global/international/planet-2/report/2010/3/teia_fsm.pdf (last accessed on 27 June 2016).

16 'No, minister – a mighty Czech power company runs into criticism', *The Economist*, 8 April 2010, available at www.economist.com/node/15869464 (last accessed on 29 October 2015).

17 Ibid.

18 Ibid., see also Gregory Feifer and Brian Whitmore, 'The velvet surrender', *New Republic*, 17 September 2010, available at www.newrepublic. com/article/politics/magazine/77397/russian-aggression-the-velvet-surrender-vladimir-putin-vaclav-klaus-czech-republic (last accessed on 29 October 2015).

19 Mark Tran, 'Climate change: EU leaders reach compromise deal on emissions', *Guardian*, 12 December 2008, available at www.theguardian.com/environment/2008/dec/12/eerope-carbon-emissions-climate-change (last accessed on 29 October 2015).

20 Alongside Poland and, later on, Bulgaria.

21 'Emisní povolenky: jasné vítězství průmyslu', *Euractiv*, 12 December 2008, available at www.euractiv.cz/energetika/clanek/emisni-povolenky-jasne-vitezstvi-prumyslu-005408 (last accessed on 29 October 2015).

22 Ibid.

23 Environmental Law Service, 'Případová studie. Přílepek století aneb geneze největš ího legislativního úspěchu společ nosti ČEZ', *Brno* (no date), available at http://aa.ecn.cz/img_upload/98a9a0fe3779d35f22d-c8d93fe87df89/case_study_prilepek.pdf (last accessed on 29 October 2015); see also: Frank Bold, 'Povolenky: lidem brát, ČEZu dát', available at http://frankbold.org/resime/pripad/povolenky-lidem-brat-ČEZu-dat (last accessed on 29 October 2015).

24 For the entire series of newspaper articles issued by MF Dnes, see http://zpravy.idnes.cz/topolanek-a-lobbiste-v-italii-djr-/domaci. aspx?klic=64097 (last accessed on 2 August 2016). Other newspapers suspected its exact legal ownership to lie with Marek Dalík – lobbyist, advisor and right-hand of Mirek Topolánek. The latter allegedly spent his holidays with his family at exactly the same villa only one year later.

25 Environmental Law Service, *Případová studie. Přílepek století aneb geneze největšího legislativního úspěchu společnosti ČEZ*, Brno, no date, available at http://aa.ecn.cz/img_upload/98a9a0fe3779d35f22dc8d-93fe87df89/case_study_prilepek.pdf (last accessed on 29 October 2015).

26 Namely the National Investment Plan for the Modernisation of Infrastructure and green/renewable energy resources (Národní Plán investic do modernizace infrastruktury o do čistých technologií v energetice).

27 Environmental Law Service, *Optional Derogation: Transitional Free Allowances for Power Generators in the Czech Republic*, Brno, 2011,

available at http://frankbold.org/sites/default/files/publikace/report-on-czech-10c-application_final.pdf (last accessed on 29 October 2015).

28 www.economist.com/node/15869464.

29 www.euronews.com/2013/02/18/xyz-weekend-of-rage-in-bulgaria-as-tens-of-thousands-protest-electricity-prices; www.economist.com/blogs/easternapproaches/2013/02/bulgarias-electricity-prices; www.enerdata.net/enerdatauk/press-and-publication/energy-news-001/CEZ-settles-dispute-albania-over-power-distribution-company_29335.html.

30 31 and 27 per cent respectively; see Environmental Protection Agency, *Transportation Sector Emissions*, available at www3.epa.gov/climatechange/ghgemissions/sources/transportation.html (last accessed on 27 November 2015).

31 The other half is made up of freight trucks, aircrafts, ships and boats, as well as trains.

32 European Commission, *Road Transport: Reducing CO_2 Emissions from Vehicles*, available at http://ec.europa.eu/clima/policies/transport/vehicles/index_en.htm (last accessed on 27 November 2015).

33 According to VW's own estimates; see press release of 3 November 2015, available at www.volkswagenag.com/content/vwcorp/info_center/en/news/2015/11/internen_untersuchungen.html (last accessed on 27 November 2015).

34 Russel Hotten, 'Volkswagen: the scandal explained', *BBC News*, 4 November 2015, available at www.bbc.com/news/business-34324772 (last accessed on 27 November 2015).

35 See, for example, www.zeit.de/thema/vw-affaere.

36 Environmental Protection Agency, *Volkswagen Light Duty Diesel Vehicle Violations for Model Years 2009–2016*, available at www2.epa.gov/vw (last accessed on 27 November 2015).

37 Justin Huggler, 'German government "knew VW was rigging emissions test"', *Telegraph*, 23 September 2015, available at www.telegraph.co.uk/finance/newsbysector/industry/11884877/German-government-knew-VW-was-rigging-emissions-test.html; Julia Bradshaw, 'Volkswagen scandal: CEO Martin Winterkorn resigns over emissions deception – as it happened on Wednesday', *Telegraph*, 23 September 2015, available at www.telegraph.co.uk/finance/newsbysector/industry/11884260/European-stock-markets-set-to-open-lower-as-VW-emissions-fallout-deepens-LIVE.html#update-20150923-1130 (last accessed on 27 November 2015).

38 'Dobrindt-Kommission: Vor dieser Truppe muss VW keine Angst haben', *Der Spiegel*, 16 January 2016, available at www.spiegel.de/auto/aktuell/volkswagen-nur-industriefreundliche-vertreter-in-untersuchungskommission-a-1072255.html (last accessed on 7 April 2016).

39 Alexandria Sage, 'U.S. judge sets April 21 deadline for VW diesel fix', *Reuters*, 24 March 2016, available at www.reuters.com/article/us-volkswagen-emissions-court-idUSKCN0WQ1SK (last accessed on 7 April 2016).

40 U4 Anti-Corruption Resource Centre, *Environmental Crime and Corruption*, Expert Answer 326, Bergen/Norway, April 2012, available at www.u4.no/publications/environmental-crime-and-corruption/ (last accessed on 17 June 2015).

41 Manuela Mesco, 'Naple's garbage crisis piles up on city outskirts', *The Wall Street Journal*, 25 November 2013, available at www.wsj.com/articles/SB10001424052702304465604579218014071052296 (last accessed on 10 June 2015).

42 Graziano Abrate, Fabrizio Erbetta, Giovanni Fraquelli and Davide Vannoni, *The Costs of Corruption in the Italian Solid Waste Industry*, Carlo Alberto Working Paper No. 275, Torino/Italy, December 2012, available at www.carloalberto.org/assets/working-papers/no.275.pdf (last accessed on 29 October 2015).

43 UK Environmental Law Association, *Urgent Need for Environmental Reform in Northern Ireland*, 14 May 2004, available at www.ukela.org/rte.asp?id=10&pressid=20 (last accessed on 12 June 2015).

44 Criminal Justice Inspection Northern Ireland, *A Review of the Northern Ireland Environmental Agency's Environmental Crime Unit*, Belfast, May 2015, available at www.cjini.org/CJNI/files/77/776ee5fc-b3c0-4759-8fbe-18a72a8f31e5.pdf (last accessed on 12 June 2015); Europol, *Europol Threat Assessment: Environmental Crime in the EU*, The Hague, November 2013; Christopher Mills, *A Review of Waste Disposal at the Mobuoy Site and the Lessons Learnt for the Future Regulation of the Waste Industry in Northern Ireland* ('Mills Review'), Department of the Environment Northern Ireland, November 2013, available at www.doeni.gov.uk/niea/mills-review-december-2013.pdf.

45 See, for example, United States District Court, Southern District of New York: *United States v Carmine Franco*, Indictment, 15 January 2013,

available at www.justice.gov/archive/usao/nys/pressreleases/November13/
PeterLeccontePleaPR/Franco,%20Carmine%20et%20al.%20Indictment.
pdf (last accessed on 12 June 2015); Waste Management World, *Waste
Mafia Charged in New York*, 17 January 2013, available at www.waste-
management-world.com/articles/2013/01/waste-management-mafia-
charged-in-new-york.html (last accessed on 12 June 2015).

46 State of New Jersey Commission of Investigation, *Industrious
Subversion: Circumvention of Oversight in Solid Waste and Recycling in
New Jersey*, New Jersey, December 2011, p. 2.

47 See, for example, United Nations Environmental Programme, *Illegally
Traded and Dumped E-Waste Worth Up to $19 Billion Annually Poses
Risks to Health, Deprives Countries of Resources*, Nairobi, 12 May 2015,
available at www.environmental-expert.com/news/illegally-traded-
and-dumped-e-waste-worth-up-to-19-billion-annually-poses-risks-
to-health-deprives-c-484298 (last accessed on 12 June 2015).

48 For more information and specific cases in the renewable energy sector see, for example, www.renewableenergyworld.com/articles/print/
volume-16/issue-3/wind-power/corruption-hit-as-italy-cleans-up-
wind-sector.html; www.legambiente.it/temi/ecomafia; www.telegraph.
co.uk/news/earth/energy/renewableenergy/7981737/Mafia-cash-in-
on-lucrative-EU-wind-farm-handouts-especially-in-Sicily.html; www.
occrp.org/en/blog/2047-the-environmentally-friendly-mafia; www.
waste-management-world.com/articles/2011/12/crime-magnet-
new-jersey-s-waste-recycling-industry.html (all last accessed on 29
October 2015).

49 Lavorgna and Sergi, 'Trade secrets'.

50 Note that the article quoted states that this price was €180 for a kwh –
we highly doubt this, as that would be grossly overpaying, and assume
that it is for Mwh – which would still be significantly higher than what
is paid in the rest of Europe. Article quoted: Nick Squires and Nick
Meo, 'Mafia cash in on lucrative EU wind farm handouts – especially
in Sicily', *Telegraph*, 5 September 2010, available at www.telegraph.
co.uk/news/earth/energy/renewableenergy/7981737/Mafia-cash-in-
on-lucrative-EU-wind-farm-handouts-especially-in-Sicily.html   (last
accessed on 8 November 2015).

51 Borsa dell'Innovazione e dell'Alta Tecnologia, *Focus on Renewable
Energy in Sicily*, no date, available at www.ice.gov.it/export_sud/
Sicilia_DEF.pdf (last accessed on 8 November 2015).

52 Craig Morris, 'Why is UK wind power so expensive?', *Energytransition. de*, 29 April 2015, available at http://energytransition.de/2015/04/why-is-uk-wind-power-so-expensive (last accessed on 8 November 2015).

53 Squires and Meo, 'Mafia cash in on lucrative EU wind farm handouts'.

54 Steve Robson and Hannah Roberts, 'Italian police seize more than £1billion in assets from Sicilian wind farm magnate because of alleged links to mafia', *Daily Mail*, 3 April 2013, available at www.dailymail. co.uk/news/article-2303549/Italian-police-seize-1billion-assets-Sicilian-wind-farm-magnate-alleged-links-Mafia.html (last accessed on 8 November 2015).

55 'Energy tycoon gets four-year jail term', *Ansa.it*, 8 February 2015, available at www.ansa.it/english/news/general_news/2015/02/05/energy-tycoon-gets-four-yr-jail-term_00c4fce6-0b8c-41ad-b499-c31b067e996b.html (last accessed on 8 November 2015).

56 F. Garea and R. Méndez, 'Tax agency uncovers alleged wind farm pay-off scheme in Castilla y León', *El Pais*, 20 April 2015, available at http://elpais.com/elpais/2015/04/20/inenglish/1429523798_153803.html (last accessed on 8 November 2015); Doreen Carvajal, 'With wind energy, opportunity for corruption', *New York Times*, 13 December 2009, available at www.nytimes.com/2009/12/14/world/europe/14wind.html?_r=0 (last accessed on 8 November 2015).

Chapter 11: A Challenge to the West

1 Rasma Karklins, *The System Made Me Do It*, M.E.Sharpe, New York, 2005. Karklins makes a powerful analysis of individual dilemmas in the post-communist world.

2 In addition, organisations with more specialist agendas working on other issues with high importance for the fight against corruption are doing invaluable work, such as Global Financial Integrity, Tax Justice Network, Publish What You Pay, Open Corporates, the Open Knowledge Foundation, LobbyControl and Corporate Europe.

Bibliography

Abramoff, Jack, *Capitol Punishment: The Hard Truth About Washington Corruption*, WND Books, Washington, DC, 2011.

Anderson, Perry, 'The Italian disaster', *London Review of Books*, 22 May 2014.

Andreasen, Marta, *Brussels Laid Bare*, St Edwards Press Ltd, Yelverton, 2009.

Bartlett, Jamie J., *The Dark Net*, William Heinemann, London, 2014.

Black, William K., *The Best Way to Rob a Bank is to Own One: How Corporate Executives and Politicians Looted the S&L Industry*, University of Texas Press, Austin, 2005.

Bonneau, Chris W. and Melinda Gann Hall, *In Defense of Judicial Elections*, Routledge, New York, 2009.

Brady, Hugo, *The EU's Court of Auditors: Europe's Sleeping Giant?* Centre for European Reform, 6 June 2014.

Cabinet Office (UK), *PROTECT: Increasing Protection Against Serious and Organized Crime*, October 2013.

Center for the Study of Democracy, *Organized Crime in Bulgaria: Markets and Trends*, Sofia Bulgaria, 2007.

Chartered Institute of Building, *A Report Exploring Corruption in the UK Construction Industry*, London, September 2013.

Chayes, Sarah, Thieves of State, Why Corruption Threatens Global Security, 2015.

Cockcroft, Laurence, *Global Corruption: Money, Power and Ethics in the Modern World*, I.B.Tauris, London, 2012.

Collins, Ronald and David Skover, *When Money Speaks: The McCutcheon Decision, Campaign Finance Laws and the First Amendment*, Scotus Oak Park, Illinois, 2014.

Corporate Europe Observatory, *Chemical Conflicts: Inadequate Independence Policies for EU's Expert Risk Assessors*, Brussels, 2014.

Corporate Europe Observatory, *The Crusade Against Red Tape: How the European Commission and Big Business Push for Deregulation*, Brussels, 2014.

Corporate Europe Observatory, *The Firepower of the Financial Lobby*, Brussels, 2014.

Corporate Europe Observatory, *Life Beyond Emissions Trading*, Brussels, 2014.

Cronin, David, *Corporate Europe: How Big Business Sets Policies on Food, Climate and War*, Pluto Press, London, 2013.

Dickie, John, *Cosa Nostra: A History of the Sicilian Mafia*, St Martin's Griffin, London, 2004.

Dickie, John, *Mafia Republic: Cosa Nostra, 'Ndrangheta, Camorra 1946–Present*, Sceptre, London, 2013.

Dzehlkova, Rositsa, Philip Gounev and Tihomir Bezlov, *Countering Police Corruption: European Perspectives*, Center for the Study of Democracy, Sofia Bulgaria, 2013.

Eigen, Peter, *Das Netz der Korruption*, Campus Verlag, Frankfurt, 2003.

European Commission, *Report from the Commission to the European Parliament and the Council: Interim Report on Progress in Bulgaria Under the Co-operation and Verification Mechanism*, Brussels, 2012.

European Commission, *EU Anti-Corruption Report* (COM 2014) (with 28 country studies), Brussels, 2014.

European Parliament (PES513.067v02-00), *Report on Organised Crime, Corruption and Money Laundering*, 2013.

Europol, *EU Serious Crime and Organised Crime Threat Assessment*, The Hague, 2013.

Europol, Financial Intelligence Group, *Why is Cash Still King?*, The Hague, 2015.

Felbab-Brown, Vanda, *Focused Deterrence, Selective Targeting, Drug Trafficking and Organized Crime: Concepts and Practicalities*, International Drug Policy Consortium, February 2013.

Foster, Christopher, *The Corruption of Politics and the Politics of Corruption, Public Management and Policy Association*, London, 2001.

Friends of the Earth Europe et al., *Dirty Deals: How Trade Talks Threaten to Undermine EU Climate Policies and Bring Tar Sands to Europe*, Brussels, 2014.

Gounev, P. and V. Ruggiero, *Corruption and Organized Crime in Europe: Illegal Partnerships*, Routledge, London, 2012.

Gradel, Thomas J. and Dick Simpson, *Corrupt Illinois: Patronage, Cronyism and Criminality*, University of Illinois, Chicago, 2015.

Head, Simon, *Mindless: Why Smarter Machines Are Making Dumber Humans*, Basic Books, New York, 2014.

Hirschfeld, Katherine, *Gangster States: Organized Crime, Kleptocracy and Political Collapse*, Palgrave Macmillan, Basingstoke, 2015.

Horel, Stephane, *Unhappy Meal: The European Food Safety Authority's Independence Problem*, Corporate Europe Observatory, Brussels, 2013.

International Institute for Democracy and Electoral Assistance (IDEA), *Handbook on Funding of Parties and Election Campaigns*, Stockholm, 2001.

Ivković, Sanja Kutnjak and M.R. Haberfeld, *Measuring Police Integrity Across the World: Studies from Established Democracies and Countries in Transition*, Springer, New York, 2015.

Johnson, Simon and James Kwak, *13 Bankers: The Wall Street Takeover and the Next Financial Meltdown*, Vintage Books, New York, 2010.

Klein, Naomi, *This Changes Everything: Capitalism vs the Climate*, Allen Lane, London, 2014.

Krishnan, Chandrashekhar, *Tackling Corruption in Political Party Financing*, Edmond J. Safra Center for Ethics, Working Paper No. 43, Harvard Law School, 8 May 2014.

Lavorgna, Anita, 'Organised crime goes online: realities and challenges', *Journal of Money Laundering*, 18(2), 2015, pp. 153–168.

Leamer, Laurence, *The Price of Justice: A True Story of Greed and Corruption*, St Martin's Press, New York, 2013.

Lessig, Laurence, *Republic, Lost* Twelve Hachette Book Group, New York, 2012.

Lewis, Michael, *The Big Short: Inside the Doomsday Machine*, Penguin Books, New York, 2010.

Martin, Iain, *Making it Happen: Fred Goodwin, RBS and the Men Who Blew up the British Economy*, Simon and Schuster, London, 2010.

Mayer, Jane, 'Covert operations: the billionaire brothers who are waging a war against Obama', *New Yorker*, 30 August 2010.

McLaren, Richard H., 'Corruption: its impact on fair play', *Marquette Sports Law Review*, 19(1), 2008, pp. 15–38.

Meacham, Jon, *Thomas Jefferson: The Art of Power*, Random House, New York, 2012.

Mollen, Milton, *Report: Commission to Investigate Allegations of Police Corruption and the Anti-Corruption Procedures of the Police Department*, City of New York, New York, 7 July 1994.

Mungiu-Pippidi, Alina, *The Quest for Good Governance: How Societies Develop Control of Corruption*, Cambridge University Press, Cambridge, 2015.

Naim, Moises, *Illicit: How Smugglers, Traffickers, and Copycats Are Hijacking the Global Economy*, Heinemann, London, 2005.

National Commission on the Causes of the Financial and Economic Crisis of the US, *The Financial Crisis: Inquiry Report*, Public Affairs, New York, 2011.

Nield, Robert, *Public Corruption: The Dark Side of Social Evolution*, Anthem Press, London, 2002.

O'Brien, Justin, *Fixing the Fix: Governance, Culture, Ethics and the Extending Perimeter of Financial Regulation*, Edmund J. Safra Center for Ethics, Harvard Law School, 2014.

OECD, *Foreign Bribery Report: An Analysis of the Crime of Bribery of Foreign Public Officials*, OECD Publishing, Paris, 2014.

Play the Game, *Sports Governance Observer 2015: The Legitimacy Crisis in International Sports Governance*, October 2015.

Plender, John, *Capitalism: Money, Morals and Markets*, Biteback, London, 2015.

PricewaterhouseCoopers with the University of Utrecht, *Public Procurement: Costs We Pay for Corruption (Identifying and Reducing Corruption in Public Procurement in the EU)*, 2013.

Rajan, Raghuram G., *Fault Lines: How Hidden Fractures Still Threaten the World Economy*, Princeton University Press, Princeton, 2010.

Rose-Ackerman, Susan and Bonnie Palifka, *Corruption and Government: Causes, Consequences and Reform*, Cambridge University Press, 2016.

Savona, Ernesto U. and Michele Riccardi (eds), *From Illegal Markets to Legitimate Businesses: The Portfolio of Organised Crime in Europe. Final Report of Project Organised Crime Portfolio*, Università degli Studi di Trento, 2015.

Schotland, R.A., 'Judicial elections in the US: is corruption an issue?', in Transparency International, *Global Corruption Report 2007 (Corruption in Judicial Systems)*, Berlin, 2013.

Shelley, Louise, *Dirty Entanglements: Corruption, Crime and Terrorism*, Cambridge University Press, 2014.

Shepherd, Joanna, *Justice at Risk: An Empirical Analysis of Campaign Contributions to Judicial Decisions*, American Constitutions Society for Law and Policy, Alabama, 2013.

Skogan, Wesley and Kathleen Frydl, *Fairness and Effectiveness in Policing: The Evidence*, National Academic Press, Washington, DC, 2004.

Sorkin, Andrew, *Too Big to Fail*, Penguin, New York, 2009.

Stewart, David O., *The Summer of 1787: The Men Who Invented the Constitution*, Simon and Schuster, New York, 2007.

Streb, Matthew J, *Running for Judge: The Rising Political, Financial, and Legal Stakes of Judicial Elections*, New York University Press, New York and London, 2007.

Tansey, Rachel, *Fracking Brussels: A Who's Who of the EU Shale Gas Lobby*, Friends of the Earth, Brussels, 2014.

Teachout, Zephyr, *Corruption in America: From Benjamin Franklin's Snuff Box to Citizens United*, Harvard University Press, Massachusetts, 2014.

Thurber, James A. (ed.), *Obama in Office*, Paradigm, Boulder, 2011.

Thurber, James A. (ed.), *Rivals for Power: Presidential-Congressional Relations*, Rowman and Littlefield, Maryland, 2013.

Thurber, James A. and Antoine Yoshinaka (eds), *American Gridlock*, Cambridge University Press, New York, 2015.

Transparency International, *Exporting Corruption: Progress Report 2015: Assessing Enforcement of the OECD Convention on Combatting Foreign Bribery*, Berlin, 2015.

Transparency International, *Lobbying in Europe: Hidden Influence, Privileged Access*, Berlin, 2015.

Transparency International (UK), *Corrupt Capital: Is the UK Turning a Blind Eye to the World's Dirty Money?*, London, 2015.

Transparency International (UK) (Defence and Security Programme), *Organised Crime, Corruption, and the Vulnerability of Defence and Security Forces*, London, 2011.

United Nations Office on Drugs and Crime (UNODC), *Crime and its Impact on the Balkans and Affected Countries*, 2008.

Van Meurs, Wim and Alina Mungiu-Pippidi, *Ottomans into Europeans: State and Institution-Building in South Eastern Europe*, Hurst Publishers, London, 2010.

Vogl, Frank, *Waging War on Corruption: Inside the Movement Fighting the Abuse of Power*, Rowman and Littlefield, Washington, DC, 2012.

Warren, Elizabeth, *A Fighting Chance*, Scribe, London, 2015.

Zucman, Gabriel, *The Hidden Wealth of Nations*, University of Chicago Press, Chicago and London, 2015.

Index